AN
UNRECOGNIZED
CONTRIBUTION

The Metropolitan Methodist Church Bicycle Club. Even some doctors believed that women would be sexually aroused on bicycle seats and urged women to "eschew modern dangers." There was also concern about the apparel that women wore to ride bicycles: balloon pants or long pants.

AN
UNRECOGNIZED
CONTRIBUTION

Women and Their Work in 19th-Century Toronto

ELIZABETH GILLAN MUIR

DUNDURN
PRESS

Publisher: Kwame Scott Fraser | Acquiring editor: Kathryn Lane | Editor: Susan Fitzgerald
Cover and interior designer: Karen Alexiou
Cover image: Anglican Women's Training College Toronto, Church of England Deaconess House, before 1903. From left to right: Mrs. Hillyer Boyd; Fanny Cross, head deaconess; Frances Victoria (Fannie) Clute; and Miss Connell. With permission of Anglican Archives, P7902; background: rawpixel/Freepik.com

Library and Archives Canada Cataloguing in Publication

Title: An unrecognized contribution : women and their work in 19th-century Toronto / Elizabeth Gillan Muir.
Names: Muir, Elizabeth Gillan, 1934- author.
Description: Includes bibliographical references and index.
Identifiers: Canadiana (print) 20220250790 | Canadiana (ebook) 20220250839 | ISBN 9781459750029 (softcover) | ISBN 9781459750036 (PDF) | ISBN 9781459750043 (EPUB)
Subjects: LCSH: Women—Employment—Ontario—Toronto—History—19th century. | LCSH: Women employees—Ontario—Toronto—History—19th century. | LCSH: Women—Ontario—Toronto—Biography. | LCSH: Women employees—Ontario—Toronto—Biography. | LCSH: Women—Ontario—Toronto—History—19th century. | LCSH: Women—Ontario—Toronto—Social conditions—19th century. | LCSH: Women—Ontario—Toronto—Economic conditions—19th century. | LCGFT: Biographies.
Classification: LCC HD6100.T6 M85 2022 | DDC 331.4/09713541—dc23

We acknowledge the support of the Canada Council for the Arts and the Ontario Arts Council for our publishing program. We also acknowledge the financial support of the Government of Ontario, through the Ontario Book Publishing Tax Credit and Ontario Creates, and the Government of Canada.

Dundurn Press
1382 Queen Street East
Toronto, Ontario, Canada M4L 1C9
dundurn.com, @dundurnpress 🐦 f 📷

To all women: May you dream big and achieve your dreams.

CONTENTS

PREFACE

— • —

P arthenogenesis: an uncommon word not likely to be found in pocket-sized or abbreviated dictionaries. The *Concise Oxford Dictionary* (1949) defines it simply as "reproduction without sexual union," from the Greek word for *virgin* — *parthenos*. *Webster's New Collegiate Dictionary* (1949) is somewhat more detailed: "Reproduction by the development of an unfertilized egg. *Natural* parthenogenesis typically involves the development of eggs from virgin females without fertilization by spermatozoa. It occurs chiefly in certain insects, crustaceans, and worms."

While parthenogenesis is connected to females, on reading histories, especially early histories of Toronto, one could be forgiven for wondering if males were suddenly reproducing themselves. Perhaps one should think in terms of *virogenesis*, a newly invented word from the Latin word for *man* — *vir* — for few histories mention women at all. It takes time, extensive reading, and research to find any women, and then to collect all the references, in order to end up with a reasonably full story.

The following chapters, then, have evolved over time, through searching out nineteenth-century women in Toronto from various early historical works. Not only are women, half the adult population, generally missing, but their writings — diaries, poems, novels, and so on — have not been considered important enough to be saved to any large degree. One is hard pressed to find many early Canadian women's diaries, although we know they existed, as women traditionally kept diaries.

The commonly accepted thesis is that "women [in the 1800s] usually stayed at home. They cleaned the house and cooked and sewed. They didn't often go out to work and many girls didn't go to school. Women ... worked as servants ... [or] as governesses."[1] While this brief description of women in the 1800s may be true in a few cases, it tells only a small part of women's story. Research indicates that life for many women in Toronto in the nineteenth century was much more interesting and varied. Some women had incredible careers.

In the following chapters, there is a glimpse of women's lives in the nineteenth century in Toronto.

CHAPTER 1

TORONTO: A "NEW WORLD" CITY

T here had been cities flourishing in the "New World" for decades — such as Mexico City, New York City, and Quebec City — by the time Elizabeth Posthuma Gwillim Simcoe (1762–1850) and her husband, John Graves Simcoe (1752–1806), the first lieutenant-governor of Upper Canada, arrived at the north shore of Lake Ontario. This was the future site of Toronto, the proposed capital of the province of Upper Canada, but in 1793, the Simcoes saw nothing but trees. True, there were the ruins of a very small French trading post, Fort Rouillé, which had been built in 1751 and burned down in 1759. But as the saying went, the trees were so dense that a squirrel could jump from tree to tree from Windsor in the west of the province to Cornwall in the east without once touching the ground.

The Simcoes were on a scouting trip, John Graves in a bateau with seven other officers, and Elizabeth in the sloop *Onondaga*. Other locations had been considered for the provincial capital — Niagara, which was then called Newark, and Kingston — but John Graves liked the natural protected harbour of the future site of Toronto, bounded on both sides by rivers two miles (three kilometres) apart. As Great Britain had just lost the United States' seaboard colonies in the American Revolutionary War, John Graves envisioned

Painting by Elizabeth Simcoe, looking west from the mouth of the Don River.

a splendid new British territory in their stead. He immediately had twelve log houses built near the muddy banks of the Don River. Ten were for his military cohort and the rest of his party, and two were for First People who still lived in the area — at least two families of Mississaugas.[1] Elizabeth, the two young children whom she had brought to Canada, and their nanny would live in copious tents that had once belonged to the British explorer Captain James Cook.

John Graves named the future city York, and he also gave the two rivers names from English geographical locations, the Don in the east and the Humber in the west. There is a story that the city was to have been called Dublin. In fact, a map from 1796 shows the proposed survey of the "Township of Dublin, renamed the Township of York," detailing the lots along the waterfront from the Humber River to the east beyond the Don. However, the nineteenth-century historian and Anglican rector Henry Scadding was quite definite that the whole area — lake, river, fort, and so on — was called Toronto from the late seventeenth century.[2]

In any event, the new settlement would soon be known as "Muddy Little York"; it was barely thriving at first. Mary Warren Baldwin Breckenridge/ Breakenridge (1791–1871), who emigrated from Ireland with her family in 1798, when she was only seven, later remembered that at the time she found it "composed of about a dozen or so houses, a dreary dismal place, not even possessing the characteristics of a village. There was no church, schoolhouse or any of the ordinary signs of civilization."[3]

The famous adventurer and author Anna Jameson (1794–1860) described it in her writings as "a little ill-built town … [with] some government offices, built … in the most tasteless, vulgar style imaginable." The fact that she was no longer enamoured of one of the government bureaucrats who worked in one of those "tasteless" offices may have had some bearing on her reaction. Jameson, however, was never reticent about sharing her opinions.[4]

However, another Irish-born early settler, Frances Browne Stewart (1794–1872), also thought poorly of it. In 1822 she wrote in her diary:

> The town or village of York looked pretty from the lake as we sailed up in a schooner, but on our landing, we found it not a pleasant place, as it is sunk down in a little amphitheatre cut out of the great bleak forest. The lake in front is full of rushes which have been cut and left to decay in the shallow water, causing it to be very unhealthy…. Fever and ague are common…. A deadness hangs over everything.[5]

John Graves Simcoe's official secretary and aide-de-camp, Colonel the Honourable Thomas Talbot (1771–1853), who had come to Canada with John Graves, agreed in 1803 that it was fit only for "a frog-pond or a beaver meadow."[6]

Very rapidly, though, the settlement took on the aspects of a proper community. Mary Warren Baldwin Breckenridge's mother "found York had vastly changed" in the seven years she spent in the United States after the Baldwins had settled in York: "There were a church, a gaol, a lighthouse building and many nice houses, and the woods between the garrison and town fast disappearing."[7] After she settled in York for a short time, Frances Stewart decided that it was a very clean town and the "surrounding countryside very beautiful," although some time later for some unknown reason, she would describe it as "vile" and "odious," but not dark or gloomy in the hot summer months, "when gloomy would have been refreshing."[8]

In 1832 William Cattermole, the land agent for the Canada Company trying to attract immigrants, described it as "flourishing" and "beautifully situated," with the "society ... equal to any provincial town in Britain," but obviously he had an agenda; and C. Pelham Mulvany, writer and great fan of the Upper Canadian government, thought it handsome, "reared as by enchantment in the midst of a wilderness."[9]

But many must have considered it a worthwhile place to live. Settlers came by the score:

- United Empire Loyalists from the United States, escaping the penalties for siding with the British during the Revolutionary War and eager to receive their free allotment of land in Canada, even though it might be dense forest that had to be cleared manually by saw and axe; people described as "the first body [of immigrants to Canada] numbering ten thousand ... the most cultured class of American society";
- men and women from England and Scotland, singly or in boatloads as part of organized emigration programs, all of them dreaming of a better, more prosperous life;
- Americans, bringing their skills and talents to a new land for new opportunities, attracted by the fertile lands of Canada;
- people of colour from the south, fleeing from servitude and maltreatment; and
- toward mid-century, thousands of Irish, destitute and ill as a result of epidemics, the potato famine, and indifferent landlords, hoping just to survive.[10]

It was not until 1834, however, that the new settlement, consisting then of 9,254 men and women, was declared a city and renamed Toronto, supposedly after the Mohawk word *tkaronto*, meaning "where there are trees standing in the water." The name *Taronto,* spelled with an *a,* also referred to a channel of water through which Lake Simcoe to the north discharged into Lake Couchiching, and was recorded on one of Samuel de Champlain's maps as early as 1615.[11]

From the beginning, women played a major role in the growth and prosperity of the new centre. From 1796 up to the very early 1800s, the records of the early patentees of the town and the township — that is, those people who gave in their name to receive a lot of land — contained names of more than twenty women, such as the well-to-do Elizabeth Russell (1754–1822). She had accompanied her half-brother, Peter, a member of John Graves Simcoe's executive council who succeeded Simcoe after he went back to England. Women were not as free as men in Victorian Toronto; they were prevented from participating fully or even at all in certain occupations and professions. Yet they soon established a vast number of businesses and gradually became part of much of the professional and business life in the city.[12]

CHAPTER 2

WOMEN IN NINETEENTH-CENTURY TORONTO: THEIR WORK AND STATION

———————— •◦• ————————

n Toronto's Methodist churches of the late nineteenth and early twentieth centuries, women filled out shorter marriage registers than men: there was an extra line for "Occupation" for men. It was evidently assumed by some at that time that women did not work, or if they did, their work did not count. But throughout all the nineteenth century, women did work, often to exhaustion, both inside their homes and outside in businesses and professions.[1]

Early settler life was never easy. After the land was cleared and shelters built, mainly by men, women were required to look after the gardens and conserve enough food to last the family over the harsh winters. Early on, there was an unwritten division of labour on the farm. Women were expected to care for the cows, milk them, and make butter and sometimes even cheese; the dairy was their preserve. They fed the fowl and gathered the eggs. They made soap, candles, and often potash. They sheared the sheep and looked after the bees. Sometimes they made maple syrup or helped with boiling the sap. And, generally, they cooked the meals, baked the bread, spun flax and wove wool, sewed clothes, washed them, and darned socks, all without electricity or running water inside the house. They were supposed to be familiar with herbal lore in the absence of medical facilities and doctors; the wife of the first lieutenant-governor, Elizabeth Simcoe, noted the remedies she used herself, such as catmint as a "stomatic" and sweet marjoram tea for a headache. Virtually every day in her 1845 diary, Hannah Delvina Peters Jarvis reported that someone in her family or group of friends was ill, suffering from a headache, a toothache, a fever, sore and aching joints, swollen legs or feet, or a sick stomach. Doctors were usually not readily available, and by today's standards, medicine was fairly primitive if and when doctors could be fetched. Women also had to care for their several children, sometimes being the only schoolteachers the young children might have. In the early backwoods, one tried to be as self-sufficient as possible.

The Canadian historian Isabel Skelton tells a story that was handed down in one country district:

> In the early days of cradling [cutting grain with a scythe], a certain Mr. C. was noted for always being behind with his crop. His brother-in-law, who had finished his, thought he would walk over, some six miles distant, and see how Mr. C. was coming on. As he approached his sister's home, he saw the said C. sitting up on the fence smoking.
>
> "Good morning, C., and how are you getting on with your crop?"
>
> "Oh, very slow, very slow — But we can't expect anything else when there is just her and me."
>
> "Why don't you get to work at it, then?"
>
> "Sure, what would be the good of me cutting it down sooner than she can tie it up?"[2]

The letters and diaries of early Upper Canadian women tell the stories of their constant hard work and fatigue. Mary Warren Baldwin was forced to drag hay up a hill to feed all the cattle and sheep, even though she was terrified of animals and described as a "delicate sixteen year-old."[3] In one of her letters, Elizabeth Russell noted that they ate their "own Mutton and Pork and Poultry" and they grew their "own Buck wheat and Indian corn and have two

Oxen got two cows with their calves and plenty of pigs and a mare and Sheep."[4] At the time, she would have helped with most of their farming tasks unless they were fortunate enough to have several competent servants. She wrote that they had not yet made butter, but would soon.

In 1818 a Mrs. David Darling in Trafalgar Township, forty miles (64 kilometres) from York, carried a tub of butter through the bush to the York market, sold it to buy a metal logging chain, then carried the heavy chain back to her home, an eighty-mile (128-kilometre) trip.[5]

There were, of course, none of the appliances that would appear in the next century. In her diary of 1845, Hannah Delvina Peters Jarvis writes that on January 14, the day after it was "snowing fast," some sheets were washed "at [the] river" by the women.

In 1823 Frances Browne Stewart wrote in her diary about her parents' condition:

> The life of hardship and toil became almost unbearable, it
> was impossible any longer to hide from their friends that a
> farmer's life, in the far off forest, was not only unprofitable,
> but almost unbearable from hardships unnamed. The great
> length and severity of the winter, and great labour and anx-
> iety connected with the clearing of the land was trying to my
> father's physical strength, unequal to the labour required by
> the pioneer in the backwoods.[6]

However, farming was central to the new community. Even after urbaniz-ation and industrialization in the core of the city with the coming of the rail-roads, farming continued on the outskirts. In the late 1800s and early 1900s, the most common occupation that men listed on the marriage registration form for the eastern Toronto Methodist churches was still farming. Obviously their wives and other family members would be helping with the farm work, too.[7]

Hunkering down in their little eighteen-by-sixteen-foot log house after a hard and discouraging day's work or in desperation in the face of the upcom-ing winter, some of the women — and the men — would perhaps have cringed at this upbeat description of Upper Canadian farm life:

Thus do the receding forests, the smiling farms, yielding their abundant crops, the comfortable homestead, with on either hand the well replenished barn or fold-yard, garnished with life, in the full and broad proportions indicative of munificent and careful husbandry; the smiling, contented look of the proprietor, as he contemplates their increase, and counts the profit from their sale.[8]

As the twentieth-century historian Edwin Guillet noted, it was a time when perseverance amid discouragement was the rule.

From the beginning of the fledgling community of York, detailed records were kept annually of all the residents — their names and often their occupations — but the information was not always accurate or complete. At the beginning, male residents were "press-ganged" or "volunteered" to take on various community tasks, such as assessor, overseer of "highways," or town clerk. It was the duty of the town clerk to list all the residents each year. It was a sign of regard and trust to be elected to these tasks, but it was often a burden, and one could be appointed *in absentia* and fined if the tasks were not completed. Hence, the volunteer town clerk might ride past a residence where no one was at home and fail to come back a second time to gain accurate information about the occupants. Sometimes the "volunteer" would spell a name "creatively," or was ill-educated and could not spell. Thus we cannot be certain of the accuracy of this data, but it is a good indicator of the early makeup of York and, later, Toronto.

The following sections describe women listed in the directories in the very early years, then in the 1830s, the 1850s, and finally the 1880s and 1890s.

Early 1800s

Even in the early years, the city directories listed a number of widows. Men were never listed as widowers, but only by their names and occupations. Whether being highlighted as a widow was a sign of respect or a signal of availability, one can only guess; the format continued for years. But in the city directories from 1796 to the early 1800s, many women were apparently living as widows at addresses on their own; in 1805, when there were just over two hundred men and women listed in the directory, six women were listed as heads of families. There was an exceptionally high number of widows in 1813, possibly as a result of the 1812–1814 war. Notably, in 1813, the population of York and the surrounding district had shrunk to only 720, *half* the population of 1812. In 1813 sixty-two men were killed in the war, with others missing, wounded, or taken prisoner.[9] Many of the widow-led residences listed had a number of occupants, mainly children. For example, the widow Stanton's house had seventeen occupants, twelve of them children. Perhaps it was an early orphanage or boarding school, or even the widow Stanton's large father-less family. The year with the greatest number of single women as a percentage of the total population was 1814 — again, possibly because of war widows.[10]

1830s

As the community of York expanded and became more urbanized, profession-als, or at least companies with paid workers, produced the directories with more complete information. In 1833 a number of women were listed as work-ing outside the home. However, many women still apparently lived on their own without an occupation, some of them listed as widows or spinsters, the latter designated *Miss.* Some were listed just as *Mrs.*, obviously widows, too. One wonders how they existed financially. The most common occupations for women that year were milliner and dressmaker, boarding house propri-etor, and schoolteacher or small school owner, mostly for very young girls or "ladies." The girls' schools generally offered English reading, writing, and arithmetic, as well as homemaking skills. Women were also often connected to shops, mainly of dry goods or groceries, but it is impossible to know whether they owned the shops or were simply employed to work in them.

Some of the working women lived at the same address as a male with the same last name but in a different occupation; evidently it was deemed ne-cessary for some couples or families to have two salaries even then. In a few cases, though, a woman and a man with different last names and each working in a different occupation lived at the same address. Perhaps one of them was renting space. Other female occupations listed that year were washerwoman, midwife, teacher of Oriental tinting, mistress at Upper Canada College, housekeeper, and stay maker. But most curious of all was a Mrs. Anderson, who was listed with "entertainment and grocery" as her occupations.[11]

The contemporary writer George Walton assessed the various boarding houses that year, noting that only seven were "respectable." Of these, only one was owned by a woman, Mrs. Hall. The other boarding houses, he wrote, were "of inferior description," presumably most of those owned and operated by women.[12]

In her memoir of her trip to Toronto in the late 1830s, the adventurer Anna Jameson noted that there were "two ladies in Toronto who [had] conservatories" at that time, "a proof of advancing wealth, and civilisation, and taste…. One of them had the kindness to send me a bouquet of hot-house flowers while I was ill this last time." Likely the conservatories were part of their residences, though, and not a commercial venture.[13]

1850s

Almost twenty years later, the 1850 directory followed a similar pattern, except that there were many more interesting and varied vocations outside the home for women. Again the most common occupations listed involved sewing in some form — seamstress, dressmaker, "tailoress," and milliner, as well as shirtmaker. Operating a boarding house or a beer shop, inn, tavern, or hotel was also very common. It was quite clear that the women owned the inns, taverns, and hotels they were associated with, and did not just work in them, as the women were listed as "prop." There was evidently not enough room on the line to spell out *proprietor* or *proprietress*! That year, the compiler considered eight of the boarding houses worthy of listing separately by name, noting that there were others.

Again, many women were listed as owning schools or teaching in them, and one woman was engaged as a music teacher. Also again, a number of women either owned or worked in shops — confectionary shops, small grocery stores, fruit shops, fancy goods stores, and a wool shop. Seventeen women were listed as hucksters, or small variety-store workers, suggesting that they were, indeed, the owners of the shops. Two women were listed as "market women," and one as a "potato dealer." Louisa Hyde is listed as owning a grocery store, and presumably, there were many other women owners who were not named as such.

There were "monthly nurses," women who cared for a woman for a month or so after childbirth; midwives; a "doctress" (presumably a midwife or monthly nurse); and a woman who worked at the lying-in (maternity) hospital. There were women in a number of other jobs: an upholsterer, an organist, an office keeper, and several "milk women," perhaps women who owned or worked in commercial dairies, although most Toronto dairies were not in operation until the late 1800s. (At that later time, more than twenty women owned Toronto dairies and two of those women also owned a grocery store.)[14] There were shoe binders, a brick maker, a housekeeper, and one woman who worked in an exchange office. And, of course, there were women who worked in laundries and several washerwomen, and, again, a stay maker.

Lamb's Blacking and Glue Factory. After a fire destroyed the factory in 1888, it was never rebuilt. The Lambs' son Daniel operated the factory after Mr. Lamb died, although some sources claim that Mrs. Lamb was in charge for a time.

One important business that appears to be missing from the directory but was mentioned in other histories of the time was Lamb's Blacking and Glue Factory, established in the early 1800s by Peter Rothwell Lamb (1809–1864), but possibly owned in the late 1860s by the widowed Jane Evans Lamb (1812–1899) and one of their six children, son Daniel; it had an international reputation.[15] It was not unusual for businesses to be passed on to wives in the event of the male owner's death. The woman managed the business and was sometimes mentioned in the directory along with a son or sons. Perhaps women were not considered capable enough on their own without a male, even if only a young son. The historian C. Pelham Mulvany noted that Mr. Daniel Lamb "and his mother," the widow of the original founder, looked after the factory after Mr. Lamb's death. When his father died, Daniel would have been twenty-two, well able to look after the factory, although he was busy as a member of the city council along with his other activities.[16] There are different dates listed for the establishment and closure of Lamb's factory. It is likely that Peter Rothwell Lamb arrived in Toronto in 1834 and established the factory in 1848, producing stove blacking, glue, and possibly a tannery, eventually in twelve buildings which burned in 1888. Lamb also co-founded the Unitarian Church and the Riverdale Zoo, and Daniel is credited with establishing the public waterworks on Toronto Island. The smells from the factory were intolerable. A columnist suggested that they drove the residents out of the nearby graveyard.

Another Toronto woman who wasn't included in the street directories is the widow Ruth Fellows Adams (1800–1864), who applied for a patent for a "reverse cooking stove" in June 1854. She was granted patent number 492 on January 20, 1855, the first patent granted to a woman inventor in Canada. Originally from New Hampshire, Ruth married the itinerant (travelling) Methodist minister Zenas Adams in 1826. She bore eleven children from 1827 to 1844 as Zenas, who was in charge of the Toronto Methodist circuit, travelled around Upper Canada. Unfortunately the drawing of Ruth's stove has not survived, although the description has; perhaps she had developed and used such a stove to care for her large family and the surprise guests that Zenas might have brought home from his circuit travels.[17]

In a competing street directory, one woman was listed as a merchant and another as a saleswoman. Mrs. Bilton owned a respected fruit, fish, and oyster

Mrs. Douglas Hair Works on Page's Block on Yonge Street, Toronto. Charles Page was a dry goods importer, and the block from 184 to 194 Yonge Street became known as Page's Block.

depot that had been founded by her husband in 1862 but was operated by her after he died in 1869. It was considered "high rank of its class." Joseph Copley, a "dealer in hair goods," was "assisted" by his wife, "a Miss Midgley, from England." Jahn and Schwenker also owned a hair works, established in 1882; the business was formerly owned by Mrs. Ellis.[18]

Jane Cleghorn was the Cleghorn of Cleghorn and Son, a fruit, oyster, and fish shop. Mrs. L. Royle owned Royle's Dye Works. Mrs. Jessie Knowles was the Knowles of Knowles and Son, selling hardware, paints, and house furnishings. And in 1874, the three-storey brick Palace Store on one of the main streets was occupied by Mrs. Kelley, where she and her husband, Charles, sold Berlin wools, embroidery, ladies' fancy articles, and other dry goods. Evidently she rented the building, but the store may have been very profitable, for there were several large ads for her business throughout the street directory listings. The ads alternated between her name and her husband's, although C. Pelham

Elizabeth Cuthbert's house in present-day Cabbagetown, Toronto. She was one of many women who owned fancy goods shops.

Mulvany listed Mrs. Kelley as the owner. Mrs. Kelley was also listed as the owner of a school of art.

Women often staffed tollgate booths on roads and bridges. In 1877 Margaret Deniord was the gatekeeper at toll number one on Mill Street, later called Broadview Avenue. Later, in 1894, a teamster ran through that same tollgate without paying, and the gatekeeper at the time, Mrs. Rowan, gave chase in an early motor car. The police apprehended the offender, who then paid the toll.[19]

1880s and 1890s

About thirty years later, in 1880, a historian noted that there were 1,617 female domestic servants and 263 male domestic servants that year, but none of these appeared in the list of residents in the street directories. In many cases, they would be living with their employers, but for some reason, they were not recorded. No servants were listed in the 1833 or 1850 street directories either, although there are stories of the rapid turnover of settlers' servants, both young women and men. In fact, almost every householder reported that it was often impossible to find a female servant, and Anna Jameson noted that "almost all the servants are of the lower class of Irish emigrants, in general honest, warm-hearted, and willing," but did not know "how to serve properly." One source suggests that female servants were paid about a guinea a month along with room and board, while Jameson reported that they gave their own "man-servant eight dollars a month, ... the cook six dollars, and ... the house-maid four," but that this was at the lower end of the wage scale for "good and experienced servants."[20]

At that time, the position of servant was not necessarily degrading, al-though it has been suggested that for a woman it was slavery and only one step above a prostitute; there was an unsubstantiated rumour that the servants' registry that women staffed later in Toronto was in fact only a cover for recruit-ing women for prostitution.[21] Many poor women, however, would travel to the new land on their own only if they were certain of obtaining employment when they arrived. Often, for a young woman, employment in a household would lead to marriage, or at least to some form of training. In many cases, the mistress was able to offer limited home-schooling. Sometimes, though, the young woman was discouraged and returned to her birthplace very quickly.

For a man without sizable funds, working on a farm to help to clear another settler's land, or indeed to maintain it, was the only way he could save enough money to purchase his own lot. Living on the farm or in the house and receiv-ing room and board was the fastest and easiest way to accumulate savings.

The historian Eric W. Sager suggests that domestic service, at least for women, was an occupation of short duration and high turnover and that by 1901, 38 percent of working women were servants, experiencing "long hours, lack of freedom, loneliness, and vulnerability to exploitation and abuse," as well as being poorly paid.[22] That, however, seems like an extremely high per-centage, given the different occupations and vocations available to women and the difficulties many women had in finding a female servant.

The Toronto newspaper, the *Globe*, estimated that by 1868, of the 27,000 women in the city, 5,000, or almost one-fifth, were supporting themselves by earning their own living. This would have been even higher by 1880, as the new city was flourishing. The increase in the number of women who held jobs outside the home at that later time would have kept pace with the population increase, and the great variety of jobs listed in the street directories and available to some women was staggering. As before, several women — widows and spinsters — lived on their own with no listed occupation. The method of recording the women had become more formulaic, though, suggesting that men "owned" the women, symbolically at least. When they were single, women were listed with their maiden names, but after their marriage, they became known only as the husband's wife. If they were widowed, the listing reverted to their first name, but still noted them as the husband's wife. For example, *Miss Mary Brown, spinster,* would become *Mrs. John Jones* on marriage, and then on widowhood, would be listed as *Mrs. Mary Jones, widow of John.* Her maiden name had disappeared, but John Jones remained, even after death — unless, of course, she had remarried.

Again, by far the most common occupations were related to sewing: dressmaker, seamstress, "tailoress," milliner, and mantle maker, with the addition of more exotic activities such as silver and gold embroiderer, ostrich feather dyer, embroiderer and fancy worker, carpet weaver, corset maker, shirtmaker, costumer for theatre, lace dealer, and ladies' shoulder brace manufacturer. Butterick dress patterns for women had become available in 1866, and one woman retailed those. (Men's and boys' patterns had been the first to be created, three years earlier.) And as a result of technology, there were two sewing machine operators; sewing machines had been developed as early as the 1840s but were perhaps not widely available in Canada. C. Pelham Mulvany notes, however, that by 1876 Singer had become a household word, and 262,316 sewing machines were sold by the Singer Company that year. Women were also involved in selling clothes second-hand and in retailing children's wear. For example, in the February 3, 1896, issue of the *Globe,* Mrs. J. Philipps advertised her infants' outfits for sale, with short dresses for only fifty cents. Her shop was on College Street.

Shopkeeping was the second most frequently cited occupation, but again, whether the women owned the shops or worked in them was not usually specified. A number of women were hired to work in factories or to serve the public in stores. In 1868 the *Globe* reported that saleswomen were well paid; their wages averaged from $250 to $300 a year.[23] Possibly, salaries would have been higher in 1880. In 1885 D. McCall & Co., wholesale dealers in millinery, mantles, and fancy dry goods, employed about 150 "girls" among their staff; W.A. Murray & Co. hired "none but the most experienced ladies ... to cater to the wants of a discriminating, purchasing public," but what the public bought is not noted; Anson and Stone, dry goods merchants, had 25 salesmen and ladies involved in manufacture; A.W. Cooper employed a sales staff of 5 ladies and salesmen, selling staples, fancy dry goods, and dress and mourning goods; Petley and Petley, dry goods merchants, hired salesmen and ladies, with a number of "girls" working on the third floor all day; G.W. Dunn employed 14 salesmen and ladies to sell fancy goods; J.H. Shearer, also dry goods merchants, had a staff of 8 "salesmen and ladies"; and Robert Parker owned a steam-dye works and employed 13 males and 21 females. The oldest dry goods shop, however, had been established in 1861

The Vermilyea Corset Company, owned by Hannah Hulett Vermilyea, who hired women for all the positions in the factory — likely more than 350. It produced thousands of corsets every week.

by a woman, Mrs. Halliday, who came to Toronto in 1860; it was noted that the store was well-known. She had two sons associated with her in the business, Alex and John.

The Crompton Corset company hired young ladies, who "followed patterns." At least three corset factories were owned by women in Toronto: Catherine Bondidier and her sister Mary; Hannah Hulett Vermilyea (1847–?, the Vermilyea Corset Company); and Fannie M. Holmes (?–1906, the Corset Specialty Company). Hundreds of women staffed these factories, working as machine operators, office workers, bookkeepers, salespeople, designers, seamstresses, and forewomen. The factory work was very tiring. It required women to sit in one position for hours at a time in a hot environment because of the steam machines used in the production of the garments.

A few women owned confectionaries. Mrs. Lumsden's Confectionary was one of the most popular. Indeed, the street corner where her shop stood was known as "Mrs. Lumsden's corner." Much to the delight of the children in those days, she stocked peppermint pastilles, sugar sticks, marzipan figures, and other treats such as gingerbread hearts. Henry Scadding remembered her, not only because of the delectable sweets she sold, but because his school books were published by Lumsden and Son in Glasgow. Scadding doesn't say whether it was the same family or simply a coincidence. Another woman, Mrs. M. Carrick, owned a bakery and confectionary on Bay Street.[24] Elizabeth Dunlop advertised her King Street confectionary, where she sold preserves as well as catering for a variety of events including weddings.

Women were part of, in some manner, an assortment of other shops: house furnishings, stationery stores, general stores, hardware stores; grocery shops; fruit stores; dry goods and fancy goods stores; variety stores; bookstores; crockery, china, and glass stores; hair goods stores; and other confectionaries. One woman was listed as a butcher; she operated her trade along with her husband. Another woman, Mrs. Swift, had a butcher shop at Queen and Leslie Streets in the 1890s, and there were three "dairy women." Also in the east end, Mary Chambers had a grocery store on Kingston Road after her husband died. She is listed in the 1877 city directory. Othman Manthie's widow, Harriet, had a grocery store on Kingston Road in 1873, and Ellen Elwood, John Elwood's widow, owned a grocery store in Leslieville the same year.

Women still owned a number of boarding houses, taverns, and hotels. They were also involved to a large degree in education, either as teachers or as owners of schools, or both. Other occupations listed for women were watchmaker; gardener; brick manufacturer; bookkeeper; sign painter; "stamping," which was usually listed in connection with fancy goods and embroidery; news depot; tinware; boots and shoes; hairdresser; brush manufacturer; paper bag manufacturer; coal, wood, and ice dealer; toll operator; postmistress (Mary Sedman Trench was the postmistress in 1898 in East Toronto); gatekeeper; baker; cook (a Mrs. Chapman cooked for the garrison at Fort York, according to the well-known early settler Ely Playter, but that could have been a different cook); manageress; "burnisher"; and photo colourist. One woman with the unlikely name of Mrs. T. Rothschild was involved in some way in importing and exporting furs, diamonds, and jewellery. There were washerwomen and laundry women, and at least two women owned the laundries where they worked.

The medical profession was slowly becoming less male: two Toronto women had become doctors and thirteen women were listed as nurses. There were still monthly nurses and midwives, and one woman was a "medicine worker," perhaps working in a drugstore, although the first female pharmacist in Toronto did not graduate from the University of Toronto until 1883.

Six hundred and twenty-four women were noted as paid workers in group homes and institutions, as matrons or other workers, a group not mentioned in directories earlier. And as before, there were very few female servants listed, although six women worked at a "servant registry" indicating a booming business. There were seven chars, fourteen caretakers, one maid, one waiter, and one "lunch room" worker (or owner) listed, all female. Perhaps most of those were hired through the registry.[25]

With a careful reading of J. Ross Robertson's densely worded volumes on the history of Toronto, *Landmarks of Toronto*, one can find a number of references to women's shops and businesses in nineteenth-century downtown Toronto. For example, in a tour of King and Bay Streets, he mentioned that the Misses Lyons had a fancy store; Mrs. M.A. Higgins sold fancy goods; Mrs. J.F. Lyons was a modiste (upscale dressmaker or milliner); Miss Bolster and others were cooks and confectioners; Mrs. Nicholas Strange was a broker

Bell Telephone switchboard operators and their supervisor at the Toronto head office.

and sold second-hand clothes and gave free gossip ("what Mrs. Strange did not know of every family in Toronto from 1830 was not worth knowing"); Mrs. Lepper sold fruit; Misses Mary and Maria Bate were fashionable hairdressers; and Matilda Haas sold embroidery.[26] The Bate sisters' ads were in newspapers.

The telephone was a fairly new invention, and working as a Bell Telephone switchboard operator quickly became an option for women. Several women were working there by 1880, but it was not deemed a particularly safe occupation. In the early 1900s, the new Department of Labour documented a devastating case against the Bell Telephone Company. It was not paying high enough wages to the women compared to the cost of living, and it was thought that the telephone switchboards where they worked were giving them frequent shocks, especially the long-distance operators, resulting in hospitalization, heart failure, and deafness. Some of the women had to work nine hours a day and were paid for only five.[27]

There were other hazards for working women. In 1867 the Toronto *Globe* expressed concern over the plight of women: "There is another class of female labour whose earthly prospects ... are not so bright, these are the widows and orphans." The Bureau of Industry reports and the Royal Commission of 1889 also noted problems for female workers. The commission reported that "women and children may be counted on to work for small wages ... and to work uncomplainingly for long hours." It is also not known if the women listed as dressmakers in the directories worked at home, or if they worked in one of the dressmaking shops where women often fainted because they were "obliged to work in a standing position" and without "proper ventilation." There were obviously serious downsides to the progress women had made in increasing opportunities for salaried employment outside the home.[28]

There were many opportunities for women on the land, although these often involved back-breaking work as well, such as market gardening and brick making. The soil around the Don River Valley and to the east of the river was especially suited to these industries. Left over from the last glacial age, the sandy loam was ideal for horticulture, and the glacial clay deposits contained little organic matter and few pebbles, resulting in smooth bricks. As more communities passed fire laws ruling out the construction of new wooden buildings, bricks were greatly in demand in the province. It was a business that demanded that all the family pitch in; even small children could carry a single brick mould to the drying area.[29] Mary Gapper O'Brien (1798–1876), an immigrant who lived initially in Vaughan Township north of the city, and who visited York on many occasions, commented as early as 1836 that "large brick houses of three and four storeys are taking their place everywhere." Earlier she had written that "it seems to be all suburb ... formed by low scattered houses." Another visitor to York in the 1830s noted that brick was in common use, and in 1831 the writer George Henry remarked in his *Emigrant's Guide* that "a distinguishing feature in the town of York is the numerous substantial brick dwelling-houses."[30]

Although most of the brickyards were held by men, women owned them, too, sometimes inheriting them after their husband's death. In 1869 Jane Morley owned a brickyard in what is now called Leslieville in East Toronto, as did Ada Wagstaff, possibly inheriting hers; the Wagstaffs and Morleys were prominent brick makers in the east end.[31] At least one woman, Emily Walker, owned a shop making brick moulds as well as wheelbarrows and wagons.

In his *History of Ontario*, Alexander Fraser reported that 44.5 percent of the land in the "eastern section" of the township was considered first-class land for agriculture. Consequently there were a number of successful market gardens, and women inherited those, too. After her husband, George, died, Catherine Manus Cooper looked after her seven children and a market garden in Leslieville. (A Mrs. Manus owned a small hardware shop for many years; perhaps it was a relative.) George and Catherine had bought seven acres (2.8 hectares) on what was then called Pape's Avenue. Leslie Creek, one of the Toronto city and area creeks that were later filled in, ran through their property, providing a good source of water for the garden. Elizabeth Sedgwick was a market gardener on the same street in 1869 with her sons, William, Joseph, and Albert. Irish-born Elizabeth Coghlin Logan looked after their market garden after her husband, John, died. Earlier, Elizabeth had driven their wagon with its produce to the market and sold the vegetables while John had remained at home, cultivating. She was well aware of the business.[32] Another widow, Mrs. Flynn, gardened at Colbert Place in 1873, and in 1869, Mrs. Love gardened also in Leslieville.[33]

Toronto annexed much of the land in the east end in 1884, the fiftieth anniversary of the incorporation of the city, and these agriculturalists and brick makers became an integral part of the municipality.

CHAPTER 3

EARLY SETTLERS

A s well as Indigenous people, a few settlers lived in the Toronto area before the Simcoes arrived, such as the squatters William Holmes Peak/Peake and George Crocker, who had homes in the Don Valley as early as the 1780s. Peake was a fur trader who later sold lime, which was used for foundations, and he claimed to be the first settler in York. He and his wife, Margaret, had seven daughters and three sons, and by 1842, fifty-seven grandchildren and nineteen great-grandchildren. Evidently there were enough fish, animals, and plant food to sustain them well. John Coon, a sergeant in the Butler's Rangers, had a house on the Don River, apparently living on his own in a house surrounded by pines. Elizabeth Simcoe visited him and watched him split large blocks of pine to make into shingles. And Parker Mills had a farm close by with a household of two males and five females. In her book of documents of early Toronto, the librarian-historian Edith Firth reproduced a list of 115 men and 97 women who lived in the Township of York in the year 1797.[1]

However, little is known about the other women who lived there before the official beginning of the settlement of York, when one of the first women to arrive was Elizabeth Simcoe. Although Sarah Ashbridge immigrated to

Toronto the same year, Elizabeth must have been there first, as she notes in her diary that when the Ashbridges entered the bay in their boat, they blew a "blast on a big [sea]shell" which they had brought with them and used later as a dinner horn. In fact they had brought two shells. When they blew on the shells, ducks flew up by the thousands from the marsh and the lake. Evidently Elizabeth witnessed this.

Elizabeth had some contact with Sarah Ashbridge, for Elizabeth received seeds for "callibash," a long melon also known as bottle gourd, from the Ashbridges.[2] She also rode out to the Ashbridges' home on occasion to have tea with them.

As Catharine Parr Traill wrote in her well-known *The Backwoods of Canada*, immigrant settlers needed to practise prudence and economy to succeed.[3] Most of the early women settlers described below did succeed, but it was hard work.

Sarah Ashbridge (?–1801)

A widow from Pennsylvania, Sarah came with two sons, Jonathan and John; two married daughters, Elizabeth Wilcot and Mary McLure; and possibly an unmarried third daughter, Hannah, who died in Toronto in 1844. They settled east of the Don River and built first a shanty, then a log cabin, and later a duplex close to the lake on a large tract of land they obtained, even though they were not United Empire Loyalists. The Ashbridges had been Quakers in the United States, but for some reason, possibly neighbourhood quarrelling or because he had owned and sold a Black woman and had been a distiller, the father, Jonathan Ashbridge, had been disowned by the Chester Quaker Meeting there; he died in 1782 either in battle or from battle wounds.[4] The sons farmed their new land in Upper Canada and became respected "pathmasters"; that is, volunteers designated to supervise the construction of the early roads. Initially the family subsisted adequately on food such as fish and waterfowl from the lake and pigs they raised. They earned money from selling ice from the bay in the wintertime for home refrigeration.[5]

Anne Murray Powell (1755–1849)

Anne Powell, wife of the chief justice the Honourable William Dummer Powell, was at first part of the charmed circle of the initial Toronto administrative bureaucracy, even with her background. The daughter of a struggling Scottish physician, Anne was taken to Boston in 1771 by her aunt Elizabeth and established in a millinery shop there, first as the seamstress and later as the manager. But milliners were considered by Anne to be of "low social status," and all her life, she remembered the "irreparable humiliation" of those years. She had also eloped with William Dummer Powell, the son of a prominent merchant, but in spite of these "social embarrassments," Anne's position in Upper Canada, where her husband became a judge, was quite "high" and she became a self-designated arbiter of class standing. In a letter in 1805, she noted that newcomers to York were no addition to their society. "Indeed I have no intercourse with them," she wrote to a friend in New York City. She went on at length to describe various social slights and bad manners — principally when and whether or not people had returned social calls.[6]

The large home of Hannah and Secretary William Jarvis, 1795–1818.

In 1830, in a letter to her friend George Murray, she described the first York Bazaar, which would be held every year in the 1830s, noting that her contribution had been "two netted caps" that were very much admired. But the more important aspect for her appeared to be that the bazaar "speaks well of ... the increase of the number of respectable families."[7]

Anne appeared to be totally obsessed with social standing, probably because of her experiences in Boston, but unfortunately for her, worse was to follow. Her husband's career in Upper Canada ended badly, and her daughter Anne chased after John Beverley Robinson, lawyer, politician, and later lieutenant-governor, who was sailing to England with his new wife. In the end, her daughter Anne died in a shipwreck off the coast of Ireland in a later ship. Anne Sr.'s husband died in 1834 after mental decline; she became deaf and crippled with rheumatism; and one of her granddaughters was divorced for adultery, the first divorce in Upper Canada, bringing more disgrace, in her mind, to her family.[8]

Hannah Delvina Peters Jarvis (1763–1845)

The wife of William Jarvis, the first provincial secretary and registrar, Hannah Jarvis was not particularly happy in York, even though when her house was built it was the largest one in the community. She had difficulty finding good servants — she had three, more than anyone else — and she noted that the country lacked a healthy climate, all far below her customary standard of living. She wrote:

> This is one of the worst places for Servants that can be — they are not to be on any Terms.... We cannot get a Woman who can cook a Joint of Meat unless I am at her Heels — and at the price of seven, eight & nine Dollars per Month.... I have a Scotch girl from the Highlands, Nasty, Sulky, Ill Tempered Creture ... the place is very unhealthy ... a vast number of Persons have died from ... feavor ... We have not had one Night's Sleep for this Month Past.... Mrs.

Hannah Delvina Peters Jarvis with her daughters Maria Lavinia and Augusta Honoria Jarvis. Oil on canvas by American artist James Earl, 1791/2.

Simcoe ... looks like a walking skeleton.... [As for the governor] his health is much impaired, and his eyes and skin are as yellow as saffron and he is peevish beyond description.[9]

Hannah also found a tremendous lack of goods in the new country. She was constantly complaining, writing to her friends and family in England for items such as shoes, good quality calico cloth, castor oil, sulphur, and dance books.

It seems, though, that Hannah's constant unhappiness pervaded her judgment about a lot of events and people. She didn't care for Elizabeth Simcoe, accusing her *"entre nous"* of deliberately being sick in order to avoid attending public balls "to avoid Expense," which was highly unlikely, as Elizabeth loved balls and gay social affairs and had lots of money. Life was evidently against Hannah, which was Mrs. Simcoe's fault: Mrs. Simcoe's linens arrived in good condition, but Hannah's were "mildewed." Hannah claimed that people didn't like "Petecoat Laws" — that is, Elizabeth Simcoe. "I am sorry that the Governor did not come out solo," she wrote. She hoped that Simcoe and his wife would be detained in England and "a Man who is fond of Justice" sent out instead.[10]

Hannah had been born in the United States and went to England when her father's strong conservative views forced him to flee Connecticut. She met and married William Jarvis, and in 1792 his family immigrated to Upper Canada on Simcoe's recommendation. But Hannah's life did not turn out particularly happily. She detested "the little stuttering Vixon," another term she used for Elizabeth Simcoe. Hannah and her husband lived extravagantly; they were noted for their ostentation. Unfortunately, her husband lost most of his wealth, and a son — one of eight children — was jailed for murder as a result of a duel. After William died, Hannah ended up virtually destitute, living with a widowed daughter. Where once she had eight servants and slaves, now she gardened, washed, ironed, scrubbed, cleaned, mended, and cooked for herself and her daughter's family. Sometimes there wasn't even food in the house. Her diary describes her drudgery. Nevertheless, Hannah lived a long life for that time, dying at age eighty-two.

Hannah's cookbook has recently been published, showing how many products had to be made by the housewife at that time. Apart from basics such as candles and soap, there are recipes in her book for various items such as cement and paint, shoe polish, insecticides, ale, and foods such as corn pudding.[11]

Elizabeth Russell (1754–1822)

While most residents and early settlers appreciated John Graves Simcoe's attempt at fairness, his administrator, the Honourable Peter Russell, treated people somewhat differently. Russell, the Irish-born receiver general, came out a year after Simcoe, and was called "the man who would do well unto himself." As the historian Mulvany wrote, it was common for Russell to "grant himself large tracts of valuable land." Mulvany noted that "the in-iquitous system of land monopoly began to flourish," although Peter Russell has also been described in more flattering terms. But according to Mulvany, Russell felt that those on the executive council should be compensated for their inadequate salaries and unusual expenses, such as the high cost of servants.[12]

Elizabeth and Peter, her half-brother, lived together from 1786 on. They owned slaves and advertised them for sale in newspapers such as the *Gazette* and *Oracle*:

> A black woman named Peggy, aged forty years, and a black boy her son, named Jupiter, aged about fifteen years, both of them the property of the subscriber.... The woman is a tol-erable cook and washerwoman, and perfectly understands making soap and candles.... The price set upon Peggy is $150, and upon Jupiter, junior, $200. Payable in three years, with interest from the day of sale ... one-fourth less for ready money.[13]

At one time, Elizabeth had given a slave, Amy Pompadour, to her friend Mrs. Captain Denison as a gift.

A number of officials, including the secretary, William Jarvis, also owned slaves. In 1811 Jarvis accused a slave boy and a girl of stealing gold and silver out of the desk in his house. He demanded prison sentences for both of them, as well as for a free adult Black man he accused of aiding the younger couple.

At the same time, the solicitor general, Isaac Dey Gray, freed Dorinda, the slave in his possession, leaving a large sum of money for her and her heirs. John Graves Simcoe was opposed to slavery and in 1793 tried to abolish it in Upper Canada, but so many influential people were against abolition that he could only effect a compromise: There would be no new slaves in Upper Canada, and the ones already there were to be freed when they reached the age of twenty-five.[14]

SLAVERY IN CANADA

Most Canadians do not realize that the practice of enslaving African Black people happened in Canada. Enslaved people had no rights. Some owners treated them very cruelly, including inflicting physical and sexual abuse. Families could be torn apart as members were sold or given away. Lawrence Hill's *The Book of Negroes*, while fiction, provides horrific examples of the barbaric treatment that slave traders and owners inflicted on Black slaves. However, even when owners treated enslaved people less harshly, they were property, not seen as human beings.

The English slave trade of Black people is thought to have begun in 1562. While Portugal and Britain accounted for about 70 percent of all Africans kidnapped and transported to the Americas, Britain was the most dominant between 1640 and 1807. It is estimated that Britain abducted over three million African men, women, and children and brought them to the British colonies through enslavement. This practice was not abolished until 1807.

Many of the people enslaved in Canada in the eighteenth-century were brought from the United States by their owners, who were part of the United Empire Loyalist diaspora. After slavery was abolished in Upper Canada, many of the freed people returned to the United States. Although Simcoe worked to abolish slavery in 1793, it was not until 1834 that slavery was abolished in the British Empire.

In an early letter Elizabeth Russell wrote to a friend in 1799, she said that she liked "Slaying [sleighing] on the Ice on which about a mile & quarter we go across the Bay to the opposite side to the Lake ... on which there is charming riding or driving to the Length of eight miles [thirteen kilometres]," but in spite of her enjoyment she mentioned several "difficultys" — "paying a woman from three and nine pence to four and sixpence a day only for scrubbing your

Elizabeth Jane McMurray wearing a common nineteenth-century hairstyle for young women.

House, and to a man upwards 5 shillings a day for cutting wood." She found everything in York very expensive compared to what it had cost in England. She also asked her friends to send dresses and dressmaking supplies, both for "visiting afternoon" and "morning" dresses.[15] It was important to have the correct type of dress for each occasion: visiting, dances, concerts, and so on. Even fairly ordinary people such as teenaged Elizabeth Jane McMurray Turnbull took her black velvet dress for "appearing in company" when she visited her aunt and uncle in Niagara-on-the-Lake in the 1850s.[16]

In York, Elizabeth Russell and her brother first lived in a log house "consisting of only two small rooms on the ground floor," which Peter bought because it was the only one he could get. "It is quite a poor cottage," she wrote, "but it is much better than it was when we first came as then it didn't keep out the weather," surely a comedown for the Russells. Soon, however, they lived in what was termed Russell Abbey. Some called it the Palace. It was a one-storey building, but according to the historian Henry Scadding, who was a child at the time, it was of a peculiar design: "To a central building were attached wings with gables to the south; the windows had each an architectural decoration or pediment over it" giving the house a "monastic air." The historian J. Ross Robertson called it a "pretentious edifice."[17]

During the war of 1812–1814, in order to escape the conflict, Elizabeth Russell loaded her phaeton (carriage) with all sorts of "necessities," and with a servant driving, she walked with her friends — about eight men and women — four miles (six and a half kilometres) north on Yonge Street through the bush to the log house of land owner and military man Baron Frederick de Hoven/ Hoen, a friend of the Baldwins. One of the women carried a baby on her back the whole way. Three days later, they reversed their journey, just in time to prevent the American soldiers from ransacking the Russells' house. Afterwards, she "entertained" two of the American officers, perhaps forced to billet them.[18]

Peter Russell became the administrator after John Graves Simcoe left. Elizabeth Simcoe rarely mentioned Elizabeth Russell in her writings, although she did compliment Elizabeth Russell on her method of preserving cherries and the way she pressed leaves of plants in books. Elizabeth Russell had a lovely garden and was not averse to turning dogs loose on the pigs that rooted up the grass in front of her house, a problem that obviously lasted for some time, as the community named volunteer hog catchers every year.

Sarah Lord Helliwell (1773–1842)

A small cotton manufacturer, Thomas Helliwell left England clandestinely in 1817, as manufacturers were needed in England and were therefore refused permission to emigrate. That summer, his family followed. Sarah Lord Helliwell, Thomas's wife, brought the youngest five of their children — ranging in age from one to twenty-one — on her own, leaving a son to come later. A married daughter, Elizabeth, had already immigrated to Canada. Seven-year-old William wrote later of their voyage that they had "knocked about the ocean" for seven weeks, but it was more "tempestuous and dangerous" on Lake Ontario, sailing to Queenston at the western end of the lake.

Their whole voyage was one of extreme hardship. After leaving Liverpool, their ship, the *Abeona*, ran aground and then sprung a leak; they had to put back to port for three days. When they reached New York City, most of the passengers remained there to take legal action against the captain for his bad seamanship, but the Helliwells obtained a small boat for themselves and their possessions and sailed to Pelham Bay, then to Albany, then to Schenectady. There they changed boats and went to Oswego, then Lewiston after a stormy passage, and then to Queenston, Upper Canada.[19] In 1818 the Helliwells opened a store there, and in 1819, Sarah and some of the children moved to Niagara Falls, where the family rented and operated a distillery. The next year they travelled to York, with Sarah seated on a chair inside a kettle they used for the brewery.

A posthumous portrait of Sarah Lord Helliwell, brewster, 1844.

There had been mills on the Don River in York since the summer of 1779, and it was the lower mills on the east side that Thomas bought and operated after they came to York in 1820. The Helliwells added a distillery, a brewery, a malt house, and a home for themselves of sun-dried adobe bricks on ten acres in the Don Valley. There they found the pure water they needed, grain, and yeast from the hop garden that a Mrs. James Case grew nearby. They also found bears, sheep-eating wolves, and deer.[20]

The roads in the area were so bad that in the summer, when it was almost impossible to navigate over mud and stumps, the Helliwells hired a white-haired, sharp-featured hermit who lived in the valley — Joseph Tyler — to transport their beer over the river in his forty-foot canoe, *The Lady of the Don*. The canoe could hold twenty-two barrels and two people. The Helliwells had a contract to sell beer to the Fort York garrison; in 1792, each soldier was allowed six pints of beer a day, so Thomas had a steady profitable market.[21]

Thomas died in 1823, and Sarah inherited the operation. Her son William praised her as a "splendid businesswoman." Her sons were each left shares in the business, which they were to be given when they reached twenty-one. Her daughters were left more tangible goods, including money, and Mary, who had just got engaged, also received one yoke of steers, one cow and one calf, a feather bed and bedding, six chairs, one table, and other small furniture.[22]

It is doubtful that Sarah participated to any degree in the social life of the city. While a very capable woman, she did not come from an aristocratic or upper-middle-class background in England, and her concerns and personality suggest that she was more interested in her family and their businesses. In any case, she would probably not have been welcomed by some of the wives of the administrators who had become what was later termed the Family Compact, an informal group of wealthy, self-serving, powerful bureaucrats. As Anna Jameson wrote:

> Toronto is like a fourth or fifth rate provincial town, with the pretensions of a capital city. We have here a petty colonial oligarchy, a self-constituted aristocracy, based upon nothing real, nor even upon anything imaginary; and we have all the mutual jealousy and fear, and petty gossip, and mutual

meddling and mean rivalship, which are common in a small society of which the members are well known to each other.[23]

Sarah was not the only woman to own a mill around Toronto. In the north of Toronto, in what is now the community of Thornhill, a sawmill was erected in 1820 with a gristmill added later on. When it was enlarged and named the Pomona Mills, the complex was owned by a Mrs. Harris. Eventually there would be at least twenty-two mills on the Don River alone.[24]

Julia Maria Lambert (1792–1861)

Julia Lambert hadn't intended to remain in Canada, but after her older sister Susan died in 1840, she remained in Toronto with her sister's widower, the Honourable George Crookshank, as his chatelaine, and helped with the children. Crookshank's brother wrote that Julia "managed everything in such a quiet way I think it is a pleasure to be under the same roof. What an excellent wife some Blockhead has missed."[25]

Born into a well-to-do educated family in the United States, Julia began visits to York, Upper Canada, in 1821 when her thirty-nine-year-old sister married. Susan bore children in 1823, 1825, and 1829, when she was forty-one, forty-three, and forty-seven years old, respectively, a rather advanced age for beginning a family. Julia would travel to Susan's home to help out, and while she was there, she wrote a number of letters to her family in Connecticut and New York. She described the social events they participated in, such as dinners and balls. Because Crookshank was a United Empire Loyalist, a legislative councillor of Upper Canada, and receiver general of the province of Ontario at one point, there were a number of events he and his family would be expected to attend. And for the women of the élite, or the Family Compact, visiting back and forth would be almost constant. Julia, however, seemed as interested, if not more so, in governmental affairs, legal challenges, educational facilities, and the intolerable state of the roads around Toronto. She would easily have dispensed with the visiting, but as she noted, it "seems here [in Toronto] to be thought indispensable."[26]

Julia Maria Lambert. Painting by American Thomas Sully, 1814, oil on canvas.

She described York as "not as large as I expected and the houses are a good deal more scattered. The town would make much more of an appearance if it was more compact, but probably the dwellings would not be as pleasant.... There appears to be considerable style kept up tho' I cannot see the necessity," she wrote to another sister, Elizabeth Lambert in Wilton, Connecticut. The letters in the collection ceased in 1854, five years before Julia's death.[27]

Mary Sophia Gapper O'Brien (1798–1876)

Mary Gapper O'Brien had come to North America as an adventurer, but she remained as a wife. Her life was a busy one. On June 8 she wrote in her diary:

> We breakfast at six, before which I expect my little lassie [servant] to dust and arrange the parlour while I am helping the children to dress, skimming the milk, and looking at the cows and poultry. The latter, now that the hatchling season is here, require a more experienced hand than Willy's [farmhand] to adjust all their affairs. After breakfast I arrange all my household affairs and give orders for the day's proceedings so as to avoid as much as possible future interruption. Then I complete the business of the dairy and give Willy his reading lesson, the little damsels meanwhile furbishing in their department.... This with a few minutes' gossip, brings me to about nine o'clock ... the girls read to me.... At eleven o'clock the boys come in from the field ... then we sit to lessons until dinner time — one o'clock.... After dinner I finish the girls separate lessons which continue ... into the evening.... I have unintentionally got more teaching on my hands than I intended, and my spirits sometimes shrink from it.

A cultivated Englishwoman, thirty-year-old Mary Gapper had sailed to Canada in 1828 on the *Warrior* with her widowed mother to visit two of her brothers, half-pay officers who had farms north of Toronto in what is today called Thornhill. An adventurer, she promised her sister in England that she would come back to help raise her sister's large family. However, she met an old friend of one of her brothers, Edward O'Brien, also a farmer and British half-pay officer, and after some deliberation, decided to accept Edward's offer of marriage and remain in Canada. Her life seems to have been happy, even with very few outings away from their farm — to Toronto, to church, and to visit her other brother — and of course, she taught her own and some neighbours' children.

Soon after she arrived, Mary, with her sisters-in-law, started organizing a book society in which men and women read and discussed books, similar to book clubs today. It took some months to launch; the main stumbling blocks were the cost of and access to books in Upper Canadian society, especially in the rural areas. For example, a bachelor neighbour, Squire Miles, responded to Mary's invitation to join that he had already spent many dollars that year in purchasing Paley's *Josephus*, and his neighbours were to share that expense. By October 25, 1828, she had mustered only six members. So she began a library twice, then and later on when they moved north to Lake Simcoe. These societies were open to women at a time when most book clubs were open only to men on a regular basis. Not only did she promote a book group, but later she hosted a meeting of neighbours who were organizing a temperance society.

The daughter of a clergyman, Mary was reasonably well-educated, speaking both Italian and French. When she sailed to Canada, she was learning German and teaching her nephew and niece, children of her sister Mary Sophia, who had also married a clergyman. Edward O'Brien, the man Mary Sophia married, knew Latin, French, Spanish, and Arabic.

Mary noted that on their farm, in addition to the housework, the garden and the dairy were to be her "special care." Not that she liked housework: "Domestic arrangements, I must confess, are not much to my fancy, either in theory or in practice. However, if Edward thinks that I do it well and praises me a little sometimes, I suppose I shall like it well enough," she wrote on April 26, 1829. On June 11 of that year, she wrote that she managed to milk the cows after her third attempt, and she succeeded in making butter, "sitting under the verandah and reading Milton all the time." On July 1, 1830, she recorded that she had made two puddings and a pie, baked two loaves and a cake, and made two pounds of butter, besides preparing two dinners and keeping her house in order. She was, indeed, proud of her accomplishments.

Mary and Edward continued to have a busy and active life. Around 1845 they moved to the centre of the City of Toronto, enrolling their sons at Upper Canada College. With his government connections, Edward worked in a number of interesting positions and died at the age of seventy-six. Mary lived to seventy-eight.[28]

Anne Langton (1804–1893)

A single woman of thirty-three, Anne Langton emigrated in 1837 with her parents and aunt to join her younger brother John in Canada, although she wondered seriously at times whether she should remain in the new country or return to England and stay with her older brother William and his family. Her own family had been living in "reduced circumstances" ever since her father's business had failed and they had lost their stately home; she would be going back to a life quite different from the one she had known earlier. In the end she decided to face the adventure of living in Upper Canada and spent her last years in Toronto. A talented and well-educated woman, she operated an unofficial "parlour" school in her home for neighbourhood children, teaching reading and writing. She also sketched; painted, especially miniatures; and made and played musical instruments, although little in Canada, possibly because of increasing deafness. However, she was the organist and choir director at St. John's Anglican Church for a short time, from 1852 to 1855.[29]

A very observant woman, Anne offered advice for new settlers in her letters to her older brother, perhaps hoping that William would join them. She wrote that one should have at least one thousand pounds to begin to operate a farm in Canada, and even at that, one would have to economize. She was used to having servants, but retaining them was always a problem, many of the girls being too young to have much knowledge or many skills. She noted that some of the settlers, even the wealthier ones, had given up hiring servants and looked after the work themselves. While she felt this was a good idea, and at times was forced into that position herself, she still maintained help as much as possible.

She had advice about sea travel as well, having undergone some discomfort on the packet ship *Independence*. "Bring a small mattress" she wrote; she had been tossed about on a hard surface for days. Also bring a few "basin cloths." Evidently her "wash-hand basin" had not been as scrupulously clean as she wanted. And bring some books, as the ship's books often had pages missing. And one might consider avoiding a packet ship completely, she suggested. In Upper Canada itself, the roads were in dreadful shape, as every settler commented, full of stones, stumps, and other obstacles. You will need a supply of strong shoes, she wrote; "even in fine summer weather the frost will be wet, and you can never reckon upon going any distance without encountering some spot where the water has been dammed up by some wood obstruction."[30]

She also had thoughts about the lot of women in the country. In October 1838, Anne wrote in a letter:

> I have caught myself wishing an old long-forgotten wish that I had been born of the rougher sex. Women are very dependent here, and give a great deal of trouble; we feel our weakness more than anywhere else. This, I cannot but think, has a slight tendency to sink us, it may be, into a more natural and proper sphere than the one we occupy in over-civilized life.[31]

Once when John refused to take her out in their canoe, she wrote:

> John does not like the responsibility of taking me out in one and thinks it altogether an unfit conveyance for so helpless a being as a woman. I, having a due value for my precious life, should be sorry to urge the risk of it, but I am rather glad the idea did not spring up earlier.[32]

"I am afraid women deteriorate in this country more than the other sex," she wrote in 1840; when "the elegancies of her person become her chief concern and pride, then she must fall, and be contented to be looked upon as belonging merely to the decorative department of the establishment and valued accordingly." And on another day: "I have sometimes thought, and I may as well say it, now that it is grumbling day — woman is a bit of a slave in this country."[33]

Anne also commented on the widespread destruction of trees in the country. So many trees were burned in clearing the land and especially in keeping warm. "We burn, on average, about two trees *per diem*.... In a general way, I think two fifths of each tree is chopped into chips, a mountain of which accumulates about the yard, and is very difficult to get rid of." And if people burned their maple trees, she pointed out, they had to go without maple sugar, their only form of sweetener.[34]

Mary Wickson Armstrong (1819–1881)

When she was fifteen, Mary Wickson left her home in England, along with her parents and eight siblings, and immigrated to Upper Canada. Her father was a corn merchant and a chandler, a dealer in wax and candles, and appears to have moved quite often. In Toronto in 1834, her father became a butcher. Three years later, Mary married Philip Armstrong, who had immigrated a few years earlier as well. His father had died just before Philip was born, and his mother managed on weaving cotton until she passed away. Philip first married Mary Calvert; they had three children, but the first two died in infancy. Then Mary died in 1837, only twenty-nine years old. When nineteen-year-old Mary Wickson and twenty-nine-year-old Philip married in 1837, he was a widower with a young daughter, Anne. He, too, became a butcher on Toronto's main street. The next year, Mary and Philip had a son, Thomas. Ten years later, when Anne was eighteen, she married Robert Pallett, another butcher.[35]

There were a number of butchers in York and early Toronto. In 1828 there were twenty-two listed in the market building alone, one for every hundred residents. It has been suggested that Toronto earned its name of Hogtown because it raised so many hogs, producing lots of peameal bacon; on the other hand it might have been a pejorative name from those envious of the benefits of the city!

Philip, however, was not only a successful butcher but a small farmer as well. Mary took care of the poultry and the dairy; at the market she sold calves, chickens, eggs, lard, butter, vegetables, and aprons she made herself. She named her cows: Daisy, Short Horns, Butter Cup, Shamrock; it must have been difficult to have them slaughtered or sold. She bought fruit trees and roses with the money she earned at the market.

Philip gradually became more involved in the life of the city. He became a judge at agricultural shows and helped to plan the first Industrial Exhibition in Toronto, held in 1879. Unfortunately he died before it took place. He had also become a justice of the peace. By this time, their son, Thomas, was a doctor; he and his wife, Fidelia Jane Maughan (1845–1928), had six children. Other members of Mary's family were also entering middle-class occupations. Her younger brother, Samuel, became a barrister and solicitor; another brother,

Arthur, had studied for the ministry in the Congregational Church and also taught at their theological college, the Canadian Congregational Theological Institute. (The Congregational Church had an extremely popular preacher in the 1880s, attracting an average Sunday attendance of around twelve hundred, with about five hundred being turned away.) A brother, John, owned a large slaughterhouse just outside the city limits.[36]

It was only in 1859 that Mary began her diary — or at least the one that survives. But this was far from leisure time; Mary still had a household to care for. Her stepdaughter had died, and she was caring for her child, eleven-year-old Mary Ann Pallett; her son the medical student; her brother, Samuel; and perhaps the four farmhands that Philip required for his burgeoning farmlands. But Mary and Philip were becoming more prosperous. They had their own carriage; previously Mary had to take the omnibus to travel downtown. They were able to buy some "good" furniture, including black-walnut pieces and a small table for over seventy dollars, even though it was at a bailiff's sale.[37]

Mary's diary describes a relatively happy, uneventful married life of a middle-class Torontonian of the 1850s and 1860s. Her husband now and then displayed a bad temper, but that seems to have been her only problem. Unlike most women of her day, she had only one child of her own, but she spent time with her grandchildren. She helped her step-granddaughter with needlework, as her mother had done with her. She bought more goods from shopkeepers as the years advanced rather than having to spend time producing the items she needed herself. She had housekeeping help, as did many women. She enjoyed reading and was able to buy books, but her sight was affected by years of sewing in the dim light of the fireplace. She belonged to the Wesleyan Missionary Society and attended lectures sponsored by the Temperance Reformation Society and on other subjects. On many Sundays she went to church twice. It seems that small happenings were the main interests in her life; almost every day when she was keeping a diary, she recorded how many eggs her hens had laid. She watched the birds on her farm and identified them; she noticed which trees were in leaf or in bloom, which flowers had grown. Her concerns were varied, but very local.[38]

Jennie Fleming (1843–1942)

Women living in outlying areas might visit Toronto shops to find goods for their own stores. In 1869 Jennie Fleming travelled south from her home at Kilsyth near Owen Sound, to Toronto to purchase items she would then sell in the general store she co-managed with her two brothers, William and Charles, although her particular skill was bookkeeping. The idea that early settlers managed to become totally self-sufficient is a romantic ideal. Most settlers had to visit stores for many of their provisions and other materials, so the store owners needed to keep a wide variety of supplies such as textiles, clothing, sewing items, shoes and boots, hardware, livestock, lumber, and imported groceries, as well as alcohol. The most sought-after items were those that later on were still the most common: tea, tobacco, sugar, and cotton. The historian Douglas McCalla has calculated that in the 1820s, there were 470 merchant shops in Upper Canada, one for every 349 people, a ratio that was fairly consistent throughout the nineteenth century.[39]

Jennie's parents had emigrated from Scotland in 1843; Jennie was born in Canada. She later became an advocate of women in politics, business, industry, and social work, attitudes held by women as the century progressed. She never married and devoted her time to her nephew and her two nieces; her volunteer work, especially as treasurer in the local Woman's Christian Temperance Union (WCTU); and her church, the Disciples of Christ, where she taught Sunday school for many years. She also became the national secretary of the WCTU, the treasurer of the provincial missionary board of her church, and a member of the Browning Reading Circle, the Women's Art Association, and the Owen Sound Horticultural Society. She lived to be almost one hundred, spending her last years in Owen Sound.[40]

Jennie took part in the work of the family farm, and had her own special section: an orchard and vineyard on four acres. She travelled to Great Britain with her family and helped build a cottage near her home. She was energetic and filled her time with interesting activities. Jennie's trip to Toronto may have been one of many; her surviving diary covers only a few years. But she had a long list of public places she wanted to visit, suggesting that this trip was somewhat extraordinary: the art gallery and library at the Toronto Normal

School, Osgoode Hall, the grounds at the asylum, the flowers and shrubbery at Trinity College, the Mechanics' Institute and School, James Parochial School, University College Museum, the Commercial College, Trafalgar Castle in Whitby, and the Methodist Church in Oshawa. Apart from shopping, her main purpose, however, was to participate in a Disciples of Christ conference in Bowmanville. In her diary, Jennie described another trip she took in 1871 to Marquette, Michigan, on the shore of Lake Superior.[41]

Susanna Strickland Moodie (1803–1885)

In 1831 Susanna Strickland married Lieutenant John W.D. Moodie; they immigrated to Upper Canada the next year from England. John had wanted to go to South Africa. Susanna opted for Canada, a decision she must have often regretted. She is best known for her books *Roughing It in the Bush* (1852) and *Life in the Clearings* (1853), which describe the innumerable hardships she and her family endured in their new country and their almost constant financial problems, which she believed were the result of circumstances beyond their control, simply bad luck. As she wrote at the end of *Roughing It in the Bush*:

> If these sketches should prove the means of deterring one family from sinking their property, and shipwrecking all their hopes, by going to reside in the backwoods of Canada, I shall consider myself amply repaid for revealing the secrets of the prison-house, and feel that I have not toiled and suffered in the wilderness in vain.[42]

Susanna and Catharine Parr Strickland Traill were sisters; both married half-pay officers of the British army and both immigrated with their husbands to Upper Canada. They came from a refined and educated background to join their brother, Samuel Strickland, in the uncultivated woods of Upper Canada.

When Susanna first saw her new farm and home in the Upper Canadian bush, she was terrified, and "her eyes were brimming with tears." She had been sent ahead of her husband with her new baby and a servant while her husband was to follow with the luggage. Her driver had been reckless and daring, but when she arrived at the "dilapidated old doorless shanty, just then doing duty as a cattle pen," she begged the driver to stay. But the "driver laughed loud at her fears, cracked his whip and drove away." Susanna sat down with her maid and child in the middle of the filth and watched the rain coming in through the walls, the roof, the door-opening, and the windows. Soon, however, they had a shelter of evergreen boughs on the edge of a creek, and with the protection of a blazing fire to keep the mosquitos away, they stayed there until their shanty was raised.[43]

However, Susanna wrote plainly about the conditions of many log houses:

> Public newspapers and private letters ... talked of log houses to be raised in a single day, by the generous exertions of friends and neighbours, but they never ventured upon a picture of the disgusting scenes of riot and low debauchery exhibited during the raising, or upon a description of the dwelling when raised — dens of dirt and misery, which would, in many instances, be shamed by an English pig-sty.[44]

Susanna wrote in order to earn money for their survival, and she painted birds and butterflies on the fungi that grew on the trunks of maple trees. These she sold as well as her stories, and they earned enough money "to buy shoes" for her little children. She and Catharine had both earned money by writing in England earlier. But writing was never that profitable. As Catharine wrote:

> I am now old, I am four score years of age. I believe that I have not been altogether a useless member of the community though I have reaped very little pecuniary benefit from my literary labours, my yearly income being very small, but I would like to do something more for Canada my adopted country before I am called to my rest.[45]

Susanna was the sixth daughter of a previously successful London businessman who became bankrupt. She was a golden-haired, beautiful child, the last daughter after Catharine Parr. Their father ensured that all the girls learned literature, history, the classics, arithmetic, and some science in their home school. Their mother taught them the usual arts of the gentlewoman: deportment, needlework, sketching, and household management, as well as religion and morality. The two girls were very different in personality, although very close friends. Catharine, or Katie as she was called by friends, was cheerful, loving all people and loved in return, and interested in nature. Susanna was the total opposite: moody, willful, and very intense.[46]

On July 1, 1832, Susanna and John sailed on the brig *Anne* from Leith, Scotland, with seventy-two steerage passengers, for a long voyage of sixty-two days. Catharine and her husband, Thomas, sailed a week later from Greenock on the brig *Laurel*, the only passengers on the cargo ship. They arrived in Quebec City first, but Catharine contracted cholera, which was spreading rapidly that year. Fortunately, she was nursed back to health by her Montreal landlady's compassionate sister.

Life was not easy for John and Susanna. John was not used to hard physical labour and he was not very strong. He was also too trusting and honest to survive well in the Upper Canadian bush. It wasn't long before he had lost most of his money in bad investments and ill-advised land purchases. Susanna was too intractable in her relationships with those who were from a "lower class" than hers. Unfortunately, as William Cattermole noted, in the bush, it was absolutely "indispensable" to be on good terms with one's neighbours, and Susanna often didn't get along with hers. She described her first neighbours as rude, "unnurtured," dirty, and a bunch of savages whom she feared. As the writer Audrey Morris noted, "Upper class snobbery on one side was met with lower class snobbery on the other, and at no time was any attempt made at understanding." For example, Susanna refused to sit down with the hired help at mealtimes in a one-room cabin; as a result, she became very lonely and unhappy. Soon after settling on their new farm, she wrote in verse in the form of a man talking to his sweetheart:[47]

> Oh can you leave your native land,
>   An Exile's bride to be, —
> Your Mother's home and cheerful hearth,
>   To tempt the Main with me? —

Across the wide Atlantic,
   To trace our foaming tack,
And know the wave that heaves us on,
   Will never bear us back?

And can you in Canadian wilds
   With me the harvest bind,
Nor feel one ling'ring sad regret
   For all you leave behind?
Can lily hands unused to toil,
   The woodsman's wants supply —
Nor shrink beneath the chilly blast,
   When wintry storms are nigh?[48]

Finally, John was offered a job in Belleville as a sheriff. They would survive financially — just. John had to buy clothes to send to them before Susanna and their three boys could move to town; they had sold everything they had in order to exist. Susanna was frightened by the move, although obviously relieved. Described as tall and dark, thin, and intense with deep-set eyes when she came to Canada, seven years later she claimed she looked coarse and weathered from the hard work and constant exposure to sun and wind. She declared that she was "no longer fit for the world," that she looked twice the age she was at thirty-six, and that her hair was sprinkled with grey. But both John and Susanna lived a good long life — John to age seventy-two and Susanna to eighty-two, when the average life expectancy was in the forties for both men and women. After her husband's death, Susanna lived with friends or with her son Robert or daughter Katie in Toronto.[49]

Fortunately these women's diaries or small writings have been saved and can provide us with snapshots of their everyday activities and some of their problems. Other women described in the next chapter, who were in Toronto or the area for only a short time as part of their tours, leave us with a different understanding of the difficulties facing women.

CHAPTER 4

ADVENTURERS

W omen have been world travellers since the beginning of recorded history, oftentimes disguised as men, sometimes alone or with their partner, and other times in groups. Missionary women were particularly well-travelled. A few writings of early women travellers have survived, such as that of the Spanish nun Egeria, who travelled to the "Holy Land" around 381 and wrote an account of her trip; the fourteenth- and fifteenth-century English mystic Margery Kempe (1373–1438), who travelled around Europe and the "Holy Land"[1] and wrote of her travels in *The Book of Margery Kempe*, which may have been the first book in English; and numerous Quakers who travelled in the seventeenth and eighteenth centuries in Britain and around the world and recorded their adventures. Perhaps the most travelled woman in Western history was the British Methodist missionary Dorothy Ripley (1767–1831), whom some sources say crossed the Atlantic Ocean nineteen times, although other accounts list nine crossings, mostly alone. In either case, she became a seasoned traveller.[2]

The American writer and professor emeritus Thomas Philbrick notes that "intrepid eccentric" Victorian women were a special breed of travellers, journeying around the world and then producing public accounts of their trips.

For example, Isabella Bird, the first female fellow of the Royal Geographical Society, went to countries such as Tibet, China, Korea, Hawaii, Japan, Egypt, Australia, and New Zealand, as well as Canada and the United States. Whereas young twentieth-century women did the traditional European tour, young well-to-do Victorian women were often sent on a North American trip. Philbrick's description of women who travelled — women such as Anna Jameson — as "eccentric" can, of course, be challenged, but certainly they had to be "intrepid." One wonders why they persisted, given the discomfort and dangers of both land and sea travel. In her 1830 sea crossing in the ship *Friends*, the Methodist missionary Elizabeth Blake Peters (1801–1894) managed to keep her food down, but she could not bear the stench and taste of the drinking water on the ship. "If we could get fresh water, I should not at any time dislike a sea voyage," she wrote. Because it was stored in wooden casks the drinking water soon became contaminated, and vinegar was added to "alleviate" the taste, odour, and pollution.[3]

Anna Jameson described part of her sea voyage on the ship *Ontario* in 1836:

> I can give you no idea of the Hurly-burly of the elements, the shrieking of the winds thro' the rigging, the roaring of the waves which broke over the ship and poured into the cabin.... The Captain ordered some mattresses and pillows on the deck. I was carried upstairs and laid down; I fainted continually but persisted in remaining, as the air was my only chance.[4]

Three nineteenth-century adventurers are described in this chapter. They are no Victorian shrinking violets.

Elizabeth Posthuma Gwillim Simcoe (1762–1850)

Elizabeth Simcoe was not an adventurer in the sense of a women who travelled around the world on her own, yet she regarded her trip to Upper Canada as an exciting adventure. Much can be gleaned about her from her diaries and other people's recollections. The historian C. Pelham Mulvany described Elizabeth as "a very amiable and attractive lady of thirty-one." The Duc de la Rochefoucauld described her as a "woman of sense … and (she) fulfills all the duties of a mother and wife with the most scrupulous exactness." She was termed by another historian as charming, with "winning manners." Henry Scadding described her as having "superior intellectual endowments." In Upper Canada, she acted as her husband's unofficial private secretary, helping him not only socially, but also by making plans and maps for his use, and the first outline plan of the new settlement of York.[5]

Not everybody liked her, however, and some suggested that what Elizabeth wanted, Elizabeth got. One Niagara resident wrote, "Everybody are sick at York — but no matter — the Lady likes the place — therefore every one else must."[6] Her husband, John Graves Simcoe, appears to have adored her, though, and apparently he had a very romantic streak. Once, when she was coming back from Quebec City on her own and he was waiting for her at Kingston, he wrote this poem to her:

> Twice six revolving years the Sun his course
> Thru yonder azure plains, diffusing joy
> Gladness and light, has discontinuous moved
> Since thou, Eliza, ever flowing source
> Of happiness domestic, dost employ
> My wedded thoughts, most honoured and most beloved!
> And if the gathering clouds of fleeting Life
> Arise, thy presence soon illumes the Scene
> And pleasure draws from elemental strife!
> And now when night and absence intervene
> O may my wishes wing Thy speedy way
> Return thou source of Joy, return thou source of Day.[7]

The historian Mulvany was obviously biased in favour of John Graves Simcoe and his government. He considered that time to be Toronto's golden years:

> Then none were for a party,
> Then all were for the state,
> And the rich man helped the poor,
> And the poor man helped the great.[8]

It was a rather rosy picture of the early settlement, although many immigrants believed, quite falsely, that they were coming to an egalitarian society where there were "no masters and no pecking order."[9] As Mulvany himself wrote, there was, at the beginning of York, an "amount of wealth and refinement not often to be found in the society of pioneer cities," well-illustrated by the Simcoes. But his verbal portrait of Elizabeth Simcoe was consistent with that of most others who met her.[10]

Elizabeth had grown up in Devon, England, an orphan from a baby, albeit a wealthy one, cared for by her mother's sister. She was well-educated; spoke French and German and, in addition, read Spanish and Italian; enjoyed music; and sketched and drew well. Her family tree could be traced back through King Henry I to William the Conqueror. When she was sixteen, she married her cousin, John Graves Simcoe, a man almost twice her age, but she was excited about their posting to the wilds of Canada. She was a natural traveller with an enquiring mind about her environment, seemingly unfazed about living in a tent. Not only did she have two children with her — Francis, a boy of three months, and Sophia, a girl of two — but she would have a new baby girl, Katherine, during her stay, both girls dying soon after Katherine's birth. Elizabeth was, however, also accompanied by a French chef, a nurse, a maid, and "a mountain of luggage."[11] Her first winter in York was so cold that water that spilled beside her stove froze immediately — although she was the envy of others for having a stove in her tent. She had left four daughters at home in England in the charge of a friend, and it is largely because of her diaries, which served as letters back home to them, that we know so much about life in the country at that time.

As well as an amateur cartographer, Elizabeth was an artist, painting or drawing people she met or places where she travelled, but never drawing anyone or any place she didn't like. She was interested in the flora and fauna of the new country and constantly roamed the Don River Valley, searching for plants she had never seen before, or ones that she recognized. She had an un-bounded curiosity and watched Indigenous people fish and the local people farm. She was interested in food, and we know from her diaries that raccoon tasted like lamb if eaten with mint, that bear tasted like pork, that wolf was barely edible, and that gooseberry sauce was tasty on salmon. She concluded that the women in Canada were better educated than the men, who "take care of their Horses ... and leave the management of their Affairs to the women." She also noted the lack of servants, "which are not to be got." One winter it was so cold that Anishinaabe women came to her for bread; the Anishinaabe hunters could not track the deer and they were starving.[12]

Elizabeth enjoyed her time in Upper Canada so much that she cried the day she left, to the point that she was unable to see some of her friends to say goodbye. She took mementoes of her stay back to England: sleighs, a canoe and paddles, bows and arrows, and Indigenous clothing, symbols of her Canadian adventures.[13]

Anna Brownell Murphy Jameson (1794–1860)

Anna Brownell Murphy was born in Dublin to poor parents, an Irish mini-ature painter and his English wife. She married Robert Sympson Jameson in 1825 after an on-again, off-again romance. Appointed attorney general in Upper Canada in 1833, later vice-chancellor and the first Speaker of the Legislative Council, Robert pleaded with Anna to join him in the new coun-try; he felt the need for a partner, a chatelaine for social engagements.

A constant traveller, writer, and feminist, Anna eventually went to Toronto in the mid-1830s, but it appears that she spent most of her time away from Robert and soon returned to England alone with a separation settlement of three hundred pounds a year. When he died, Robert left her nothing in his will. During her time in Canada, she travelled around the country and into the United States over two months, meeting with Indigenous people and jour-neying by canoe and bateau, a keen spectator of her surroundings and the people she met. She even rode the rapids at Sault Ste. Marie, earning the respect of the "Otchipways" (Ojibwe) and the name Was-sa-je-wun-e-qua, "Woman of the Bright Stream." Anna was particularly taken with Indigenous people, especially Jane Johnston Schoolcraft (1800–1842), who was part Ojibwe and part Irish and whose Ojibwe name was Obabaamwewe-giizhigokwe, "Woman of the Sound the Stars Make Rushing through the Sky." Jane, who was an American writer, and her husband, geologist and ethnologist Henry Rowe Schoolcraft, published *The Literary Voyager*, a magazine wholly focused on the Ojibwe people. Later Anna wrote three small volumes of her observations of her trip, *Winter Studies and Summer Rambles*, with critical comments.[14]

Called a pretty lady of fashion, Anna evidently charmed nearly all those she met; numerous early writers and historians quoted her extensively. A famous Welsh sculptor, John Gibson, executed a bust of her for the South

Portrait of Anna Jameson.

Kensington Museum in London, England. Henry Scadding, whose writings are virtually devoid of information about women, was captivated by her. She "was unattractive in person at first sight," he wrote, although her features were "fine and boldly marked." But it was her "originality and independence of judgment on most subjects," her "capacious memory," and her "fascinating" conversation that made her an "enchantress." She also sang well and sketched "with great elegance." Her early studies had been in modern languages and Oriental literature.[15]

But her rejected husband, Robert, was not without his admirers, also. It was reported that his "conversational powers" were admirable; he was an intimate of the British poets Robert Southey, William Wordsworth, and Samuel Taylor Coleridge. Coleridge's son, Hartley, dedicated three poems to Robert. He was described as a "man of high culture," an amateur artist of no ordinary skill. It was in their house in Toronto that Anna wrote the preface to her book *Characteristics of Women*, and her three-volume *Winter Studies and Summer Rambles*.

Anna was uncomplimentary about Toronto after she arrived, when she stepped ankle-deep into winter mud, with no one to meet her. The historian C. Pelham Mulvany wrote, "Vice Chancellor Jamieson's [sic] clever but flighty Irish wife ... never forgave Muddy Little York for splashing her dainty *bottines* and snow-white stockings in the first day of her arrival." However, Anna noted that Toronto was well-supplied with books and could boast an intellectual society. She also confessed that her inauspicious beginning in the city was her own fault, as she had been repeatedly warned not to travel there in winter. Although it was said that Torontonians never forgave her for her remarks, it appears that she was never without fans.

It was not just the winter mud Anna took issue with. She also wrote that Upper Canada was mismanaged, its people depressed, and Canada destined only to become "the inexhaustible timber-yard and granary of the mother country." Canada, she wrote, was suffering from an earlier "total absence of all sympathy on the part of the English government."[16]

On January 16, 1838, Anna was burning up with fever. She had contracted the ague, which her maid called the "hager." A swamp at the mouth of the Don River attracted *Anopheles* mosquitos, which were responsible for spreading a mild form of malaria, although it would be years before it was recognized that the source of the malady was not "disease-producing vapours" but the small biting insects.[17]

In the winter when she was in Toronto, Anna was generally cold. "The ink freezes while I write," she wrote, "and my fingers stiffen around the pen; a glass of water by my bed-side, within a few feet of the hearth ... kept burning all night long, is a solid mass of ice in the morning. God help the poor emigrants who are yet unprepared against the rigour of the season!" But Anna generally ate and lived well. In Toronto in 1837, a year of scarcity of food, she lists the foods on her table: beef, mutton, pork, black bass, whitefish, venison, quail, pheasant, snipe, and woodcock. She lacked vegetables, though, writing that she had only potatoes. "Those who have farms near the city or a country establishment of their own, raise poultry and vegetables for their own table," she remarked. She was living in the fashionable suburbs, perhaps a distance from the market.[18]

Isabella Bird Bishop (1831–1904)

Isabella Bird was so famous that a hundred years after her death, an American company named a line of clothing after her. While she was alive, her books sold to such an extent that she was able to support poor fishermen in the Scottish Highlands with her royalty cheques; she also supported numerous charities. Her fame began after she wrote books about her travels — the first adventure in Hawaii published in 1875 — and gave various lectures in Great Britain on social, political, and religious issues. She wrote seven other travel narratives. She was the first female fellow of the Royal Geographical Society.[19]

Advised by her doctors that travel would improve her health, twenty-three-year-old Isabella sailed from Liverpool for North America in 1854 on the 1,850-ton Cunard paddlewheeler *Canada*, with 167 other passengers. Her father had given her one hundred pounds for the trip, and she returned home when her money was on the verge of running out, five and a half months and 2,000 miles (about 3,200 kilometres) later — she had ten pounds left. In her eclectic travel accounts, she describes details and dramas such as violent storms during lake crossings, shopping habits, North American fashions, hotel and hospital laundries, travel on various conveyances, and other sometimes hair-raising adventures. In Canada, she visited Nova Scotia, Prince Edward Island, New Brunswick, and Quebec, as well as cities in Upper Canada.

Isabella's parents were not well-to-do, but she was reasonably well-connected: the head of the Church of England, a lord mayor of London, and the reformer William Wilberforce were all in her family background. Her father, a lawyer, had studied for the Church of England priesthood after his first wife died. Isabella's parents had lost a son, and her father was determined that Isabella would be healthy. At age four, she rode a horse, accompanying her father on long trips into the country; her mother taught her school work to the point that at age seven she was reading the history of the French Revolution. The family moved to many different parishes because her father insisted that his parishioners abandon all work on Sundays; the men and women in his churches preferred not to attend church under those conditions, and so there were often few parishioners to pay his salary.[20]

Tiny four-foot-eleven-inch Isabella, however, was not healthy. She had a tumour removed from her lower spine, and she suffered bouts of depression and fever; hence the recommendation that she undergo a sea voyage. She had written articles for local journals, so it was not surprising that she wrote extensive letters back home during her travels, which were later published. It was common for women of her day to keep diaries. Methodists in particular were enjoined to keep journals, and Methodist itinerant ministers were required to write them. Although Isabel was not a Methodist, the custom was widespread.

She visited Canada twice after her first tour, travelling extensively throughout the United States, spending a month in the Canadian woods, and undertaking a tour of the Canadian north, a year's journey of two thousand miles (about 3,200 kilometres). In 1866 she went to North America again, this time visiting the Scottish settlers in Canada whom she had helped financially to settle.

Anna M. Stoddart, a prolific writer and a biographer of Bird's, observed her at her mother's funeral:

> The memory of a small slight figure dressed in mourning is
> still vivid — of her white face shining between the meshes
> of a knitted Shetland veil; of her great, observant eyes, flash-
> ing and smiling, but melancholy when she was silent; of her
> gentleness and the exquisite modesty of her manner; and,
> above all, of her soft and perfectly modulated voice, never
> betrayed into hardness, or even excitement but so magnetic
> that all in the room were soon absorbed in listening to her.[21]

Soon after her mother's funeral, Isabella accepted a marriage proposal
from an Edinburgh doctor, John Bishop, but unfortunately he died soon after
they were married. She decided to become a medical missionary, and after a
course in emergency-room nursing, she set out in 1889, at age fifty-seven, for
Pakistan. Establishing a medical mission at Islamabad in honour of her husband, she travelled across Iran, coming home in 1891. Then, following a course
in photography, she toured the Far East with a cumbersome camera and the
equipment to develop photos; this her last trip.

Isabella had very little to say about Toronto in 1854, finding it a town with
handsome buildings, suburban residences with gardens and shrubberies, and
a relaxed people not running "hurry-scurry." It was a very English city with
"those sure tokens of British civilisation, a jail and a lunatic asylum." It was just
too much like home, she noted. She also confirmed that the town had been
called Toronto before John Graves Simcoe changed the name to York. She
noted "healthy and progressive commercial prosperity" with wharfs crowded
with freight and passenger steamers. She remarked that the Sabbath was observed admirably, largely because of the high number of Scottish inhabitants.
Her main criticism was of the hotels, which she found "of a very inferior class,"
especially compared to those in the United States, although she found the language of recent immigrants "far from prepossessing." It was due, she thought,
to the fact that new immigrants felt equal to all: "Here I haven't to bow and
cringe to gentlemen of the aristocracy — that is to a man who has a better coat
on than myself," a recent immigrant wrote. Isabella's enthusiasm for Toronto
was also toned down when she found her neck, hands, and face stinging and
swollen from the bites of innumerable mosquitos.[22]

It is evident that Toronto was already on a list of desirable places to visit by adventurous travellers, although when they arrived, it struck them as a fairly nondescript city, a safe destination for single female travellers.[23]

Clarence C. Strowbridge, who edited one of Isabella's travel books, credited her with being the greatest of all Victorian women travellers. She had the four most important qualities for travel, he wrote: curiosity, courage, determination, and strength, both physical and emotional.

CHAPTER 5

THE DE GRASSI GIRLS AND OTHER SPIES

W hile it would be decades before women were allowed into the Canadian military, they did participate in wars behind the scenes as information gatherers and spies. Perhaps the best-known Toronto women were two teenaged girls.

The De Grassi Girls

One night in December 1837, William Lyon Mackenzie, a Scottish-born journalist, politician, and reformer, gathered with other disgruntled Toronto residents at Montgomery's Tavern on Yonge Street to lead a rebellion against the incumbent conservative government. He had been plotting it for some time.

That same night, Captain Philip De Grassi, a recent settler in Toronto, who had a background in the military in Italy and Great Britain and was sympathetic to Great Britain, rode on horseback from his east-end home to the downtown government offices, along with his two preteen or teenaged daughters, Charlotte and Cornelia. He offered his services against the rebels in any way he could. De Grassi suggested that he might "ascertain the number of rebels" gathering at the tavern that evening. Yet it was his young daughters who were dispatched to do the dangerous task of spying. As he later wrote in his memoirs, Cornelia offered to ride to Montgomery's Tavern with the excuse of looking at sleighs at the millwright's shop next door:

> One of my daughters about 13 years of age, accordingly, who was a capital rider rode out under pretence of wishing to know the price of a sleigh, went to a wheelwright's shop close to Montgomery's Tavern, and being suspected, was taken prisoner by some of the rebels who ordered her to dismount. To this she demurred and during her altercation with her captors MacKenzie [sic] came with the news that the Western Mail was taken. Amidst the general excitement my little girl had the presence of mind to urger [sic] her horse and ride off at full speed amidst discharges of musketry. A ball went through her saddle and another through her riding habit.[1]

Cornelia sped south down Yonge Street, and was taken immediately to the governor general. She informed him that she had counted far fewer rebels than the government had suspected were gathered, and so the governor general gratefully operated on this new advice, defeating the rebellion decisively before it really began. As De Grassi reported later, "My poor child was the means of saving Toronto."

In fact, both of De Grassi's daughters were involved in that evening's escapades. On their way downtown, they had narrowly escaped being harassed by a group of rebels, but Charlotte rode ahead to distract them while Philip and Cornelia took another route. Charlotte managed to convince the rebels that she was harmless, and they all escaped. Later, Charlotte was slightly injured as she was riding home alone, but she managed to warn the officials that the Don Bridge had been set on fire by the rebels, and it was soon extinguished. The story of the girls' heroic actions appeared later in the *New York*

Albion, but nowhere else, even in Toronto. That De Grassi could not remember that both daughters were part of these events is not really strange, as they happened some time before he wrote his memoirs. And though it seems peculiar that two young girls were out riding late at night, girls that young were sometimes engaged as servants at that time, and sometimes married when not much older. They were treated as adults when they turned sixteen.

What does seem irresponsible, though, is that De Grassi would allow his young daughter to ride into an armed rebel camp at any time. Historians record the girls' ages as ten and thirteen or thirteen and fourteen. But whatever their ages, De Grassi appears to have been consistently foolish. He built a sawmill just after he arrived in Upper Canada and he cleared land intending to farm, but he had no knowledge of either occupation, and neither succeeded. He brought with him to Upper Canada ploughs unfit for the Canadian countryside, thirty-six cowbells, and six hundred sheep bells, which he must have been intending to sell for a profit. Some of his livestock was stolen, and he was cheated by a miller. His house and its contents were destroyed by fire, although that would not have been his fault. But probably he had been a much better soldier than settler.[2]

Later the two De Grassi girls married Americans — Charlotte, Mr. Bacon, and Cornelia, Mr. Mathewson. Their story was recovered years afterward, but the "facts" might have been embellished.[3]

Another woman, a Mrs. Ross from a nearby tavern, was thought to have put out a fire on a Don River bridge that was set by the Mackenzie rebels. Unfortunately, her knee was severely injured and the toll keeper at the bridge was shot to death. One wonders if there were two fires on Don River bridges set by the rebels or if it was the same incident![4]

Another story passed down over the years involved a small girl during the 1837 rebellion. Some of the rebels took refuge at a house belonging to John Milne, but one of his neighbours wondered who the people were and sent his "little girl" over on an errand. The girl reported that they were strangers, the neighbour alerted the government officers, and the rebels were captured. Was this a different version of the same story?[5]

However, over the years, a number of women reportedly used stealth, ingenuity, and strength to assist British soldiers against the Americans — especially during the war of 1812–1814 between the United States and Great Britain. That conflict had a direct impact on the small community of York: battles were fought in Upper Canadian streets, British soldiers and Canadian militiamen were wounded and killed, and much of York settlers' property was damaged or irrecoverably lost.

A Mrs. Gessean is credited with saving the life of William Hamilton Merritt, a young British captain imprisoned at Lewiston in the United States. Pretending to sell butter to the American army, Mrs. Gessean managed to slip Merritt's father's parole (pass) to him, allowing him to walk home through enemy lines. Also, a woman called Sarah Willott was able to give the British army the position, size, and state of the American army at one point, informing the British that the Americans were planning to attack Fort Erie. In both cases, the women's actions were helpful to the war effort but were never generally publicized. In another instance, a Mrs. Defield was standing in her doorway with a child when she saw an American soldier about to stab British lieutenant-colonel James FitzGibbon. She quickly put the child down, wrenched the sword out of the American soldier's hand, and managed to hide it in her house, saving FitzGibbon's life.[6]

As Isabel Skelton wrote:

> At the outbreak of hostilities [the American Revolutionary War] it was the policy of both sides to leave their women and children behind on their farms and estates, while the men mustered for the fray.... The women were able to render their party great practical aid in this way. In one sense they became part of a very efficient spy service throughout the length and breadth of the land. General Marion's advice to the women ... is typical of the demands the military leaders made upon them: to "... keep up communications and send information to the men in camp."[7]

Like the De Grassi girls' actions, however, most of these women's heroic moments are not embedded in official records. The historian Cecilia Morgan suggested that these physical acts of bravery did not conform to the feminine ideal of "helplessness and passivity." Wartime service, she points out, was a masculine activity. It may be, of course, that these stories are what are jokingly called "alternative facts" today, or are very much embellished events that are more fiction than fact.

Laura Ingersoll Secord (1775–1868)[8]

The Laura Secord story, which many Canadians know well, is another example of how fact and fiction, legend, and tradition are so intermingled that it is difficult to know where truth ends and fairy tale begins. Supposedly, Laura Secord was another heroic woman who helped the British forces during the war of 1812–1814, in her case by travelling some distance to pass on a conversation she had overheard, giving the British information about the American troops' military plans.

Before sunrise, on a sweltering hot Tuesday, thirty-eight-year old Laura Ingersoll Secord left her convalescing husband, James, and her four/five/six children, and on bare feet, walked twenty miles (thirty-two kilometres), part of the way with her cow/sister-in-law/niece/oldest daughter, through rattlesnake- and mosquito-infested swampland, brambles, and thorns or dense forest thick with wolves/bears/lynx, and crawled on a slippery log over a swollen river to warn British lieutenant James FitzGibbon of an impending surprise attack at Beaver Dams by the Americans under the command of Colonel Charles Boerstler. The hazards that Laura had to surpass would have put *The Iliad* and the *The Odyssey* to shame.

Laura Secord did exist. Born in Massachusetts, Laura came to Upper Canada in 1795 with her father and his children from three marriages. About two years later, she married American-born merchant and militia volunteer James Secord. James was wounded in 1812 at the Battle of Queenston Heights.

Curiously, contemporary reports, histories, and newspapers make no mention of Laura Secord and her incredible journey on June 22, 1813. The first written references we have are notes from Lieutenant FitzGibbon in 1820 and 1827 supporting petitions from the Secords to the government asking for a military pension or some other form of remuneration as compensation for

Laura's daring effort. FitzGibbon noted that Laura had indeed been valuable in making victory possible at Beaver Dams.

After the war, and especially after James's death in 1841, Laura and her family needed money. But it was not until 1860, when Laura petitioned the Prince of Wales, the future Edward VII, who was visiting Upper Canada at that time, that she received government money. When the prince returned to England, he had one hundred pounds sent as a reward — equivalent to one thousand dollars today in purchasing power. It was also about that time that stories, poems, songs, and plays started to appear extolling Laura's contribution to the British successes in the war of 1812–1814. Every writer seemed to try to outdo the previous one, embellishing the treacherous terrain that Laura had to cross to warn the British. Toronto historian and writer Sarah Anne Curzon (see chapter 8) turned her story into a well-received drama, making Laura Secord a household name.

However, "A Ballad for Brave Women," by the nineteenth-century Canadian writer Charles Mair, may be one of the best-known poems about Laura Secord, although not the earliest:

> She tript over moss-covered logs, fell, arose,
> Sped and stumbled again by the hour, till her clothes
> Were rent by the branches and thorns, and her feet
> Grew tender and way-worn and blistered with heat.
> …
> One moment she faltered. Beware! What is this?
> The coil of the serpent! the rattlesnake's hiss!
> One moment, then onward. What sounds far and near?
> The howl of the wolf! yet she turned not in fear.

Historians agree that Laura probably made a trip to warn the British about an American attack. She may have been accompanied by someone for part of the journey. She would not have started out barefoot, although she could have lost her shoes along the way. It is highly unlikely that she went through swampland, but a twenty-mile walk just through the woods at that time would have been tiring and difficult.

It is not clear how Laura knew of the approaching attack. It is likely that American soldiers were billeted in her house and she somehow heard them talk about their plans. Accounts disagree on the details. One historian notes that there are more versions than "varieties of chocolates included in a Laura Secord [chocolate] Sampler." Indeed, Laura's own account of the story over the years kept evolving.

It is not at all certain that Laura's efforts were necessary. It may be that one of the Indigenous people warned FitzGibbon before Laura arrived at his camp. But what is quite certain is that there was no cow in Laura's walk. The wealthy civil servant, soldier, and author William Foster Coffin (1808–1878) was the first to write a cow into the story of Laura Secord. Coffin felt that taking a cow to a different pasture would have given Laura an excuse to leave her home and safely pass American soldiers.

In the early 1860s, there were threats of another war between Canada and the United States. As well, Confederation was being deliberated. In his 1864 work, *1812, The War and Its Moral: A Canadian Chronicle,* Coffin aimed to provide Canadians with the heroic legends he thought were necessary for a common nationalism. Laura was one of his "heroic women."

The twentieth-century Canadian journalist Pierre Berton suggested that Laura's story underlined "the growing myth that the War of 1812 was won by true-blue Canadians — in this case a brave Loyalist housewife who single-handedly saved the British Army from defeat." When Dr. George Bryce, president of the Manitoba Historical and Scientific Society, spoke to the Canadian Club in Winnipeg in 1907, he called Laura Secord "a study in Canadian patriotism." Over the years, Canada was looking for Canadian heroes and heroines.

As Mair wrote:

> Ah! faithful to death were our women of yore.
> Have they fled with the past, to be heard of no more?
> No, no! Though this laurelled one sleeps in the grave,
> We have maidens as true, we have matrons as brave;
> And should Canada ever be forced to the test —
> To spend for our country the blood of her best —

When her sons lift the linstock and brandish the sword,
Her daughters will think of brave Laura Secord.

Versions of Laura Secord's story continue to appear. In 2017 an American short film was planned to tell Laura's story "as seen through the eyes of the cow." At least three Canadian children's books have been written, one about Laura's childhood and a "pet cow, Peg." Laura Secord and her mythical cow continue to be two of Canada's most popular heroes.

There were other ways in which the women in the community of York supported the fight against the American invasions. In 1813 again during the war of 1812–1814, the "Patriotic Young Ladies of York" made a special banner for the Third Regiment of York Militia. In a special ceremony presenting it, Anne Powell remarked that she hoped it would become "a kind of remembrance of the unlimited confidence which they placed in the efficacy of the Militia's protection." Historian Ceceilia Morgan has pointed out, however, that the banner, rather than symbolizing women's labour as a contribution to the war, showed the women's dependence on the men for protection. Afterwards, Powell was upset that the militia gave the banner back to the women for them to protect it from being destroyed during battle.[9]

CHAPTER 6

WOMEN AND RELIGION

R eligion was endemic in Upper Canada. For example, much of Mary Gapper O'Brien's diary is concerned with her attempts to have churches built close to the various places she lived. However, she compared York to Yankee towns: "[York] did not cut so gay an appearance as the Yankee towns," she wrote in her diary on October 16, 1828, "from the absence of the spires which always abounded there. At York there are but two." According to entries in Ely Playter's diary from 1856 to 1858, he often attended the Methodist Church and became a lay (non-ordained) preacher, but he was also at various other denominational churches, presumably to find a church that appealed to him — although his lifestyle as a bon vivant is not one that would suggest a deep interest in religion.[1]

Schools were expected to open and close with Christian prayer, and it was recorded provincially how many schools followed that requirement. In 1885 seventy-six schools opened and closed with prayer, and the school inspector hoped that the next year the number would be higher. Only forty-seven schools repeated the Ten Commandments every day. As the writer of *The History of Toronto and the County of York* noted about the need for religious practice in the schools, "a regard to the Moral Law lie [*sic*] at the foundation of individual and social happiness, and there can be no security for our country's prosperity and well being without them."[2]

Women were at the centre of religious and moral training — that is, in the home. As the highly respected Methodist *Christian Guardian* and other religious newspapers hammered home in every issue, women had their place, and it was especially not in church pulpits: "The wife is not expected to go into the field, the workshop or the counting house." "To the middling class of life there is no female accomplishment more valuable than housewifery." Another paper, the well-read weekly *Christian Advocate* pointed out, "Women preach the precious gospel by sewing gloves and moccasins, knitting mittens, making baskets and brooms."[3]

As the prominent nineteenth-century Primitive Methodist preacher William Antliff (1813–1884) said in a public lecture in 1856, "*Home* is the mother's immediate sphere, and vast is the influence of a pious and intelligent mother in that sphere." While he maintained that women were equal to men and should be educated as well as men, he emphasized that "women's is the privilege of making her husband happy and honoured." In Antliff's denomination, though, numerous women had been extremely active in the church, *outside* the home, in the early years of that group's existence, both in Great Britain and in North America.[4]

Methodists

John Wesley (1703–1791), the inadvertent founder of Methodism, only gradually accepted women in leadership positions. He had not intended to begin a new denomination but, because he took church services outside the church building to where the people worked, he was no longer welcome in the Church of England where he had served as a priest. He set up a new church structure, which was later called Methodism. In addition to regular church services, he organized small bands of two to four people where they could discuss their spirituality, and classes of a dozen or so where adults could learn more about their faith. Both bands and classes were separated by gender. This, of course, gave women responsibilities and opportunities as leaders of the women's classes;

when the classes became popular and grew exceptionally large, the women leaders were thrust into positions as public speakers, and eventually preachers. Noting how capable and effective these women were, Wesley eventually encouraged and supported them with practical advice and educational resources. Wesley's mother, Susanna Annesley Wesley (1669–1742), had been progressive for her time: she believed that girls should be taught to read and write before they learned housework. Wesley would have been influenced by this. And as Wesley had preached, "The conversion of sinners is the work of God, and whoever is the instrument of doing this work is the servant of God. And we must not forbid a one," opening the door to effective women as well as to men.[5]

As a result, hundreds of single and married Methodist women travelled around the British and Irish countrysides preaching and ministering to thousands of men and women, setting up bands and classes, organizing Sunday schools, conducting religious revivals, building new churches, and even beginning a theological college. The women became so popular that male preachers admitted to jealousy. Because of this, in 1802 and 1803, and again in 1835, the male Methodist ecclesiastical hierarchy in Ireland and England passed motions that virtually prevented the women from preaching. By this time, Wesley had died, no longer able to protect and cheer on the women. Frustrated by the legislation, many of these women turned to other more liberal but orthodox versions of Methodism that had begun in the early nineteenth century, two of the better known being the Primitive Methodists and the Bible Christians. Both of these groups sent missionaries to Upper Canada: the Bible Christians to the area around Cobourg and Peterborough, two dynamic centres east of York, and the Primitive Methodists to York. In their early years, both denominations respected and encouraged women preachers.

Ann Atkinson Lawson, a bonnet maker and gifted singer with seven children; Mrs. Nathaniel Watkins; and Mary Ann Lyle (1797–1862) all preached in York (later Toronto) in the Primitive Methodist Church and on circuits in York Township. Mary Ann Towler and her husband, William Towler, had immigrated to the United States from England in 1846, but after William died the next year, Mary Ann moved to Toronto. There she opened a school in 1848 and preached on special occasions. The last extant record of her work is of an anniversary sermon she preached in 1851.[6]

SUNDAY PLAN of the Brampton Mission. —Upper Canada.—1836.

Beware of False Prophets—Matt. vii. 15.

PLACES OF PREACHING.	HOURS	OCTOBER. 2 9 16 23 30	NOVEMBER. 6 13 20 27	DECEMBER. 4 11 18 25	PREACHERS
Willington's	10½	— . A — BC —	A — C . .	A . J —	A. W. Lyle
Smith's	2	— AS — C —	AT — F .	A . D —	B. D. Berry,
Churchville	6	— A — — .	A — — .	A . — —	c. M. Smith
Hemphill's	10½	A . . F — AS	— BT — A	— R . A	D. W. Lawson
Springfield	3	A . 1 . . A	— B — AC	— R . A	E. W. Smith
Streetsville	6	A . 1C — A	— B — A	— B . A	F. T. Turley
Whitsall's	10	— D — 1C —	F . B —	U . . S —	G. M.A. Lyle
Paisley's	2	— . D — 1T	— . BC —	. C . R —	H. M. Watson
Churchville †					
Clarago's	2	F . R — F	— DC — J	. F . G	
Woodhill's	10	C . 2 — D	— AC — C	. A . D	REFERENCES.
Rains,	2	C . 2 — D	— AC — C	. A . D	
Albion	6	— . 2 — —	— A — —	. A . —	c. Collection.
Nichols's	10	U . J — B	— C — NC	. D . B	s. Sacrament.
Heglar's	2	R . — — B	— — — BC	. . A B	T. Tickets.
Tecumseth	10	— . — 2 —	B — AC —	R . A —	
Loyd Town	6	— RS — 2 —	RT — A —	B . A —	

A Day's Meeting will be held at Streetsville, Oct. 16th, No: 1 D F G. Quarterly meeting at Loyd Town Oct. 9th. At Hemphill's Oct. 30th. And the preparatory Quarter-day at Lawson's Nov. 24.

The Primitive Methodist Sunday preachers plan for the Brampton Mission, showing Mary Ann (M.A.) Lyle's name, although there is only one preaching spot for her: 2:00 p.m., December 25, 1836, at Clarago's. She was also to participate in the Day's Meeting at Streetsville, York Township, on October 16, 1836.

Mary Ann Lyle and William lived in Etobicoke in the west of Toronto in a one-room shanty with their four children. In 1837 they earned a combined salary of $288, which was to cover all their household and living expenses, even the maintenance of a horse. In comparison, a journeyman printer in Toronto took home $416 for the year 1836 and had earned even more a year earlier, and in 1832, an Anglican (Church of England) clergyman in Toronto received from one hundred to three hundred pounds per annum or 3,000 to 9,000 Canadian dollars in today's currency.[7]

The first Canadian edition of *Doctrines and Disciplines* for the Primitive Methodists, published in 1833, demanded a frugal and simple lifestyle, but possibly not as frugal as the Lyles'. No Primitive Methodist was allowed to attend "vain and worldly amusements," waste their time in public houses, buy "unaccustomed" (luxurious) goods, or be dishonest. Male travelling preachers had to wear single-breasted coats, plain waistcoats, and their hair in a "natural" form. Female travelling preachers needed "plain dress." A single male preacher was paid from four pounds, four shillings to five pounds, seven shillings a quarter, or from $67.30 to $85.60 a year. A woman received two pounds, ten shillings a quarter or $40 a year. A married man earned twice the single man's salary, but if his wife carried on his business while he travelled, he received less. The assumption was that women were quite capable of looking after business concerns, and did. All the itinerants received room and board.[8]

Some of the preachers had their own private incomes as well. Canadian-born Jane Woodill (1824–1893) and her husband, Isaac Wilson (1825–post 1901), who was born in England, bought an organ themselves for a local congregation, and later offered five hundred dollars of their own money to a neighbouring Wesleyan Methodist Church so that the congregation could repair its roof. The well-connected journalist George Brown and the parliamentarian D'Arcy McGee were among Jane's father's friends, so the family was well-connected.

Jane Woodill's parents had emigrated from England to York in 1819 and moved north a few years later. And when Jane was only eighteen, her name appeared on the Etobicoke (west Toronto/York) Primitive Methodist circuit plan, the list of all the various preaching places on that circuit along with the names of the preachers involved. She married a first cousin, Isaac Wilson; both became popular preachers in their area. Jane always dressed in sombre brown, grey, or black and preached wearing a plain bonnet without any decoration. She cared for the sick and the poor and had a reputation of being a good, fearless nurse. She was the only person who would help a neighbouring family who all fell ill with scarlet fever. She thought nothing of riding thirty miles (forty-eight kilometres) on Sundays on her spotted horse, Toby, preaching two or three times, and then riding back home to her five children and her husband, who had been looking after the local Sunday school.[9]

The 1840s and 1850s were the zenith of Primitive Methodism around Toronto. There were new church openings, prayer meetings, field meetings, ticket meetings, and camp meetings. According to historian E.C. Kyte, the Primitive Methodist Church in Toronto was known as the "match factory" because so many young people met their future partners there.[10] By the middle of the century, however, the place of women was changing in that denomination.

Gradually, many male preachers would not accept women in that same role, believing that femininity and preaching were simply not compatible. In the 1850s, James Garfield (1831–1881), later president of the United States, a country considered to be more progressive than Canada, wrote:

> There is something about a woman's speaking in public that unsexes her in my mind, and how much soever I might admire the talent, yet I could never think of the female speaker as the gentle sister, the tender wife or the loving mother.[11]

As the century progressed, the women, referred to as "ladies," tended to serve tea after meetings with male ministers, instead of being the minister. On the 1856–1857 Toronto circuit plan, there were no female preachers listed, and only one class was to be led by a woman, Sister Kent. A woman pointed out in an article in the Primitive Methodist *Evangelist* that she was a missionary in the nursery. In 1860 the "Ladies Department" of the *Christian Journal* described the position of women as one of "curiously subordinated equality." Women were expected to function in their proper sphere, that of housewife, mother, and spiritual guardian of the home.

When Mary Ann Lyle died in 1862, in her sixty-sixth year, the funeral procession was said to be more than a mile long. Four male minsters conducted the funeral service, and one of her sons-in-law called her a "prophetess" but no mention was made of her preaching. He admitted that his mother-in-law occasionally "expounded the Word" but that she was always "modest and diffident." Another son-in-law said apologetically that she "frequently addressed assemblies" but that "only a sense of duty ... could have overcome her natural diffidence and nerved her for this work." Both sons-in-law were Primitive Methodist preachers.[12]

Although there were no preaching appointments for Jane Woodill Wilson in her later years, a plaque in the brick church on their farm does admit that she was "for 40 years teacher preacher and class leader."

About this time in 1865, a photograph was taken of approximately fifty "Bible Christian Church members" in Bowmanville, just east of Toronto. This was the other Methodist group in Upper Canada that permitted and

Portrait of Eliza Barnes Case (Mrs. William), Methodist missionary, by John Wycliffe Lowes (J.W.L.) Forster. No date, oil on canvas.

encouraged women preachers. However, the photograph is of only men. Perhaps it was from a specific male members' meeting or outing, but one wonders where the women were.[13]

It was from the Methodist movement in the United States that several women went north to work on the Wesleyan Methodist missions near York in the early nineteenth century. One of the most prominent was Eliza Barnes (1796–1887), who had been born in Boston and travelled north in 1827, when she was about thirty. Even though she was a capable organizer, a fiery preacher, an effective teacher, and a successful fundraiser, William Case (1780–1855), a Methodist minister who was head of the missions, refused to sit on the platform with her when they were on the same program. Eliza was constantly travelling around Upper Canada and back into the United States to teach, preach, fundraise, supervise the women's missions, and set up women's sewing societies. She was responsible for at least one religious revival in or near Toronto. A traveller, Henry Cook Todd, wrote in his 1840 notes on Canada that "a female missionary by the name of Barnes ... visits her friends periodically, stays some short time, then repairs to her hut in the wilderness.... She is continually employed in visiting, either by canoe or sleigh, a dozen missionary stations, scattered over a circuit of several hundred miles."[14]

There were other women who worked in York and the area around the city as class leaders, prayer leaders, preachers, and teachers for the Methodists, such as Irish-born Margaret Bowes Taylor (1806–1859), sister of John George Bowes, who was several times mayor of Toronto. Margaret was a class leader in 1833 and likely earlier, when there were twelve Methodist male class leaders and Margaret. The American Ann Dulmage Coate McLean (ca. 1777–?) held religious meetings for women in her house and travelled with her husband, the itinerant Samuel Coate, on his circuit in Upper Canada. Susannah Farley Waldron (1802–1890) and Hetty Ann Hubbard (1796–1831) were missionary teachers, "extremely gifted," both from Massachusetts. There were at least a dozen more women who were actively involved in some way. The teachers received a salary, and though it was always less than a man's, it would have been appealing to women at that time. In 1832 the women teachers at the missions earned twenty-nine pounds, five shillings, 75 percent of the male teacher's wage but more than the Primitive Methodist women itinerants, although salaries fluctuated from year to year.[15]

Hetty Ann Hubbard died in 1831, soon after she married William Case; two years later, Eliza Barnes married the widowed Case. Eliza recorded in her diary on August 6 of that year that her "trials were neither few nor small"; seven days later, her diary reads very simply, "Tuesday I went in company with Mr. Case to Belleville, where I stopped until the 28th. There we were married." It was not until August 30 that Mr. Case had a familiar appellation in her diary: "my dear husband." However, it was not uncommon to address one's future or new husband in formal terms. It is recorded that thirty-seven-year-old Eliza "settled down" immediately after her marriage. She still led Methodist classes, but there is no record of any preaching. As the Methodist *Christian Guardian* noted in 1828, women were to promote Christianity by the "eloquence which flows from subjection." Equality, the newspaper said, would result in "perpetual strife." And as Case's colleague, the Methodist George Ryerson repeated to the Dorcas Society in New York City in 1831, ladies preach the precious gospel by sewing gloves and moccasins, knitting mittens, making baskets and brooms.[16] In the proceedings of the mission meetings, there is no mention of the missionary women being extensively involved anymore.[17]

There were Dorcas Societies in a number of the churches, that is groups of women who "procured" or made clothing for the poor. They were called Dorcas Societies after a woman named Dorcas described in the Holy Bible (Acts of the Apostles 9:36–42) as sewing garments for charity and giving to others. In the 1850 Toronto street directory, Dorcas Societies were listed at the Baptist Church on Bond Street and at the Wesleyan Methodist Church, where eighteen women were listed as members of a Dorcas Society Committee.

While Methodists initially considered Upper Canada a missionary enterprise, Canadians, too, became missionaries to other foreign lands. One such woman, Dr. Susanna Carson Rijnhart (1868–1908), is described in chapter 9, "Professionals."

There were other Methodist churches in Toronto, such as the African Methodist Episcopal (AME) and British Methodist Episcopal (BME) Churches. The AME was named the Grant AME in honour of Bishop Abram Grant. It was formed in 1816 in the United States as the first independent Black denomination and the oldest formal institution of African Americans. By 1840 the first AME conference was organized in Canada and the first meeting held in Toronto. But concerned about slave-catchers from the United States, most of the churches became BME churches. However, with the end of slavery in the United States in 1865, many of the BME churches decided to be joined to the American AME again.

A few women have been connected to the AME church in Canada. A Sister Taylor is mentioned in the 1850s, but no other women have been found in available material for the nineteenth century.[18]

Methodism was not the only denomination in Canada in which women at times held roles virtually equal to men. Both the Society of Friends (the Quakers) and the Salvation Army offered women the opportunity to travel, preach, and hold administrative positions in the nineteenth century. The Baptist churches offered fewer possibilities.

Quakers (Society of Friends)

In the Canadian Society of Friends, or Quakers, itinerant ministers were considered the most powerful preachers. According to the historian and writer Arthur Dorland, they were "the makers and leaders ... men and women of unusual spiritual power." In fact, Dorland claimed, without any previous knowledge or having met a person before, they could often speak to that person's spiritual condition.[19]

From the seventeenth century on, hundreds of female Quaker ministers travelled around the world, preaching in meeting houses, town halls, courthouses, and other public spaces. Between 1649 and 1660, of the 300 Quaker preachers identified in England 220, or more than 73 percent, were women. Many other women were clerks, elders, or missionaries in the denomination. As well, by the nineteenth century, Quaker women were spearheading movements for women's suffrage, the abolition of slavery, prison reform, peace, and other areas of social change around the world.

The Quaker religion had begun in England in the late 1640s when George Fox (1624–1691) came to believe that every person possessed the true light within them, the light of Christ. Margaret Askew Fell Fox (1614–1702), George's wife, was considered the co-founder of what was at first called "Children of the Light" or "Friends of the Truth." According to George, "the light is the same in the male and female," hence women and men were considered equal. As Margaret wrote in her short pamphlet, *Womens* [sic] *Speaking Justified, Proved and Allowed of by the Scriptures*, "Though we be looked upon as the weaker vessels, ... God, whose strength is made perfect in weakness ... can make us good and bold."[20] However, contemporary Canadian Quaker historian Robynne Rogers Healey points out that "Quakerism did not *allow* women to shape their world — it *expected* that they, like men, would do so." Quaker women, she notes, also "claimed their role as the keepers of the faith, within both the local faith community and the extended transatlantic Friends community."[21]

Early Yonge Street Quaker meeting house.

Quaker women began travelling to the United States, among other countries, in the seventeenth century in spite of the dangers of sea travel, the inadequate diet on board the sailing vessels, and the length of a voyage. Some of them experienced near mutiny on board ship, storms, shipwrecks, and being delivered to countries far from their desired destination. Yet they were given official sanction to travel by their home church, and they kept on, singly and in couples. It was from the United States, however, that they first travelled into Upper Canada, mostly in the nineteenth century.

There was always great excitement when a well-known Quaker from another country travelled around Ontario. At least half of these visitors were women. For example, in 1834, Hannah C. Backhouse (1787–1850), from England, visited Canadian meetings, promoting Bible study among the Quakers and beginning the First Day School movement (Sunday schools), which eventually spread throughout all the Society of Friends. In 1833 she met some resistance to her ministry in Ithaca, New York, evidently from other ministers: "In a few places they refuse women's preaching; yet it is but rare they do so; the ministers are too dependent on the people. And the people receive it [women's preaching] willingly."[22] A few of the Quaker women, however, were accused of unfeminine behaviour by the wider community as well, of being "immodest, brazen, arrogant, and obstreperous."[23]

Another well-known Quaker visitor, Priscilla Hunt Cadwallader/ Cadwalader (1786–1859) from Indiana, had little formal schooling but was able to read the whole Bible when she was only six because of home-schooling. A travelling Quaker minister, she visited every Friends' meeting on the North American continent before she was thirty-seven, with an extended visit to Upper Canada in 1823 and 1824. There she spoke about the public ministry of women, indicating that there was some hostility to women preaching within the Quakers themselves. She noted that she had read the Bible from beginning to end and had found only support of women's preaching, resulting in converting some men to her point of view. Like the other Quaker ministers, she listened for the "Master's" leading, believing that God would lead her where she had to go.[24]

Perhaps the most famous Canadian Quaker was Dr. Emily Jennings Stowe (1831–1903), the first female doctor in Canada; her biography is in the section on Toronto doctors in chapter 9. Several other well-known Canadian female Quakers are remembered by men and women in their churches today.

Alma Gould Dale (1854–1930) was one of the later but best-known travelling ministers. Her parents had settled in Uxbridge, forty miles (sixty-four kilometres) northeast of York, and Alma was born there. Her father became a prominent businessman owning mills and promoting railroads, as well as a wealthy landowner. He was elected to the Legislative Assembly of Ontario in 1854 as a Reformer. Described as unusually talented, Alma excelled as a public speaker, sang competently, and was an excellent horsewoman. Her spirited pair of cream horses, which she drove in all kinds of weather, became something of a legend. She was witty, fluent, an efficient bookkeeper, said to be a jack of all trades. The writer Arthur Dorland described her as a "woman of striking appearance and boundless energy" who "affected a mannish, tweedy style of dress which was very smart, but was also unconventional, especially for a Quaker minister." She was also such a good carpenter that she remodelled the meeting house at Quaker Hill, north of Toronto, by removing the partition separating the men's and women's sections and changing the entrance doors. In 1880, at the age of twenty-six, she became a Quaker minister. Like other Quakers in the area, she worked closely with Methodist churches, and in 1884, she was put in charge of the Sunday school class at her neighbouring Methodist church; she more than doubled its class size in a few years. Many Sundays she also preached in Methodist churches and helped with other Sunday schools.[25]

In 1898 Alma left for Manitoba. It was thought that this was a way of separating from her husband, Thomas, who had been a disastrous partner, involved in several bankruptcies. She travelled widely, speaking in Canada, England, and New Zealand. Alma died at seventy-six in England where she had been in charge of a Friends' church.[26]

The minister Eliza Spofford Brewer (1811–1894) travelled around Canada, the United States, England, and Ireland, and was especially interested in prison reform in Canada. Hannah Jane Reazin Cody (1832–1902) was involved in the Women Friends Missionary Society. Sarah Wright Haight (1746–?) was active in the ministry even though she had twelve children to look after as well. She preached the funeral sermon for Joshua Doan, a Quaker revolutionary condemned to death after taking part in the Upper Canada Rebellion of 1837.[27]

Serena Minard (1839–1912) was a delegate to the World's Convention of the Woman's Christian Temperance Union (WCTU) in London, England, in 1895. She had been brought up a Presbyterian in New York, but was acknowledged as a Quaker minister in 1879 in Canada. Described as exceptionally sweet and "winsome," with a quick response and a sense of humour, she confided that she at first had great difficulty speaking in a Quaker meeting of worship. She would stand with downcast eyes, scarcely daring to face the people. But once she heard a voice say, "Lift up thine eyes," and after that she was able to face her audience with self-confidence.[28]

Eliza H. Varney (1829–1915) was another excellent Quaker minister. Just before she rose to speak, she would remove her Quaker bonnet, showing a white lace cap covering her hair. She spoke clearly and forcefully and was well-received. When the members saw her loosening her bonnet strings, they knew she was getting ready to speak and one could feel "a ripple of expectancy" in the meeting.[29]

American Elizabeth Leslie Rous Wright Comstock (1815–1891) came to the Toronto area in 1854 and remained for three years. She had been very active in the Underground Railroad and in prison reform in the United States, and when she returned, she was acknowledged a minister. In her "Early Impressions of Canada — 1854–1857," she remarked that "they say that in Canada, it takes a very short time to learn how to farm, and if a man is willing to work, he cannot help succeeding, so little labour being required to make a farm produce the necessities of life … with a previous knowledge [of farming], he may soon get rich." Whether all of the Toronto area farmers would have agreed with this is debatable. Elizabeth also noted that she enjoyed the "bright, clear, bracing air" of winter. "It makes one feel all alive," she wrote.[30]

The first Quaker meeting house in the Toronto area was north of Toronto, reached from the city along a "bush road … through dense untracked forests of pine and ash and maple…. It was so rough that incoming settlers were forced to take their canvas covered wagons apart and drag the several sections up the steep hills by strong ropes passed around the stems of saplings." It was the first worship building north of Toronto, built in 1804. The first four overseers were two men and two women, Sarah Rogers and Edith Phillips, and among a list of other early overseers were the names of three women: Martha Armitage, Ann Pearson, and Sarah Lundy. A Yonge Street School opened two years later; Quakers had always supported and encouraged education.[31]

The Salvation Army

On June 11, 1882, Mr. and Mrs. Freer, members of the Salvation Army known as "Salvationists," held a meeting in McMillan Hall, a nondescript building at the corner of Yonge and Gerrard Streets in the middle of downtown Toronto. That year marked the beginning of the Salvation Army in Canada; the month before, two male Salvationists had held a meeting in London, Ontario. Mr. and Mrs. Freer, a blacksmith and his wife, were recent immigrants to Ontario from England. A shy man, Mr. Freer was a powerful and forceful speaker, as if he were hammering in his forge while on the stage. But few were converted. The Army workers were used to receiving harassment, taunting, ridicule, and even physical abuse. But this was discouraging. They pleaded for help from the United States and England, and finally, in August of that year, Captain Annie Shirley and Captain Charles Wass left their New York headquarters for Canada, Shirley to work in London, Ontario, and Wass to work in Toronto. The results were dramatic; so many joined the Army in both cities that several outposts had to be established in addition to the downtown Toronto corps. Members of several prominent families helped fund the organization, even if they didn't join: a Moses hardware merchant, City Commissioner Coatsworth, deputy-chief of police Archibald, and one of the wealthy Gooderhams.[32]

The Salvation Army had unofficially begun in 1865 when Catherine Mumford Booth (1829–1890) and her husband, William Booth (1829–1912), a Methodist New Connexion preacher, organized a Christian mission in destitute areas of London, England. William preached in the "unsavoury" areas of the city, while Catherine, a feminist writer, speaker, and mother of eight children, preached to the rich, asking for money to support their ministry. By 1878 their mission had evolved into the Salvation Army, with William as the general and Catherine as the "mother," both considered co-founders of the new Protestant social activist denomination.

One of the Army policies was that there was to be no difference between men and women as to rank, authority, or duties: "Women shall have the right to an equal share with men in the work of publishing salvation," the rule read. Catherine claimed that women were not morally or naturally inferior to men, that there was no biblical reason to deny women the right to preach. It was not just in the Christian ministry that she sought this equality, but at home as well. She wrote:

> How can it be expected that a being trained in absolute sub-
> jection to the will of another, and taught to consider that
> subjection her glory, as well as an imbecile dependence on
> the judgment of others, should at once be able to throw off
> the trammels of prejudice and sound judgment which are

indispensable to the proper discharge of maternal duties?...
Never until she is valued and educated as a man's equal will
[marital] unions be perfect and their consequences blissful.[33]

But while there was equality, one senior officer explained that it was a democracy "up to a point." The Army gets things done fast, he explained, which is one reason it has adhered to the military format for more than a century.[34]

By May 1883, there were more than a dozen corps throughout Ontario, and on the twenty-fourth of that month, the Salvation Army's first Canadian headquarters building, constructed by the Army, was opened in Toronto. Twenty-five men and women comprised an officers' council, eleven of them women: Captain "Irish" Annie Maxwell, Captain Nellie Ryerson Ludgate, Captain Emma Churchill Dawson, Captain Mrs. Freer, Captain Wood, Captain Abby Thompson, Lieutenant Bessie Glannigan, Lieutenant Minnie Leidy, Captain Theresa Hall Wass, Captain O'Leary, and Lieutenant Nellie Kaiser.[35]

Their progress was so great that by the fall of 1884, sixty-two corps were operating in Canada, although some sources claim there were even more. Many of their representatives gathered in Toronto for a congress that they called a "great Council of War." There were bands and parades, religious services, and many converts. As the Salvation Army had explained years before in England:

> Many of our methods are very different to the religious
> usages and social tastes of respectable and refined people,
> which may make these measures appear vulgar, that is, in
> bad taste, to them; but this does not make them wrong in the
> sight of God.... And if it can be proved from the results that
> these methods lay hold of the ignorant and godless multi-
> tudes ... we think they are thereby proved to be both lawful
> and expedient.[36]

But during the Salvation Army meetings and afterwards, there were frequently "murderously-meant" attacks by irate parents, relatives, and rabble-rousers. Children who had attended the meetings were turned out of their homes for "disgracing the family." Workmen were dismissed from their jobs for joining the Army. Hot pans, knives, forks, and crockery went flying in all directions as dangerous missiles at their meetings and during their parades. Once, two young Canadian Salvation Army girls were almost killed and had to be rescued by soldiers. One convert in Toronto, affectionately nicknamed "Shouting Nelly," married one of the male converts, effectively preventing her mother from forcing her to stay at home.[37]

Still, their religious activities persisted. Slightly more of the converts to the Army were women who had been servants, homemakers, or dressmakers. The men who joined were labourers, farmers, or skilled and unskilled workers. They were generally in their twenties when they became officers; almost all were under forty.[38] As the historian Lynne Marks suggested, "If facing the choice between drudgery in a factory or in someone else's kitchen or the life of a Salvation Army officer with its sense of high spiritual calling, relative freedom and male and female companionship, it is not surprising that many women chose to become officers."[39]

By the late 1880s, the Canadian Army was ready to begin its "rescue" efforts. A woman experienced in this work, Staff Captain Jones, was sent from England to Toronto to direct this program. A plain building of brick and stone in downtown Toronto became the site for the "reclamation of fallen women." But Staff Captain Jones found the work more difficult in Canada than in England: the prostitution trade operated undercover in Toronto. It wasn't long, however, before there were new buildings across the country for young girls who needed help, along with modern hospitals and homes for children and the aged. In 1890 the Army set up a "Prison Gate Home for Men"; they met prisoners newly released from jail and took them to a special home where they helped them re-enter society and find suitable work. The Army taught them new skills such as how to bake bread, which was then supplied to all their institutions in the city, and how to make boots for sale. There were homes for rescued babies, some dreadfully mutilated. There were Army officers who spent their days and nights locating missing persons, part of their Missing Person's Bureau. In 1893 the League of Mercy was set up — eleven women made up a charter group of "modern Samaritans" who visited prisons and hospitals when they were needed and requested to act as intermediaries between men and women and their relatives or authorities, and the need apparently was

Salvation Army All Women's Band in 1893.

enormous. There were food depots, hostels, and homes for women. Wherever there was hardship, the Salvation Army could be found. Still today, Salvation Army recruits promise to care for the poor, feed the hungry, clothe the naked, love the "unlovable," and befriend those who have no friends.[40]

The unfortunate reality, however, was that when the men and women entered the social service work of the Army, more than a third of the women remained no more than a year, and more than 60 percent remained for three years or less. With male officers, the turnover rate was even higher — 39 percent remained in the army for no more than a year. Evidently their preference was preaching, meetings, and parades.[41]

In 1896 thirty-one-year-old Evangeline Cory Booth (1865–1950), the seventh of Catherine and William's children, arrived in Toronto as the new territorial commander of Canada. Catherine had read *Uncle Tom's Cabin* just before the baby was born and wanted to name her Evangeline after one of the book's heroines, but William didn't like that name and wrote *Evelyne* on the birth certificate. Years later, Frances Willard (1839–1898), the founder of the WCTU in the United States, suggested to Evelyne that Evangeline would be more dignified, and so she took that name instead.

Evangeline had been part of the Army since she was a child. At fifteen she became a sergeant, selling their paper, the *War Cry*, in the slums of London, England. When she was twenty-one, she was appointed field commissioner in Great Britain, and was later put in charge of officer training. She came to Canada from the United States, where she had been territorial commander; her first task was bringing refugees from Armenia. In 1898 she and a group of Salvationists headed to the Klondike, where the gold rush was in full swing. Evangeline remained in Canada until 1904, when she was again posted to the United States. In 1934 she was elected general of the whole Salvation Army denomination, the first woman to hold that position.

The Baptists

The Baptists organized their first churches in Amsterdam in 1609 and in England in 1611 or 1612. At first, women made up more than half of the membership, and they were theoretically allowed to be part of the leadership as deacons. Both John Smyth (ca. 1570–ca. 1612) and Thomas Helwys (ca. 1575–ca. 1616), considered the originators of the Baptist Church in these two countries, wrote in *A Pattern of True Prayer* that the Church was to elect, approve, and ordain deacons, both men and women. But that didn't happen in most of their churches. Women often served as lesser deaconesses, not deacons, and sometimes as widows who assisted male deacons in looking after the poor and sick. The question of women preaching and in leadership positions was often discussed at general meetings, partly because many women did speak in churches and assume leadership positions, in the face of severe criticism and both verbal and written abuse.

This was especially true in the United States, where Catherine Scott was thought to have been the first Baptist woman preaching, in 1639. Later, between 1790 and 1845, at least fifty Baptist women were documented crossing the country, preaching, presiding over funerals, visiting, and voting at church meetings, mostly in the Free Will Baptist churches and the Baptist Christian Connexion churches. The Baptist denomination was a loosely organized group of churches of various theological positions, some more conservative than others, and some more welcoming to women's participation in their religious services and administration.

Therefore, it should not be thought remarkable that a few women were prominent in Canadian Baptist churches. Nor should it be deemed surprising that there are few details available about women in these churches, given the difficult struggle to unearth women in history in general, and Black women in particular.

The First Baptist Church in Toronto/York, the oldest continuously operating church in Toronto, was organized in 1826 by twelve Black men and women fleeing the hardships of slavery in the United States. At first, they met in each other's homes and then in rental space until a small church was built in 1905. The women in this church worked in missions, visited the sick, and raised money for those in need in both Canada and Africa.

Elizabeth Williams Shadd Shreve (1826–1890/6), born to the abolitionist Abraham Shadd and his wife, Harriet, was the sister of celebrated Mary Ann Shadd, the Canadian newspaper publisher. Elizabeth was brought up in

The first permanent Baptist church in Toronto built by Black settlers.

Delaware and married George Shreve; they had several children. Delaware was initially quite hospitable to Black people, but became more inhospitable in the mid-1800s. The Shreves moved to Canada.

Initially brought up a Catholic, Elizabeth converted to the Baptist Church in Canada. In 1882 she became the first president of and a stellar fundraiser for the Women's Home Mission Society of the Amherstburg (Black Baptist) Association. She also became an itinerant minister and preacher, known as Sister Shreve, looking after the sick and collecting clothes and food for the needy, travelling by horseback around the country, preaching sermons, and undertaking other offices of the church. It was on one of these journeys that her horse stumbled. She was thrown to the ground and died from her injuries.

Mary Branton Tule (1860–1923) was a fan of Elizabeth's and wrote a poem, which was read out at her funeral:

> Dearest Sister thou hast left us:
> Gone to join the blood-washed throng.
> Though we miss thee from our number,
> We must say God's will be done.[42]

Mary Branton was born in Chatham, Ontario. Orphaned in her teens, she soon joined the First Baptist Church. She believed she was called to be a missionary in Africa, even though the Baptists encouraged Baptist couples, not single women. She went to Detroit and attended the Second Baptist Church to get a good-paying job to earn enough money for her education. She, too, became president of the Women's Home Mission Society and attended Spelman Seminary in Atlanta, Georgia, where Dr. Sophia Jones, a Black Canadian, was on the faculty. Jones had left Toronto, where she had not been accepted in a medical faculty.

Mary qualified as a missionary, sponsored by the Second Baptist Church. She preached on board ship on her way to Cape Town, South Africa, in 1896, obviously a gifted communicator.

Soon, she travelled up north to the Zambezi River, 2,400 kilometres away, through hostile Africans, poisonous insects, wild animals, inhospitable weather, impassable roads, and linguistic barriers, perhaps with another missionary, John Tule, whom she married in Scotland on her first sabbatical. On her return to Africa, she established the Mary Branton Tule School in Cape Town, with herself and John as its staff and faculty.

Before her second furlough, John died, leaving Mary a widow with limited funds for her ministry. However, she was able to finance another ten years. After a third furlough of seven years, she arrived back in South Africa to discover that Black missionaries were no longer welcome. Mary died in 1923 of malnutrition, only sixty-three years old. A poem was written for her memorial service in Canada by Harriet (Hattie) Rhue Hatchett:

> Her glad gospel armour she now has laid down,
> To receive from the Father a white robe and crown.
> May the light from her tomb cast its rays far and wide
> Till Africa's sons shall be drawn to Christ's side.[43]

A female musician who is not generally well-known in Toronto's musical circles, Hattie Rhue Hatchell (1863–1958) was a Black educator, Baptist missionary, and prolific hymn writer. She had been born to escaped slaves who had been helped on the Underground Railroad by the renowned Harriet Tubman, and her family name had been changed from Miles to Rhue to try to evade captivity after the Fugitive Slave Act was passed in 1850 in the United States. All the members of her family (parents and sixteen children) were very musical, and neighbours would flock to their house to hear them sing, especially around Christmas. They were also very religious and friendly with their neighbours, the Shadd Shreves (see above).

After graduating from high school, Hattie taught school, eventually marrying one of her oldest students, Millard Hatchett. Hattie played the keyboard melodeon and piano, and she became the first organist and choir director of the North Buxton Baptist Church in Ontario, from the 1890s onward. She was known for not allowing anyone to mumble. "Let everyone know what you are singing," she is reported to have told the choir members; also to "open up your mouth and sing like you mean it."[44]

Hattie wrote hymns, both the words and music, and other songs. Many of these were the result of spiritual visions she received while she was lying in bed at night, when she heard a man playing a silver horn up above her, with an angel in her vision as well.

Much later, her four-verse song "That Sacred Spot," published in 1913, was selected as the official marching song for Canadian troops in the First World War:

> *Refrain*: There's a Sacred Spot beyond the sea
> There's a soldier's grave so dear to me
> Holy Father will you guard it well
> O my love for him no tongue can tell
> Keep your vigil o'er it night and day.
> Guard that Sacred Spot so far away.
> God of battles will you hear my plea
> For that Sacred Spot beyond the sea.[45]

HARRIET TUBMAN AND THE UNDERGROUND RAILROAD

The Underground Railroad was a series of hiding places and safe houses, called stations, in the United States and Canada. Ordinary citizens or conductors helped ferry escaping slaves from one station to another. One of the most celebrated conductors was Harriet Tubman (ca. 1820–1913), who herself was an escaped slave. As a slave, she had been forced to do housekeeping chores when she turned five and was beaten because she was too young to be able to do them well. She was not considered sale-able because she experienced unpredictable bouts of sleeping during the daytime, the result of an injury to her forehead. Eventually she was given outdoor chores, which held her in good stead later when she became a cham-pion conductor on the Underground Railroad because of her knowledge of the outdoors and her physical strength. She was small and considered plain-looking, which also helped when she led her colleagues to freedom, first in the northern free states and then in Canada when the American Fugitive Slave Act (1850) meant that even free Black people could be press-ganged and sold into slavery.

It is thought that Harriet made nineteen trips into the southern United States to rescue upwards of three hundred slaves, many of them family. All she escorted made it to freedom, and none were recaptured.[46] Harriet is supposed to have said, "If you hear the dogs, keep going. If you see the torches in the woods, keep going. If there's shouting after you, keep going. Don't ever stop. Keep going. If you want a taste of freedom, keep going."[47]

Another exceptional nineteenth-century Black Baptist woman was Jennie Johnson (1868–1967), whose male ancestors were beaten trying to escape slavery and whose grandfather, Jacob Johnson, died as a result. Jennie herself was stillborn, but her mother, Charlotte Butler Johnson, a well-known midwife, massaged her heart, bringing her back to life. When she turned sixteen, Jennie knew that she would be a minister. In 1886 she helped found a new Baptist Church — Union Baptist Church — and when still young, led evangelistic services there every night for nine weeks. Because she wanted to become a missionary to Africa, in 1892 she went to Wilberforce University in Ohio, thought to be the oldest Black private university in the United States. In order to pay for her education, she took up "domestic work," a job most Black women tried to avoid.

Unfortunately, for some unknown reason, Jennie didn't become a missionary. She did help build Union Baptist Church, preached there, and did all the work of an ordained minister, but she was denied ordination because she was a woman. Jennie was ordained eventually, but not in Canada. The Free Will Baptist Church in Michigan, which had a history of female ordination, ordained her and she then went to Dresden in Canada to work in the Baptist Church there.

All women preachers had to have thick skins to tolerate the criticism they received from the public who supported a more domestic femininity. Yet, it is interesting that women in the Quaker Societies and the Salvation Army appear to have continued their work in Upper Canada/Ontario with little or no lessening of authority or position during the nineteenth century while the Methodist women lost considerable ground. It appears to have been a deliberate move, however, on the part of the Wesleyan Methodist hierarchy in Upper Canada. The British Anglican administrators of the new colony were concerned that all Methodists were too American and that itinerant Methodist ministers were not bona fide clergy. They perceived them as untrained, ignorant fanatics, a dangerous element, American democratic sympathizers with "noxious" principles. Indeed, the Upper Canada governing clique understood the whole system of Republican/Democratic government to be "contrary to the universal order of nature."[48] As the writer and early immigrant John Howison claimed to have observed in 1821:

> A large number of ... people ... profess Methodism, and carry their religious mania to an immoderate height. Meetings are held at different houses, three or four times a week. At some of these I have seen degrees of fanaticism and extravagance exhibited, both by the preachers and congregation, which were degrading to human nature.... [The actions of Methodists] were, in many instances, one continued outrage against decency, decorum and virtue.[49]

While the Anglican Church was not legally a state church, it was generally perceived as such. Even though the Methodists were more numerous at the time, the Anglican Church was given certain privileges such as solemnizing marriages and receiving money from the sale of the Clergy Reserves, land set aside for the church. Some other more acceptable denominations, such as the Lutherans and the Church of Scotland, were also privileged. The Methodists wanted in, too.

Compounding the negative attitude toward the Methodists on the part of the Anglican governing élite was the fact that the Methodists were gaining rapidly in numbers as the Anglicans were growing much more slowly. The *Census of the Canadas 1851–2* reported that Methodists of all stripes had grown from 77,643 members in the City of Toronto in 1842 to 211,382 in 1851, almost three times, whereas the Anglicans had not quite doubled in membership in Toronto during that same period. The most threatening aspect of this was that the Episcopal Methodists, or those initially from the United States, had increased the most — from 2,411 to 43,884 members in Toronto. This was partly because the Methodists took their religion to where the people were, and their services were suited to a scattered and secluded people, whereas many of the Anglicans expected the people to come to a church building for worship, in many cases inconveniently and inaccessibly distant.

Even with these statistics, there was a deliberate move on the part of the Methodist hierarchy to be well-liked, to be seen as not too loud, not too radical, and definitely not American. This included keeping women in their proper place, which was not in the formal ministry. And so, while women in other Protestant denominations inched their way forward, in the Methodist churches, they were pushed out of ministerial positions. It was not until 1936 that a woman (Lydia Emilie Gruchy, 1894–1992) was ordained as a minister in the Methodist Church, then a part of the United Church of Canada.[50]

The Baptists, despite their plans in the beginning to treat men and women alike, were also mixed in their approach. Some of their churches, such as the Free Will Baptists, did treat women equitably for a time, but most of them refused to ordain women.[51] However, Black women were preaching in those churches earlier than in any other denomination.

A number of instances in the Baptist missionary societies illustrate the dichotomy of women's status in religious society. If men were present at their meetings, the female president of the society would often decline presiding, leaving it to the gentlemen in the room. And the money raised by the women for their own missionary enterprises was seen by some of the men in the general mission societies as diverting funds that should have been given to the general societies.[52]

The Sisters of St. Joseph

In 1851 Mother Delphine (1813–1856) and three other Sisters of St. Joseph — Sister Mary Martha (Maria [von] Bunning) (1824–1868), Sister Alphonsus (Sarah Margerum) (1826–1855), and Sister Mary Bernard (Ellen Dinan) (1829–1901) — came to Toronto to care for an overcrowded orphanage that had been set up as a result of the recent epidemics. Parents had died on the voyage across the Atlantic to the "New World" and in the fever sheds in Toronto after they arrived, leaving scores of parentless children. Mother Delphine had recently been appointed superior of a novitiate in Philadelphia, but, in desperation, Toronto's Roman Catholic bishop, Armand-François-Marie de Charbonnel, asked to have her released from her duties there and brought to his city.[53]

The Sisters of St. Joseph had been founded around 1646 in France by six women and a Jesuit priest with the purpose of helping the sick, the poor, and the vulnerable. The sisters wore the common dress of the day, lived in a small group, and professed simple vows. They made and sold lace and ribbon to support themselves financially. During the French Revolution (1789–1799), however, Catholic orders were disbanded, and several of the nuns were either guillotined or imprisoned. But a distant ancestor of Mother Delphine, Jeanne Fontbonne (Mother St. John) (1759–1843), who had escaped execution, revitalized the community after she was released from jail.

The nineteenth-century Mother Delphine had been born in France as Marie-Antoinette Fontbonne, the eleventh child of a vinedresser and his wife. Marie-Antoinette entered the community of the Sisters of St. Joseph in Lyons when she was nineteen, and sailed to the United States with an older sister, Antoinette (Sister Fébronie), in 1836. There she was appointed head of a log cabin convent in St. Louis, Missouri, then superior of a novitiate and orphanage in Philadelphia.[54]

In Canada, the sisters cared for more than orphans. As a contemporary account noted, "Hardly had they placed their bonnets and shawls in the front room, when the Superior was inspecting, arranging, ordering from dormitory to cellar. It was not long before a complete transformation was effected." They supported themselves financially by begging in the streets and doing laundry, among other chores. They also received funds from bazaars, concerts, and picnics. In 1852 Sister Mary Martha was dispatched to Hamilton to open an orphanage there, and two sisters began teaching in St. Patrick's School in Toronto. They set up two other separate schools in 1853 and organized a mission to the nearby city of Amherstburg. In 1855 Mother Delphine began planning the House of Providence, a house of refuge open to all; over the next century it expanded to provide care, food, and shelter for more than seven hundred people at any one time. Unfortunately, 1856 brought another wave of typhus to Toronto, and Mother Delphine and some of her community, consisting by then of thirty-eight women, succumbed to the disease. Still, the House of Providence was built, opening in 1857.[55]

The sisters were heavily involved in teaching. In 1854 they established St. Joseph's Academy, a private day and boarding school for girls offering elementary and secondary studies; they also founded five Catholic girls' high schools throughout the area and three schools of nursing attached to hospitals in Toronto and Winnipeg. The St. Nicholas Home for Boys, a hotel for working boys such as newsboys and boot blacks, opened in 1868, and the sisters were asked to look after that facility. In 1871 they established a hostel for working girls such as seamstresses and teachers, Notre Dame des Anges, where they also offered courses in numerous subjects, including music and art. In 1891 they took charge of an isolation hospital during that year's diphtheria epidemic, and the next year they opened St. Michael's Hospital in downtown Toronto with twenty-six beds. They founded more hospitals across the country in the next century. Six nuns volunteered to staff the isolation hospital during the epidemic in 1891, and despite the close contact they had with their contagious patients, all the nursing sisters except the directress lived into their seventies and eighties.[56]

Margaret Brennan (Sister Teresa) (1831–1887) was the first Canadian-born member of the sisters. She became the first Canadian-born superior general in 1858, two years after Sister Delphine was a victim of typhus.

The Loretto Sisters

Mary Ward (1585–1645), an Englishwoman, was declared "Venerable" in 2009 by Pope Benedict XVI and named an "incomparable woman." In her lifetime, however, she had been censured by the Catholic Church and thrown in prison for usurping roles that "rightfully" belonged to males — the conversion of England. Then the Church described her and her Englishwomen followers as "poisonous growths in the Church of God [which] must be torn up from the roots lest they spread themselves further." Mary had established schools for girls throughout Europe; she planned to strengthen the Catholic faith in women, especially in England, by training young girls in order to influence the wives and mothers of future generations. She believed that women were mentally, physically, and morally equal to men and should have access to equal education. She also created a new order for women, the Institute of the Blessed Virgin Mary, which was non-monastic and non-cloistered. Mary's order has continued today in two contemporary orders, one being the Loretto Sisters.[57]

In 1847 Michael Power, then bishop of Toronto, asked the Loretto order in Ireland for help with his burgeoning Catholic population. Five young sisters were sent out to Canada; the youngest was Ellen Dease (1820–1889), named Mother Teresa, soon to become the superior of their tiny group. She had been raised by her grandmother in Dublin, having been orphaned when she was five years old. Educated at her grandmother's home, in Dublin, and in Paris, she spoke French and Italian and became a musician. It was not until she was twenty-five that she entered the Roman Catholic order of the Loretto Sisters in Dublin.

The *Garrick*, which the sisters sailed to Canada on, was delayed, and years later Mother Teresa confessed, "One day longer in the cherished land of our birth … was a balm to the heart." Homesick, the sisters found there was no one to meet them in Toronto and no place ready for them to stay, and the city was raging with disease. However, they soon had a small school of nine boarders where they taught language and music. A larger boarding academy they also set up advertised a course of education for "Ladies," comprised of "Reading, Elocution, Arithmetic, English, French, Italian, History, Geography, Useful and Ornamental Needlework, Music and Painting." Twenty boarders could be accommodated at twenty-five pounds per annum. Textbooks were from the Irish National School curriculum.

The young nuns were not used to Canadian weather, and disease was rampant in the city. They requested more sisters from Ireland. Within four years,

Mother Teresa was the only nun alive out of the original five, although more arrived from Ireland and postulants were attracted in Toronto.

Eventually the women taught in two kinds of schools in Toronto: convent schools for young women who could afford to pay tuition, and free schools for Catholic children, soon known as separate schools.

In 1849 the sisters announced a public examination of the "Pupils of the House of Loretto," a common happening with many schools at this time. There were public morning and evening programs; French and English dramas; musical numbers; displays of needlework, drawing, painting, and wax flowers in the classrooms; and public questioning of students on various subjects that displayed their knowledge and accomplishments. The school prospered, and other convents were opened in surrounding communities — Mother Teresa opened thirteen during her administration. Soon the sisters were attending Toronto Normal School, and needlework and china painting were no longer part of their schools' course of study.

The Loretto Sisters' strength was always education, and one of the Canadian-born sisters — Margaret O'Neil (1842–1927), Mother Agatha — worked tirelessly both to assure that the sisters themselves were well-educated in order to teach, and to establish a college for Catholic women at the University of Toronto. However, it was only in 1911 that an agreement was reached, allowing Catholic women to be enrolled formally in St. Michael's College at the university.

Perhaps the best-known sister in this order was not a Canadian educator but Mother Mary Teresa Bojaxhiu (1910–1997), or "Mother Teresa of Calcutta," who felt called to serve the poorest of the poor in Calcutta and requested permission to leave the Sisters of Loretto.

Many other orders were active in nineteenth-century Toronto, such as the Sisters of the Good Shepherd, whose facilities were set up to rehabilitate women, and the Sisters of Charity of St. Vincent de Paul. The Catholic Church was concerned that Toronto's Catholics, and especially Irish Catholics, should have support services to help them survive, keep them within the Church, and take pride in their Irish heritage. Because of their communicable diseases and abject poverty when they arrived in Toronto, the Irish were severely stigmatized, often ostracized, and their children sometimes physically abused. Prior to 1846, Toronto had a small Catholic population, but the famine immigrants rapidly increased their number to one-quarter of the city, and by 1855 the Irish made up 90 percent of Toronto's Catholics.

Sisterhood of St. John the Divine

While most religious sisters lived in Roman Catholic communities, an active convent community within the Anglican Church was established in Toronto toward the end of the nineteenth century. Ironically, in deciding to create this order, the Anglican Church was influenced by the great work that Roman Catholic sisters were accomplishing. The provincial inspector of charities, Dr. W.T. O'Reilly, pointed out that while only one-fifth of the population in Ontario was Roman Catholic, 1,557 patients were treated in Roman Catholic hospitals, compared to 3,519 patients in all other hospitals; in refuges, there were 989 in Roman Catholic institutions and only 564 in all other institutions; and Roman Catholic sisters cared for 1,651 orphans compared to 1,381 elsewhere. The Anglican Church listened.[58]

Brought up as a "high-church" Anglican and widowed in 1878, Sarah Hannah Roberta Grier Coome (1837–1921) had decided to join the Community of St. Mary in England, but Anglicans in Toronto prevailed upon her to begin a sisterhood there instead. To prepare, Hannah and a friend, Amelia Elizabeth (Aimée) Hare, entered the novitiate of the Community of St. Mary in Peekskill, New York, and spent time observing at their hospital and their missions in that state. Then, in 1884, Hannah founded a new Sisterhood of St. John the Divine in Toronto, which began activities such as meals for the poor, a dispensary, Bible classes, and sewing for churches. They followed what is known as the "mixed Religious Life," both prayer and works of mercy. At first they wore long black habits, which some of their religious colleagues found "too Roman Catholic."[59]

They undertook their first big project in the spring of 1885, when they were asked to help out as trained nurses in a western field hospital in Moose Jaw, Saskatchewan, where wounded men were brought from the North-West Resistance. Hannah, Aimée, and two postulants from the fledgling order travelled west, leaving three sisters in Toronto. The next year, they set up St. John's House, the first surgical hospital for women in Toronto; then they established a home for the aged. They have also run schools and orphanages, offered religious retreats, and made altar linens. Now they have communities in Toronto and Victoria, British Columbia.[60]

Missionaries

North American women also joined sewing or Dorcas groups or taught Sunday school in the various denominations. By the 1830s Sunday schools were common throughout Upper Canada, and they were often where children learned to read.

Many women also found great satisfaction and stimulation in missionary societies. These were some of the largest women's organizations in the nineteenth century and the first national women's groups to form. Not only were women active in the societies in Canadian churches, but they also served in foreign countries as missionaries themselves, often because male missionaries were not allowed access to the local women, who in some other lands were kept out of sight. The churches realized that the only way they could contact these "hidden" women was by sending female missionaries along with the men, and most Protestant denominations, many headquartered in Toronto, sent out female missionaries around the world.

Trying to deal with gender issues, however, sometimes had serious complications. For example, the first women the Canadian Presbyterian Church sent out to India in an effort to convert women in secluded zenanas (areas in households where women were segregated and sequestered from view) had problems. Marion Fairweather Stirling (1846–1888) from Bowmanville, east of Toronto, was a teacher who applied to the Presbyterian Church to become a missionary with a friend, Margaret Rodger. Marion had a personality that was not easy to work with on the mission field. She believed she should convert high-caste Indian men in addition to visiting women in zenanas and teaching school. There was no question as to her capability, ambition, and drive. But her attempts to convert men was the basis for gossip of unfounded sexual improprieties. Fairweather was recalled from the mission field, and despite her pleas to be posted to another location and her subsequent medical training, her missionary career ended ignominiously.[61] In spite of this experience, most of the Protestant denominations encouraged deaconesses and female missionaries.

Deaconesses

Some denominations trained women as deaconesses or church workers not requiring ordination as ministers or priests. In 1893, after a few years of preparation, the Anglican Church opened the Church of England Deaconess and Missionary Training House in Toronto to train women for church work. Gradually, over a few years, a committee hammered out what these women would do after they were trained: visiting in parishes; Bible reading; evangelistic work among the poor and the rich; caring for the poor and the sick; working in soup kitchens; making clothes and selling second-hand clothes; looking after young women in homes; caring for and correcting children; looking after crèches (nurseries for babies and young children); working in prisons; training church workers; and fostering and developing a missionary spirit. It was an impossible list.

Perhaps the most improbable part was that the deaconesses were to be volunteers. There was to be no salary and the deaconesses were to be unmarried. The amazing result was that someone did apply and offered her house for the school. Unfortunately, she was not well enough physically to undertake the role of head deaconess. Finally, a suitable woman, Fanny Cross, was selected as head deaconess and some other women applied to be students — Annie Rae and Margaret Darling. The home was opened. After their training, most of the women found positions within the Anglican Church in Canada, although poorly paid. In 1969 the school joined with the United Church of Canada's Covenant College, becoming the Centre for Christian Studies in downtown Toronto, training deaconesses in both denominations.[62]

CHAPTER 7

PROPRIETORS OF BOARDING HOUSES, TAVERNS, AND HOTELS

———— ◆ ————

The historian Edwin Guillet noted that at every crossroad in Upper Canada in the nineteenth century there was at least one tavern, and the main highway was dotted with dozens more. Even as early as 1801, the town of York boasted only seventeen shops and around seven hundred inhabitants but six taverns, or one for about every 115 people. In 1850, with about thirty thousand residents, Toronto kept a lower, but still high, ratio — 152 taverns or one for every 190 men and women, along with 206 beer shops. Liquor was always cheap and widely available.[1] The ratio of taverns to people peaked in 1829, and then declined somewhat.[2] Whisky cost about seventeen cents a gallon in the early years, too great a temptation for many. It was not uncommon for a discouraged land-clearing husband to take solace in the "stone jug" and desert his wife and family, leaving them destitute. When Anna Jameson was travelling in Ontario, she commented on the high level of drunkenness in the country. As she pointed out, there were few booksellers around but plenty of taverns. "There is a duty of thirty per cent on books imported from the United States, and the expense of books imported from England adds at least one-third to their price; but there is no duty on whisky," she wrote. She repeated the ditty,

> Men learn to drink, who never drank before;
> And those who always drank, now drink the more.[3]

A lady wrote to the *Upper Canada Gazette* that a tax was to be laid on "scolding wives." She thought that one should be imposed on drunken husbands to be equitable and just. She wrote:

> The manner in which they are to be rated is as follows: For getting drunk in the morning, £30 per annum; twice a day, £40; three times a day ... £50; every alternate day, £20; once a week, if not on Sundays, £15; on Sundays, £60; for beating his wife once a day, £200; ... coming home from the tavern drunk and beating his wife into a fit of hysterics, consumption or giving her a pair of black eyes, £700. Getting drunk and being in consequence confined to his bed a week or two, £1,000.[4]

Liquor soon caused so many problems that the Woman's Christian Temperance Union was organized around the continent; it was one of the first reform organizations in Toronto and Upper Canada.[5] Didactic "high-minded" literature became common. One example is Dr. Benjamin Ward Richardson's book for reading in schools and families, *The Temperance Lesson Book: A Series of Short Lessons on Alcohol and Its Action on the Body*, which ends with this caution:

> Believe, finally, that you yourselves will, under the rule of total abstinence, grow up strengthened in wisdom, industry, and happiness, and that your success in life will reward you a thousand-fold for every sacrifice of false indulgence in that great curse of mankind — strong drink.[6]

Initially, however, taverns, inns, and hotels were an essential part of life in Upper Canada. Innkeepers were more than innkeepers. They sometimes had to act as bankers or storekeepers, and often courts and local meetings took place in those establishments. They were the centres of social life: the first church services, council meetings, libraries, circuses, and dances were held in taverns. As one sign in a tavern noted, "Would those patrons learning to read please use yesterday's newspaper." Villages were built around them and the tavern-keeper might be the best-known and most popular person in the district. They were, of course, also stops along the way in a tedious and uncomfortable journey. And no one appreciated them more than stagecoach drivers after hours of bumping and jostling along the horrendous Upper Canadian roads.[7]

Because they were social centres, women were an integral part of the activities held in taverns. In his journal (from 1801 to 1853), settler Ely Playter records activities of a number of women in his own tavern in downtown York. The historian Julia Roberts counted forty-eight women named in Playter's diary, twenty-seven of them in some activity in his tavern. Mary Thomson lived in his tavern; Sophia Beman, a neighbouring tavern-keeper's daughter, was often in Ely's tavern, as he was courting and would eventually marry her; a "Miss T." and a "Miss B.," probably Mary and Sophia, met with Ely and other men and women to play musical instruments, talk, drink wine and tea, and read to each other in some of the tavern rooms. Of course, women worked in taverns as well.[8]

It was also common for women to own taverns, inns, and hotels, although according to Ely Playter, the profit one could make from this occupation was "trifling." However, Blanche Westlake and her brother-in-law John Hoare had a small empire that included the Royal Adelaide Inn, stables, a blacksmith shop, and adjacent farms, so some people found financial success in that trade.[9]

A poem addressed to a woman tavern owner in 1874 and quoted by Margaret McBurney, historian of taverns in Ontario, indicates how well-known and powerful an innkeeper was, male or female:

And there in whitewashed shanty grand,
With kegs and bottles on each hand,

Her face decked with a winning smile,
Her head with cap of ancient style,
Crowned arbiter of frolic's fate,
Mother McGinty sat in state,
And measured out the mountain dew
To those whom strong attraction drew
Within the circle of her power
To while away a leisure hour.
She was the hostess and the host,
She kept the reckoning, ruled the roast,
And swung an arm of potent might
That few would dare to brave in fight.[10]

Historians record a number of women innkeepers. The widow Hannah McBride was one of the first, but after her marriage in 1803, she left that occupation. In 1802 five of the tavern licences issued in Upper Canada were issued to women. In 1868, out of 201 licences issued that year, 16 went to women, almost 8 percent, and the gender of some who were awarded licences cannot be determined.[11] In 1833 a tavern licence cost eleven pounds, five shillings, while

Mrs. Margaret (Mother) McLean's tavern near Lakeshore Road and the east side of the Humber River, 1849. Mrs. McLean was the original grantee of Lots 40 and the west part of 39. Pencil drawing by F.H. Granger.

a shopkeeper's licence to sell spirituous liquor and wine in a quantity not less than one quart was only five pounds three and eight pence.[12]

Madame Vallière owned an early wayside hostelry at York Mills with help from her son and grandson, still there in 1812.[13] In 1815 a Scotsman named McLean had a tavern on the York side of the Humber River, and for many years after his death, his widow looked after it. In 1853 ownership passed to Mrs. Creighton, until it was destroyed in order to build a Great Western Hotel.

Like many of the businesses, especially market gardens and brickyards, taverns and inns passed on to widows after their husbands died. The Shamrock Hotel was owned by Thomas Lee's widow until she died in 1862. The Royal Arms had much the same fate; Christiana McFarlane inherited the hotel from her late husband and was still operating it in 1885. Jane Jordan operated the York Hotel for more than twenty-five years after the death of her husband in 1817. Mary Kennedy (Mrs. W.J. Lillis, 1869–?) owned the Eagle House in Weston after her husband, John Brasgrove Eagle, died in 1901.[14] In 1860 Mrs. Charlton inherited a tavern after her husband was killed in a fire on Shuter Street — he was a volunteer in the fire brigade — and she managed the business for two years until she remarried.

Mrs. Loden/Loder's tavern in 1844, 192 King Street East.

A brick store on King Street, built around the time of the 1837 rebellion, was a tavern in 1844 kept by Mrs. Loden/Loder, and later a dressmaking shop owned by the Misses Milligan. Next door, a Mrs. Flight kept a furniture store.[15]

Travellers often wrote casually of women as owners of inns or taverns — it was well accepted. When Anna Jameson was travelling in Ontario, she twice recorded visiting taverns, both owned by women. In one instance near a village called Stony Creek, her landlady told her of immigrating with her husband forty years earlier. They had prospered, owned three farms and several hundred acres of land, and brought up nine sons and daughters. The other occasion was on Jameson's way to visit Colonel Talbot, John Graves Simcoe's former secretary, at his new home on a cliff high above Lake Erie. In both instances, Jameson did not evince surprise at a female owner.[16] The historian Edwin Guillet, later travelling near Barrie, Ontario, found "Mrs. Barr's clearing and log inn."[17]

In 1829 Mary Gapper O'Brien once stopped for a night at what she describes as a very good inn, but with an ill-humoured barmaid. "She well nigh threw the viands at our heads because one of the company complained that the toast was burned. All of them laughed to see her make a slop basin of the fireplace," she wrote in her diary on October 20.

Jameson wrote that "the manners of the country innkeepers in Canada are worse than anything you can meet with in the United States, being generally kept by refugee Americans of the lowest class, or by Canadians who, in affecting American manners and phraseology, grossly exaggerate both."[18] In the early days of the nineteenth century, given the hostility toward Americans, it was assumed that any ill-tempered tavern-keeper must be an American. As the traveller and author Sir Richard Bonnycastle wrote on innkeepers, "If you meet with indifference and greasy meats, they are American." Indeed, census records support the fact that most tavern-keepers were American or Irish-born.[19]

Along with raising a family of thirteen children, Susanna Barnett Robinson (1825–1913) was looking after the Gladstone House at the corner of Gladstone and Queen Streets after her husband's death. It was one of the oldest continuously operating hotels in Toronto, built in 1889. Her husband, Nixon Robinson, owned the Red Lion in Kleinberg and the Globe in Yorkville, although he was also listed as a brewer. Susanna came to Canada in 1837. She was widowed with a large family before the red-brick-and-stone Gladstone was constructed. A popular and affordable hotel, it was used mainly by commercial travellers and exhibitors at the Canadian National Exhibition close by, although there were often events for artists and community groups in its bars and ballroom.[20]

In 1843 or 1849 Irish-born Bernard Short operated a brick-and-stone tavern in French-style Napoleon III on Garrison Common, but after he died in 1865, his wife, Mary (Anne) Rooney Short (1832–ca. 1898), owned and leased the complex of buildings on the corner of King and Bathurst for thirty years, as well as maintaining the inn. In 1872 she (or another Mary) married Moses Furlong and the inn became known as the Wheat Sheaf Tavern. Sources say that Mary managed it so successfully that when she died at age sixty-six, there was enough money for a substantial monument for her and her husband. It may be that Mary Rooney Short Furlong is one and the same Mary, married to

The Wheat Sheaf Tavern at Bathurst and King Streets, owned by Mrs. Short from 1866, after Bernard Short died, until 1872; thought to be the oldest existing tavern in Toronto, recently renovated and reopened (inset photo). Mrs. Furlong owned it from 1882 to 1883, after Moses Furlong died. Moses evidently bought it from Mrs. Short.

both Bernard Short and Moses Furlong. The Garrison at Fort York patronized the tavern. The Wheat Sheaf Tavern still exists in the twenty-first century, although it has recently been remodelled.[21]

One of the best-known female hotel proprietors was Catherine (Kate) Dwyer Greenwood (1822–1897), owner of the Puritan Hotel on Queen Street East, which opened in 1864. Also an ice dealer and market gardener, she operated the hotel after her husband's premature death in 1868 as the Greenwood's Hotel, even though the 1871 census reported that she was illiterate. Her husband, named for the English Puritan martyr John Greenwood, had apparently sold liquor out of their home without a licence before the hotel was built, and even after it opened, he was fined at some time for selling liquor illegally. A painter and carriage maker, John also loved to place bets. There were complaints that he kept a disorderly (that is, bawdy) house, but it may have been simply that he sold liquor illegally. Catherine and John had six children, the last born just after John's death when Catherine was forty-seven years old. She retired from the hotel in 1886 and then ran an ice cream parlour in the same neighbourhood. Sadly, there was a small ad placed by John's sister in a later *Globe and Mail* looking for the whereabouts of John Greenwood, coach painter. Perhaps Kate answered it.[22]

Another female-run hotel in the same area was Callendar's Hotel, operated by Jane Weymouth Callendar/Callender. The mother of seven children, she was solely in charge of the hotel after her husband Henry or "Hank" died in 1895. On a property measuring 150 by 500 feet, the hotel could accommodate forty guests and had excellent stables. Built in 1863, it had originally been known as Uncle Tom's until Jane and Henry remodelled it.[23]

The Rescue Tavern was kept by Mrs. Hickman in the 1850s. It sported a gigantic signboard with a sensational drawing of a mother rescuing her infant from an eagle's nest in a rocky pass at the head of some inaccessible mountains. A favourite spot for troops stationed at the Old and New Forts, it was the first place checked when soldiers were reported as being absent from their duties. Nearby, the Cooper's Arms was kept by Mrs. Julia Murphy, John Murphy's widow, and the Toronto Hotel was owned by Elizabeth Fawcett.[24]

Boarding houses, too, were kept by women, who were usually struggling to make a living. One of the most popular early boarding houses, established

Mrs. Hayes's popular boarding house at the northwest corner of King and Ontario Streets accommodated twenty guests, usually members of Parliament.

around 1812, was Mrs. Johnson Hayes's at King and Ontario Streets, where many out-of-town members of the legislature stayed when they had to be in York. Colonel Thomas Talbot always stayed at her place. A good-natured woman and a good cook and manager, Mrs. Hayes often "put on an impressive spread" if people wanted to entertain at her house. She married John Hayes, a bricklayer and plasterer, after her first husband's death.[25]

There were, of course, always some bad apples among the women owners. In 1804 innkeeper Elizabeth Ellis was convicted of keeping a disorderly house and sentenced to six months in jail and two hours on the pillory in front of the market on each of two days.

But generally, alcohol did not seem to be a problem for women. There were stories, however, that sometimes men became so discouraged in the woods and alcohol was so readily available that they left their families and ran away with alcohol as a solace. Catharine Parr Traill described a poor destitute woman with children not far from where they lived who was in that condition.

Alcohol was a fact of life at many events. Susanna Moodie described the reality of a "log house raising." The same was true of barn raisings. Many of the men went to local barn raisings not to help out, but to drink alcohol. William

Proudfoot, a Presbyterian minister in Middlesex County, raised a barn on his own property in 1833, and he reported that, while ninety men came to the three-day raising, about two-thirds of them never lifted a log, but had just come to drink. "There was such a quantity of swearing and buffoonery that the whole thing was very painful," he wrote. Yet at the bee of Robert Woodill, the father of Primitive Methodist preacher Jane Woodill, the barn went up in only part of a day, even though they served only coffee and sandwiches. Neighbours had cautioned that the barn would never be built, but as the workmen went away, they shouted, "Hurrah for the temperance barn!"[26] At that raising, there were no drunken brawls as there usually were at early bees, sometimes resulting in serious fights and fatalities.

CHAPTER 8

VISUAL, LITERARY, AND PERFORMING ARTISTS

———————⬤———————

n one sense, all Upper Canadian women were artists. They sewed patterned quilts, hooked and braided rugs, stitched samplers, knit, embroidered, and made many of their family's clothes. Of necessity, they were also engaged in what would be termed crafts today — making candles, spinning wool, and weaving cloth. Many of their artworks were quite colourful and original. A number of women had attended girls' schools where they were taught painting and drawing. Early settlers and adventurers such as Elizabeth Simcoe, Anna Jameson, Anne Langton, the Strickland sisters, Susanna Moodie, and Catharine Parr Traill were gifted artists and writers. They had been given lessons in drawing and painting as part of their "feminine" upbringing, and this became useful for some of them when they needed financial support, both in their birth country and in Upper Canada.[1]

In York, a literary and philosophical society was formed as early as 1831, as well as the short-lived Society of Artists and Amateurs; in 1834, the latter held an exhibition of 196 paintings at the legislature, its one and only exhibition. "Ladies" were admitted as subscribers to the York Literary and Philosophical

Drawing by Anne Langton.

Society on the recommendation of any two members; gentlemen needed three recommendations. The Society of Artists and Amateurs was more limited, including only one woman in its exhibition, Jemima Howard, described below.

Several nineteenth-century Toronto visual, literary, and performing artists are described briefly here. They were well-known at the time, but there were many other Canadian women who had no or limited contact with Toronto and are excluded from this chapter; and many female Canadian artists who may have been born in the nineteenth century but flourished in the twentieth are also omitted.

Visual Artists

Jeanne-Charlotte Allamand Berczy (1760–1839)

One of the earliest visual artists was Jeanne-Charlotte Allamand, who was born in Switzerland, where she learned how to paint. Her husband, Albert-Guillaume (William) Berczy, was at first a miniature artist. He and Jeanne-Charlotte exhibited paintings at the Royal Academy of Arts in London, England. However, in 1791, William was hired to recruit German colonists for New York State, which he did the next year, but dissatisfied with the arrangements, he left the group in the spring with Jeanne-Charlotte in charge. They resettled the group later, north of York/Toronto, while the Berczys themselves went to York. Jeanne-Charlotte was again left in charge of the settlement as Berczy travelled to find food and tools. Often left on her own, she used different means to support herself and her two sons, William and Charles, such as setting up a haberdashery and textile shop and organizing a school for girls where she taught drawing, watercolours, music, and languages. She painted later in life as a hobby. Her husband was also recognized in Canada as a competent writer and painter.[2]

Jemima Frances Meikle Howard (1802–1877)

Jemima Howard was the only woman to exhibit her paintings in the first and only exhibition of the Society of Artists and Amateurs, in 1834. It may have been because her husband, John Howard, was on the committee of the society and vice-president at the time, and one of the "Associated Artists."

Jemima Howard, as an older woman.

Jemima Meikel married John Howard in England; he was earlier known as John Corby. He had been a sailor for two years but found he had "an incurable liability to seasickness." Then he became a carpenter and a joiner, finally becoming a professional architect in 1827, the year he met and married Jemima. Five years later, they immigrated to Upper Canada, taking the surname of Howard from the 4th Duke of Norfolk, from whom John claimed he was descended.

In Toronto, John immediately became a teaching master at Upper Canada College and very rapidly set up a thriving architectural practice, which was involved in more than eighteen residential buildings, fifteen commercial buildings, and eleven ecclesiastical projects. Jemima assisted by preparing copies of specifications for his projects. In 1843 he became Toronto's official surveyor, later a public notary, and in 1853 a justice of the peace for a term of four years.

John bought the land in Toronto, in what is now known as High Park, which he intended as a sheep farm, and to the east, Sunnyside Farm, now the site of St. Joseph's Health Centre. On the High Park farm site, he built Colborne Lodge, a house that later became their country residence and still stands today. At first it had only three rooms, but by the time John was finished in the 1880s, the building had twenty-two rooms. The greenhouse was the last addition. John was interested in new scientific inventions, and he installed a shower and one of Toronto's first indoor flush toilets. Both John and Jemima were avid gardeners, planting orchards and gardens around the house, but keeping most of the property in its natural wooded state.

Later, the Howards gave their property to the City of Toronto, most of the present-day park, stipulating that they were to be allowed to live there as long as they wished and that there was to be no alcohol on the grounds. John became the official forest ranger for the property.[3]

Meanwhile, Jemima and John both painted, and John helped organize the Society of Artists and Amateurs. The rules for the first exhibition were that the "Associated Artists" had to exhibit more than eight paintings while the "Amateurs" could exhibit only up to eight. Jemima was classed as an amateur. The titles of her paintings are interesting: *Flowers, Wild Duck*

Shooting, Pheasant Shooting, Woodcock Shooting, Partridge Shooting, Interior of a Convent, Interior of a Monastery, and *The Tired Soldier.* All of these except the flowers are listed as painted by Mrs. Howard; *Flowers* is listed by "a Lady." But since that adds up to eight paintings, it is likely that *Flowers* was painted by her as well. And in the list of "Honorary Exhibitors," her name does not appear, but as there is the name of "a Lady," they are evidently one and the same. John's contributions are mostly architectural drawings, reproductions of masters, or paintings of Toronto buildings. One of the stars of the show was the well-known early Canadian artist Paul Kane.[4]

Jemima died of cancer in 1877 after years of pain. She was the first woman known to be diagnosed with breast cancer in Toronto. Some say that she still haunts the house. A psychic, Carolyn Molnar, claims that Jemima is a happy ghost in the kitchen, wearing an apron, while others claim they have seen her face in the windows.[5]

Mary Hastings Fitzgerald Meyer (ca. 1826–?)

Irish-born Mary Fitzgerald is the only nineteenth-century female artist recorded in Edith Firth's 1983 commemorative volume of artists depicting Toronto scenes. Her painting of an interesting view of the Don Valley shows the high wooded banks that once bordered the meandering Don River. Mary and Hoppner Francis Meyer, a painter of miniatures, married in 1852 and had two children, Hastings and Meta, although some sources record five. There are at least three surviving paintings of the city by Mary, including the one from the Don Valley of the river and the city in the distance, painted in 1855; the cupolas of City Hall and St. Lawrence Hall; and Little Trinity Church with the peninsula (later the island) in the background.[6]

In 1855 at least two aldermen moved in favour of buying Mary's five-foot-by-three-foot Don Valley painting — "such a beautiful painting and accurate view of our city executed in a masterly manner by one of our Townswomen." Alderman Gooderham voted against the motion, but two years later, when he was no longer on the council, the city bought it for fifty pounds. The *Daily Colonist* called it a "great work for a lady."[7]

The Don River with the city of Toronto in the background, viewed from the northeast. Painting by Mary Hastings Fitzgerald Meyer, 1855.

Mary won prizes for her art in 1853 as an amateur at the Upper Canada Provincial Exhibition, and between 1868 and 1885, she exhibited flower paintings in London, England, where she and her husband travelled; Hoppner had been from England originally.[8]

Agnes Dunbar Moodie Fitzgibbon Chamberlin (1833–1913)

The daughter of Susanna Moodie (*Roughing It in the Bush*) and niece of Catharine Parr Traill (*The Backwoods of Canada*), Agnes Moodie was thirty-two when her husband, barrister Charles Thomas Fitzgibbon, died. She was left with several young children and very little money. She taught herself to paint with advice from her mother and illustrated the lithographic prints in Traill's book *Canadian Wild Flowers with the Botanical Descriptions*. Published in Montreal in 1868, it was probably the first book in colour in Canada. Agnes proved to be not only a gifted artist but a successful marketer of her book. In 1870 she married Brown Chamberlin, a publisher and member of Parliament.[9]

Canadian Harebell, Campanula rotundifolia, painted by Agnes Dunbar Moodie Fitzgibbon.

Charlotte Mount Brock Morrell Schreiber (1834–1922)

English-born Charlotte Schreiber was already an artistic success when she was twenty-one, exhibiting at the Royal Academy and commissioned to illustrate several books. She and her husband and his children immigrated to Toronto in 1875, and the next year, she was elected to the Ontario Society of Artists, and then became the first woman to teach at the Ontario School of Art. In 1880 she was the first woman elected to the Royal Canadian Academy, although she was not allowed to attend meetings. Talented and energetic, she also helped found the Women's Art Association of Canada. She had studied anatomy and paid attention to detail and realism in her paintings. "The human hand, the finger nail, the foot, every portion of the living body, the parts of a flower, are divinely beautiful ... it is a joy to paint them as they are in reality," she wrote in 1895. She was not only a painter, but also an organist at St. Peter's Anglican Church. After the death of her husband, she returned to England in 1898.[10]

Alicia/Alice Killaly Turner (1836–1908)

Born in London, Ontario, Alice Killaly lived many years in Quebec City and Montreal, moving to Toronto in 1855. After her marriage in 1871 to Christopher H. Turner, a retired lieutenant in the Prince Consort's Own Rifle Brigade, she moved to England. Little is known about her early years, but it is thought that she studied art under the famous Dutch Canadian artist Cornelius Krieghoff (1815–1872).

Alice Killaly Turner.

Her known work shows Canadian scenes, such as canoe trips, frozen rivers, and Niagara Falls. Also thought to be by her are lithographs published in 1868 and signed A.K., depicting the winter adventures of Captain Busby and Miss Muffin. They provide a humorous glance at winter in mid-nineteenth-century Canada.

Mary Ella Williams Dignam (1857–1938)

Founder and initial president of the Women's Art Association in Toronto in 1892, Mary Ella worked in pastels and watercolours, and later in her career, she was greatly influenced by Impressionism. The association had earlier been the Women's Art Club, which Mary Ella began in 1886. In 1898, under her watch, the association coordinated an eight-course, twenty-four-place-setting state dinner service for Canada as a celebration of the four-hundredth anniversary of the explorer John Cabot's visit to Canada in 1497. Fourteen or sixteen Canadian female artists participated in the project, although Mary Ella was not one of them. At least nine of the women artists were from Toronto or had strong connections to the city: Martha Logan (1863–1937), Clara Elizabeth Galbreaith/Galbraith (1864–1941), Juliet Howson Burdoin (1873–1963), Margaret Irvine, M. Roberts, Justina Harrison, Lily Osman Adams/Adam (1865–1945), Jane Bertram (?–ca. 1940), and M. Louise/Louisa Couen/Cohen. Other participating women artists were from Galt, Hamilton, St. Catharines, Yarmouth, Halifax, and Montreal. The plates depicted Canadian scenes on Royal Doulton and Limoges china, with Canadian flora from strawberries to dogtooth violets and fauna from Canada geese to brook trout. The Canadian government (members of the Senate and the House of Commons) purchased the Cabot Commemorative State Service as a parting gift for Lady Ishbel Hamilton-Gordon, Marchioness of Aberdeen and Temair (1857–1939), who had been in Canada with her husband, Lord Aberdeen, the governor general from 1893 to 1898. Lady Aberdeen supported women's suffrage, and during her stay in the country, she had helped found the National Council of Women of Canada, the Victorian Order of Nurses, and the Women's Art Association of Canada. She was the first president of the International Council of Women.[11]

Lady Aberdeen. Topley photographers, date unknown. Silver gelatin print, laid down on cardboard mount.

Mary Ella later helped found the International Society of Women Painters and Sculptors and, in 1900, the first all-women's international art exhibition.

Gertrude Eleanor Spurr Cutts (1858–1941)

Gertrude worked in various media — oil, watercolours, and pen-and-ink sketches — but she is best known for her rural landscapes. She also spent time restoring old or damaged paintings.

She was born in England and exhibited her work there, but immigrated to Toronto in 1890, where she opened an art studio. She became the

Gathering of Canadian artists. Gertrude Eleanor Spurr Cutts (1858–1941) and Mary Evelyn Wrinch Reid (1877–1969), centre left, sit among a phalanx of Canadian male artists at an Art Gallery of Ontario opening. Mary Wrinch flourished in the twentieth century, known for her miniature paintings and her boldly coloured northern Ontario landscapes.

corresponding secretary of the Art Students' League in 1896. Her work was shown in the Palace of Fine Arts at the 1893 World's Columbian Exposition in Chicago, and later in several Canadian galleries.[12]

Harriet Mary Ford (1859–1938)

A Canadian by birth, Harriet Ford was known as "the Canadian New Woman." An artist, critic, lecturer, muralist, and jeweller, she became an authority on Renaissance art. Never married, she studied and travelled in Canada, France, England, and Italy. She maintained that a Canadian artist did not have to depict Canadian scenes. "It is the way a thing is painted, not what is painted, which makes a 'school' in painting," she wrote.

Harriet worked in oil, watercolour, and pastels, eventually decorating screens, furniture, and murals in private homes and public institutions. At the turn of the century, she became interested in jewellery using silver and gold and incorporating semi-precious stones. She was a popular lecturer and co-founded *Tarot* magazine, which was dedicated to the Arts and Crafts movement. She founded the Society of Mural Decorators in 1894.[13]

Sydney Strickland Tully (1860–1911)

Another member of the Strickland artistic family, Sydney was a grandniece of Susanna Moodie. She studied under Charlotte Schreiber in Toronto and in Paris, New York, England, and the Netherlands. A multi-talented woman, Sydney began her artistic career by colouring photographs and designing Christmas cards. She taught, wrote articles for the *Globe*, illustrated children's books, and worked in oils and pastels. She is best known for her award-winning painting *The Twilight of Life*, which was the first painting by a Canadian artist acquired by the Art Gallery of Ontario (then called the Art Gallery of Toronto).

Sydney's sister Louise Beresford Tully (?–1917) was also an artist. She operated an arcade-based teaching studio in downtown Toronto.

Laura Adaline Muntz Lyall (1860–1930)

Like many other Canadian artists, Laura studied abroad, especially in England and France, returning to Toronto in 1898. There she taught students for some years, becoming an associate of the Royal College of Art. She had exhibited at the Palace of Fine Arts at the 1893 World's Columbian Exposition in Chicago, and in Paris in 1894 as part of the Société des artistes français. In 1901 she won a silver medal at the Pan-American Exposition. Elected a member of the Royal Canadian Academy of Arts in 1895, she was the ninth woman to be so honoured. In 1899 she was also the first woman appointed to the executive council of the Ontario Society of Artists. Laura was an Impressionist painter, best known for her portrayal of mothers and children.

Her parents had disapproved of her career, but she eventually showed that she had great talent as an artist. She initially earned money as a schoolteacher, later teaching art to students such as the successful Marion Long (1882–1970), who is represented in collections across Canada and internationally, and Estelle Muriel Kerr (1879–1971), who is especially well-known for her paintings of children.[14]

Helen Galloway McNicoll (1879–1915)

Born in Toronto to affluent parents, Helen Galloway McNicoll went on to be one of the most influential female painters in the twentieth century in Canada. Her father was also an artist — he sketched while working with the Canadian Pacific Railway — and her mother painted china and wrote poetry.

Deaf from childhood as a result of scarlet fever, Helen learned to lip-read. She studied in England and France, but lived mostly in Montreal. She was especially known for her Impressionist style and use of light and air, painting working women in outdoor settings. She died at age thirty-four.

Mary Hiester Reid (1854–1921)

Mary Hiester Reid was one of Canada's most important nineteenth-century artists. She was certainly the country's pre-eminent floral painter. Born in Philadelphia, she was educated there and met her future husband, artist George Agnew Reid. In 1885 they moved to Toronto, where they became a powerful artistic couple. In 1893 she was one of the first women to be elected an associate of the Royal Canadian Academy of Arts, and in 1922 she was the first woman to posthumously receive a solo retrospective exhibition at the Art Gallery of Toronto (now the Art Gallery of Ontario).

Writers

Women have been writing for centuries, even though some adopted male pseudonyms, often so they would be taken seriously and not stereotyped as female. It is therefore no surprise that there were a number of women writers across Canada, and specifically in Toronto, in the nineteenth century: journalists, travel writers, poets, novelists, and historians, many of them well-known and well-respected. But perhaps the saddest story is that of Florence Deeks, who spent most of her life writing the history of the world and then fighting a losing battle against the famous British author H.G. Wells, whom she accused of plagiarizing her work. It was a David-against-Goliath plot, except that Goliath won.

Florence Amelia Deeks (1864–1959)

An Ontarian by birth, Florence attended Victoria College and then taught at the Presbyterian Ladies' College, both in Toronto. She became the historian for the Women's Art Association of Canada and recording secretary for the Toronto Women's Liberal Club. She decided to write a history of the world, but unlike most histories, hers would emphasize women's contributions. After spending years researching and writing, she submitted her manuscript, "The Web of the World's Romance," to the Macmillan Company in Canada, but they only replied months later, after a lot of hectoring, and then they returned a dirty, dog-eared copy. When H.G. Wells produced his 1,324-page *The Outline of History* soon after, Florence recognized a number of similarities with her own manuscript. She sued Wells for half a million dollars for "literary piracy." Wells had theoretically researched and written his work in eighteen months, a Herculean task. A number of prominent literary and historical scholars at universities agreed with Florence — partly because of the similarity of several historical errors in both manuscripts. Florence's brother, George, kept financing lawyers year after year and judiciary trial after trial, with Florence ending up in front of the Judicial Committee of the Privy Council in London, England, representing herself. But in the end, Florence lost her suit and Wells was legally vindicated.[15]

Mazo de la Roche (1879–1961)

Mazo was not French, but Maisie Louise Roche from Newmarket, Ontario, born of Canadian Irish and English parents. Her uncle Francis signed himself Francis J. de la Roche, and "Mazo" adopted the name. She lived in Toronto at various periods of her life, studying at the Metropolitan School of Music, the University of Toronto, and the Ontario School of Art.

She became a prolific writer, producing at least twenty-three novels, thirteen plays, and more than fifty short stories, writing her first short story at age nine. But she was best known for her Whiteoaks of Jalna series, which numbered seventeen novels spanning one hundred years, the story of a fictional family who lived in a house similar to one in Mississauga, just outside Toronto. She won a ten-thousand-dollar award for the first of the series when she was forty-eight. Mazo published her final novel, *Morning at Jalna*, when she was eighty-one.[16]

Ella Cora Hind (1861–1942)

Orphaned as a young child and having begun formal schooling only at eleven, Cora Hind eventually became a famous journalist and agriculturalist. She was born in Toronto, but her mother died when she was just two, and her father, three years later. She was brought up on a farm by an aunt and a grandfather, learning all about farming, horses, and cattle and being homeschooled. As an adult, she moved to Manitoba to teach, but because she had failed algebra, she couldn't get a teaching certificate. So she tried to become a journalist, but at first, she only succeeded in becoming a typist. She was told that the newsroom was no place for a woman. She set up her own business as a stenographer, the first one in Manitoba. Eventually she found a job as a reporter with the *Manitoba Free Press* and became the commercial and agricultural editor of the paper. She became so well-known that when she died, trading was halted at the Winnipeg Grain Exchange for two minutes in her memory.[17]

Mary Ann Camberton Shadd (1823–1893)

Educated for six years in a Quaker school in Pennsylvania, Mary Ann Shadd opened her own school for girls, teaching there for twelve years. After immigrating to Canada in 1851, she again set up a school in Windsor, Ontario. Then she became the first Black female editor and publisher of a North American newspaper. From 1853 to 1857, she published the *Provincial Freeman*, headquartered in Toronto, although her name was generally kept off the masthead in order not to alienate people who would be opposed to a woman editor. Between 1850 and 1860, the Black population in Canada increased from about forty thousand to sixty thousand, but unfortunately it was not large enough to support an abolitionist newspaper for very long. Mary Ann was constantly travelling to raise financial support, in both Canada and the United States.[18]

Born into a moderately well-to-do free Black family in Delaware, the eldest of several — possibly thirteen — children, Mary Ann believed that education, thrift, and hard work were the keys to racial equality for Black men and women, as did her father. Abraham Shadd also helped with the Underground Railroad, and her mother always kept extra food on hand for unexpected "guests." Mary Ann published a pamphlet in 1849, *Hints to the Colored People of the North*, urging Black people to stop imitating white people's materialism and to take antislavery reform into their own hands.[19]

From childhood, Mary Ann was influenced by her father's thinking, and so she was disappointed when the famous American orator and suffragette Lucy Stone (1818–1893) spoke in Toronto on March 17, 1855, and very few "coloured people seized upon the occasion to learn lessons of practical wisdom" by attending this lecture. She also believed, as did her father, that Black and white people should be integrated as much as possible, especially in schools. As a result, she faced ideological battles with other prominent Black people, especially with Mary and Henry Bibb, who believed that the only way Black people could retain their racial identity was through educational segregation.[20] The evidence, though, was on the side of Mary Ann Shadd's way of thinking. As reported in *The Refugees from Slavery in Canada West*, the Freedmen's Inquiry Commission found at the time that Black people who integrated with white settlers accomplished more and had more self-esteem than those who were segregated in communities by themselves, no matter how excellent the communities.[21]

In 1852 Mary Ann published another pamphlet, *A Plea for Emigration, or Notes of Canada West, in Its Moral, Social and Political Aspect*, encouraging immigration to Canada; she felt this country was a safe haven for free or escaped Black people, since it operated under British law. She believed this was urgent, as the Fugitive Slave Act had just been passed in the United States, requiring that slaves be returned to their owners even if they were in a "free" state. However, the Freedmen's Commission in 1864 determined that while Black people were legally safe in Canada, there was a great deal of discrimination, especially against groups of them. Black individuals were more readily accepted, it reported, although Black children were often not wanted in public schools by the other children and their parents.[22]

In 1856 Mary Ann married Thomas Cary, a hairdresser and business partner with Richard B. Richards, co-owning four ice houses that used ice frozen from local spring water and from Ashbridges Bay. They advertised that they would "convey the ice by wagon daily to within six miles of Toronto." After Cary died in 1860, Mary Ann returned to the United States and became a recruiting officer for the Union army. She later enrolled in evening law school at Howard University, eventually receiving her law degree in 1883. She cared for her own two children, along with three stepchildren from her husband's earlier marriage.[23]

Mary Elizabeth Miles Bibb (ca. 1820–1877), Mary Ann Shadd's nemesis, had a similar life story, although it appears that Bibb never lived in Toronto. However, it is thought that at one point she organized a convention or gathering on prejudice and slavery in Toronto. Also a free Black woman with an American Quaker background, Bibb was well-educated in New England schools, and she organized and taught at schools herself. She married an escaped slave, Henry Bibb, and they immigrated to Canada, settling near Windsor, Ontario. There she opened other schools for Black students. She and Henry published the *Voice of the Fugitive* from 1851 to 1853 or 1854, a four-page newspaper for Black people, although it appears that Mary was the real editor and the main person behind the operation. Henry had no formal education, and he was away for weeks at a time travelling across the United

States and Canada, speaking in support of abolishing slavery. Mary also taught Sunday school, dealt with Henry's correspondence, volunteered with refugee organizations, and at times earned money through dressmaking.

Mary and Henry were in favour of life in the country as opposed to urban living. In the cities and towns, Black children were "taught as a general thing to aspire no higher than to be boot blacks, wash women, wood-sawers, and table waiters," they wrote. They also believed that education was key to the success of Black men and women.[24]

After Henry died suddenly in 1854, Mary supported herself by operating a fancy goods store. She eventually married Mary Ann Shadd's brother-in-law, hairdresser Isaac N. Cary. The strained relations between Mary Ann and Mary Elizabeth improved with this new connection. Like Mary Ann, Isaac and Mary also moved to the United States toward the end of their lives.

Kathleen (Kit) Blake Ferguson Willis Watkins Coleman (1856–1915)

In 1889 forty-three-year-old Kit Coleman became the first editor of a women's page for the *Toronto Mail*, writing a weekly column for more than twenty years. Called "Kit of the Mail," she gave advice to the lovelorn and wrote about fashion, current events, the arts, entertainment, and whatever interested her. She was sent to Chicago to write about the World's Fair in 1893 and to London to cover Queen Victoria's jubilee celebrations in 1897.

An Irish redhead from Galway, Ireland, Kit married an Irish merchant, Mr. Willis, forty years older than she was. She immigrated to Toronto after he died but without his fortune, which he had left to his sister. She took on a secretarial job and married her boss, who turned out to be unfaithful and a heavy drinker. She began writing for *Saturday Night* magazine and then the *Toronto Mail*. She wrote travel articles and interviewed celebrities such as newspaper publisher William Randolph Hearst and actresses Sarah Bernhardt and Lillie Langtry. She dressed as a man to do a story about the opium dens in San Francisco.

Kit helped form the Canadian Women's Press Club. She became a free-lance writer in 1911, writing the first syndicated column, "Kit's Column," which she sold to newspapers across Canada.[25]

She had a third marriage, to Dr. Theobald Coleman, the company doctor for the Canadian Copper Company in Copper Cliff, Ontario. As well as newspaper writing, she published short stories and books of poetry. She was an accomplished and world-renowned woman writer. But even with her career and her belief in equal pay for equal work, it was only in the twentieth century that she supported women's suffrage, as maternal feminism was so ingrained in people's lives.[26]

Sara/Sarah Jeannette Duncan Cotes (1861–1890)

Few Canadian writers were able to break into American magazines and newspapers. Sara Duncan was first published as a poet when she was only nineteen, and her writing appeared in *Harper's Bazaar,* Scribner's publications, *The Century Magazine,* and the British *Athenaeum.* But she also wrote for the Toronto *Globe* as Garth Grafton and spent time as a parliamentary correspondent for the *Montreal Star.* In fact, she was so widely sought after, she was able to make a living as a journalist.

Trained initially as a teacher, she soon began working as a travel writer for various newspapers and as a columnist for the *Globe.* She was soon put in charge of the literature section at the American *Washington Post,* a remarkable feat for a Canadian woman. During a trip to India, she met and married an Anglo-Indian civil servant, Everard Cotes, and so she wrote under his name as well and spent her time in England, Canada, and India. She began writing novels, eventually publishing twenty-two. Her most widely received book was a fictionalized account of a trip around the world: *A Social Departure: How Orthodocia and I Went Around the World by Ourselves,* published by Chatto and Windus in 1890.[27]

Lucy Maud Montgomery (1874–1942)

The internationally famous writer L.M. Montgomery, known best for her stories of the orphan Anne of Green Gables, published twenty novels, 530 short stories, five hundred poems, and thirty essays during her lifetime. Born in

Clifton, Prince Edward Island, she died in Toronto at age sixty-seven. Lucy was raised by her grandparents, and her young life was very lonely. She created imaginary friends such as Katie Maurice and Lucy Gray, who lived in a room behind her bookcase in the drawing room.

Lucy taught school, and then studied literature at Dalhousie University. She had a job proofreading for newspapers and looked after her elderly grandmother. After her marriage to a Presbyterian minister, she wrote all her other books. In the next century, she was the most successful Canadian writer of all time, even though her books were sometimes dismissed as children's or women's books.

Her marriage was not a happy one. She and her husband both suffered from depression and they had different interests. She is reported to have said, "Those women whom God wanted to destroy, He would make into the wives of ministers." However, she tried very hard to make her marriage work, even though she felt that her husband treated women as things of "no importance." She was also challenged by an unscrupulous publisher who cheated her out of substantial royalties, and even though he was found guilty in a court of law, he still tried to avoid paying her what he owed.[28]

Matilda Ridout Edgar (1844–1910)

The historian Arlis Barclay wondered how Lady Matilda (Tillie) Ridout Edgar tolerated her domineering husband, for James David Edgar had a habit of constantly directing Matilda in all her affairs, no matter how insignificant, even to the point of reminding her to put the date and hour on every note she wrote to him, or how to give her children the maple sugar he had sent home to them. Thus, it was unusual for her to accept a speaking engagement to the Women's Canadian Historical Society in 1896 without letting him know. He found out about the engagement through a notice in the Toronto *Globe*. Barclay has suggested it may have been a deliberate survival tactic, although after James's early death, Lady Matilda was so grief-stricken that she gave up all her activities.[29]

A Toronto-born historian, Matilda began her literary career in her mid-forties after her several children were grown. She wrote about the War of 1812, and about Major-General Isaac Brock, a book that was highly praised for its accuracy and for "beauty of style." She also became involved in philanthropic causes such as the infants' home, and she was president of the Women's Canadian Historical Society of Toronto, which she and Sarah Anne Curzon founded, and acting president of the National Council of Women of Canada, supporting the campaign for women's rights.[30]

Sarah Anne Curzon (1833–1898)

Part of the Toronto Women's Literary Club, Sarah was one of the more active of the group's fifty members. She also helped found the Women's Canadian Historical Society and the Women's Art Association, as well as being a columnist for the *Canada Citizen,* a temperance and reform journal.

One of her main passions, however, was Laura Secord (see chapter 5); Sarah's story and drama helped propel Laura into a major Canadian hero. In the dramatic play that Sarah wrote, Laura's husband, James, has been invalided, wounded in the war. In an exchange of roles, he is confined to the home, caring for the family while Laura undertakes the man's role, one of heroic adventure, danger, and importance. James tries to dissuade Laura from her task, but she is insistent:

> Then will you taste a woman's common lot
> In times of strait, while I essay man's role
> Of fierce activity. We will compare
> When I return. Now, fare-thee-well, my husband.[31]

Born in England, the daughter of a wealthy glass manufacturer, Sarah received an advanced education with tutors and in private girls' schools. Even as a child she wrote stories and poetry, which were published in English magazines. She and her husband, Robert Curzon, immigrated to Canada around 1862. In 1876 she wrote what she called "Canada's first feminist play," the drama of Laura Secord, but she found it difficult to get it published at first.

However, she had poetry, essays, and stories published in a number of periodicals such as the *Canadian Monthly*, the *Dominion Illustrated*, *Grip*, *The Week*, the *Evangelical Churchman*, and the *Canadian Magazine*.[32]

Sarah suffered from Bright's disease and had to leave a job at the *Canada Citizen*, where she was associate editor; the newspaper carried an early women's page, which covered the issues of women's suffrage and access to advanced education.

Poets

Isabella Valancy Crawford (1850–1887)

A small garden park in downtown Toronto at Front and John Streets, near the CN Tower, has been named the Isabella Valancy Crawford Park. But who was Isabella Crawford? Elizabeth McNeill Galvin titled her book *Isabella Valancy Crawford: We Scarcely Knew Her* (published by Natural Heritage, 1994).

Dublin-born Isabella immigrated with her parents to Ontario around 1858. She became fascinated by backwoods life and Indigenous Peoples' stories. She began earning money selling verse and "formula fiction" after she and her mother moved in 1876 to Toronto, a city she came to view as "a demonic urban world of isolation and blindness," perhaps because they could afford to live only in boarding houses and rooms. Recently she has been considered one of Canada's finest early poets and the first to use Canadian images, although in his master's thesis, "The Growth of Canadian National Feeling as Reflected in the Poetry and Novels of English Canada," William Henry Magee wrote that of eighty-six poems in a book of her collected poems, he considered only two distinctly national in theme. He excerpted stanzas from "Malcolm's Katie: A Love Story":

> "Bite deep and wide, O Axe, the tree,
> What doth thy bold voice promise me?"

> "I promise thee all joyous things:
> That furnish forth the lives of kings!"

"For ev'ry silver ringing blow,
Cities and palaces shall grow!"[33]

Although she published only one book, her stories, novels, novellas, and long narrative poems were published and sometimes serialized in American and Canadian publications, including the *Mail*, the *Globe*, the *National*, the *Evening Telegram*, and the *Fireside Monthly*. But still she was not well-known when she was alive, and she died in poverty even though, at times, she was able to earn a living by writing. Her most popular work was "Malcolm's Katie and Other Poems" in *Old Spookses' Pass*, a long narrative poem in blank verse dealing with the love and trials of a couple living in the Canadian bush and of a war between the North and South Winds, personified as Indigenous warriors.[34]

Susie Frances Riley Harrison (1859–1935)

Susie Riley published her first poem in the *Canadian Illustrated News* when she was sixteen, using the pseudonym Medusa, which was supposedly a misreading of her signature, *S. Frances*. But she also worked as a novelist, music critic, and composer in Ottawa and Toronto under other pen names: Seranus and Gilbert King. She became the music critic for *The Week*, was considered an authority on folk music, and composed what is thought to be the first string quartet written by a woman in Canada. She wrote for *Canada: An Encyclopedia of the Country*, *Conservatory Monthly*, *Conservatory Quarterly Review*, and the *Imperial History and Encyclopedia of Music*, as well as at least six books of poetry and three Gothic novels. Unfortunately, her reputation declined even during her lifetime.

Her "September" poem reads:

I.
Birds that were gray in the green are black in the yellow.
Here where the green remains rocks one little fellow.

Quaker in gray, do you know that the green is going?
More than that — do you know that the yellow is
   showing?

II.
Singer of songs, do you know that your Youth is flying?
That Age will soon at the lock of your life be prying?

Lover of life, do you know that the brown is going?
More than that — do you know that the gray is showing?[35]

Emily Pauline Johnson (1861–1913)

A poet, writer, singer-songwriter, and performer, Pauline was born in Six
Nations territory. Her father, George Henry Martin Johnson, was a well-
educated Mohawk Clan chief. Her mother, Emily Susanna Howells, an
upper-middle-class white woman, had immigrated to the United States from
England in the 1830s, scandalizing everyone with her marriage. Pauline's
Mohawk name was Tekahionwake ("Double Wampum" or "Double Life"). She
was home-schooled and spent long hours reading English literature. When
she was about thirty, she created a Mohawk costume and toured Canada with
popular recitals of her poetry, comedy routines, and plays. One of her best-
loved poems was the melodious and delightful "The Song My Paddle Sings."
But she wrote other, harsher poetry about the treatment of Indigenous people,
such as "A Cry from an Indian Wife," and even white English audiences stood
and applauded in appreciation as she recited these.

My forest brave, my Red-skin love, farewell;
We may not meet to-morrow: who can tell
What mighty ills befall our little band,
Or what you'll suffer from the white man's hand?
...
They but forget we Indians owned the land
From ocean unto ocean: that they stand

Upon a soil that centuries agone
Was our sole kingdom and our right alone.
They never think how they would feel to-day
If some great nation came from far away,
Wrestling their country from their hapless braves,
Giving what they gave us — but wars and graves.
...
By right, by birth we Indians own these lands,
Though starved, crushed, plundered, lies our nation low.[36]

Though Pauline was living in the small town of Brantford at the time, Toronto was important to her. The cultural thinking was that nice girls didn't

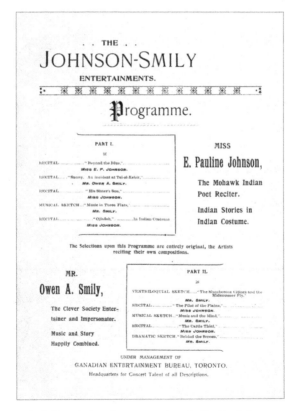

Playbill, ca. 1898, of a program given by Pauline Johnson.

act on the stage, as Pauline had wanted to do, unless they were Shakespearean actors. But Pauline became convinced that she could be a "recitalist," in the same league as preachers or writers or lecturers — not entertainers but spreading culture. Her first appearance was in the art gallery of Toronto's Academy of Music and she was overwhelmed with her reception, the star of the show.[37] Over the years, Pauline toured the country, often returning to Toronto.

Jean (Janet/Mary) McKishnie/McKishney Blewett (1862/1872–1934)

A journalist, author, and poet, Janet McKishnie (pseudonym Kathleen Kent) became editor of the Toronto *Globe* newspaper's "Homemakers Department" in 1898. She had already been recognized as a poet, winning a six-hundred-dollar prize from the *Chicago Times-Herald* for her poem "Spring," and later, in 1896, an international poetry prize. She had published her first novel, *Out of the Depths*, in 1890 and her first collection of poems, *Heart Songs*, in 1897. She also wrote for *Everywoman's World*, an early Canadian magazine. Her poetry was admired for "the directness and simplicity of theme and form and for the occasional whimsical note." The *Globe* called it "unpretentious, domestic, kindly, humorous and natural."[38]

Although she was married to Bassett Blewett when she was only sixteen or seventeen, this did not keep her from working. She gained a reputation as a "woman's poet," writing about subjects and ideas that appealed to homemakers and mothers. She was also called a "bard of common things." At age sixteen she was paid by *Frank Leslie's Popular Monthly*, a popular American literary magazine, for a simple lullaby.

Janet began a pamphlet for the Canadian Suffrage Association in Toronto in the early 1900s titled *The Canadian Woman and Her Work*, in which she advocated political and social education for both men and women in order to vote effectively, and she held up Laura Secord as the true brave compatriot:

> One need not be a seer or a prophet to discern the signs of the times. *The women* of this day and generation are in line, intelligently, methodistically *in line*, and marching on

towards the highest kind of citizenship. Seeing that they want the Suffrage, and that like the Heilan' Laddie they "do not ken how to pipe a retreat," they will likely go straight on until they get it.[39]

Musicians

A number of women taught music in their homes or in schools; some of them had been playing and taking lessons themselves for years. For example, Mrs. Lillie Yates, who apparently deserved a major heading in J.H. Beers's biographical record of prominent people in the County of York, had been studying in London, England, and Toronto under the "best teachers" and made a "great success" of her own music school in Toronto.[40]

But even more impressive in Mr. Beers's eyes was Mrs. L. Allard Chestnut, who not only won "high rank as a teacher of music," but also "displayed marked executive and financial ability as a publisher." Beers went on to say that "the ability of women to engage successfully in lines which were formerly supposed to be the special province of men has been demonstrated now so often and so variously as scarcely to need comment." Mrs. Chestnut prepared students for studying at the Conservatory of Music and had a downtown studio and a large number of "scholars." But for five years, she also published a magazine called *Varney*, which had been almost bankrupt. She not only put it back onto a sound financial footing, but also raised it to "a much higher level of literary merit." Perhaps it was inevitable that her son would work for the Canadian Bank of Commerce!

The historian G. Mercer Adam also devoted a couple of pages to female musicians because he believed that music was a female occupation: the study of music is "essentially feminine," he wrote. However, the amount of space that the early male historians gave to women does not bear this out. But Adam did list some prominent women musicians such as Clara Asher Lucas, a musical prodigy appointed to the Prince of Wales in England before she entered her teens. After she married Clarence Lucas, who was on the staff of the Toronto College (Conservatory) of Music, she came to Toronto, giving lessons on the piano to "advanced pupils only." Sarah Maud Mary Harris (1864–?) was another highly regarded pianist living and teaching in Toronto. She was also a pianist for the Toronto Choral Society. She studied abroad extensively, in France, England, Germany, and New York City.[41]

But a couple of souvenir booklets produced in 1897 and 1898, entitled *A Souvenir of Musical Toronto*, curiously written by H.H. Godfrey in the office of the Minister of Agriculture, are more helpful. Godfrey was a musician and composer, known for the military song "Hark the Drum!" For twenty-five cents the booklets could be mailed "post paid" to anywhere in Canada, Great Britain, or the United States. More importantly, they listed a number of men and women, mostly connected to various schools focusing on music in Toronto. Out of twenty-four names of "Musicians and Musical Institutions," eight are female musicians; six are music facilities or schools, many of them owned and operated by women; and the remainder, male musicians.

The schools included the following: At Miss Veals's Glen Mawr Ladies' Seminary, Miss Rahtjen, Miss Graham, and Miss Williams were among the music departmental faculty. Havergal Hall was under the direction of principal Miss Knox, who was trained in England and Scotland, but the music faculty were all male. However, Bishop Strachan School, where Miss Grier was the principal, had on its faculty of music Miss Williams, Miss Morris, and Miss Graham. Evidently some of the instructors travelled from school to school. Mrs. Neville's Private Ladies' School had Miss Norah Hillary in charge of its vocal music department. Moulton Ladies' College, under the direction of Miss Dicklow as principal, had an extensive musical department supervised by Miss Smart, and their large piano class was taught by Miss Edith Burke.

There were a number of female teachers at the Conservatory of Music. In fact, women taught music there from its beginning. Margaret Milne received her associate of the Toronto Conservatory of Music credential, graduated from a music theory course in 1893, and then a teacher's course the next year. The historian J.H. Beers reported that she then began teaching at the conservatory, but neglected to mention which subject.[42]

Mrs. Joseph Lister Cockburn Nichols, one of the first faculty members of the Toronto Conservatory of Music, taught pianoforte. She had received her musical education in Leeds, England. In 1887 she and her husband and three sons immigrated to Toronto, where her husband continued as a contractor, laying the first concrete sidewalk. The conservatory opened in 1887, and Mrs. Nichols joined the faculty the next year.

Born in Scotland and trained in Germany, Mrs. Bertha Drechsler Adamson (1848–1924) taught stringed instruments, although her specialty was the violin. She also began and directed the thirty-piece Toronto String Orchestra. All of her family members were musicians, and her daughter Lina Hayes played viola in a quartet Bertha organized. Mrs. H.M. Blight and her husband offered joint organ and vocal concerts throughout Ontario. Born in St. Catharines, Mrs. Blight trained there as well as in Toronto, and was the organist at several large churches, including the Elm Street Methodist Church

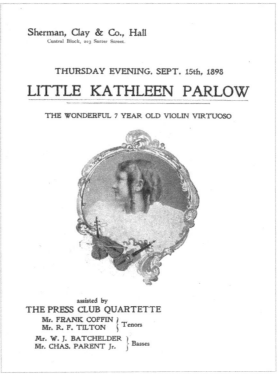

"Little Kathleen Parlow, The Wonderful 7 Year Old Violin Virtuoso," September 15, 1898, at Sherman, Clay & Co. Hall, San Francisco.

and the Bloor Street Presbyterian Church. She was also skilled at accompanying soloists, both on the organ and on the piano.

The child prodigy Kathleen Parlow (1890–1963), "the lady of the golden bow," also taught at the conservatory in the twentieth century, beginning in 1941. Born in Calgary, she had lived in the United States, going to San Francisco in 1894. In 1942 she founded the Parlow String Quartet in Toronto, her third quartet.

The pianist Fannie Sullivan began her studies with the Loretto Sisters, later teaching at the Toronto College of Music. She received several prizes, including the Torrington Organ Scholarship, a gold medal for general proficiency, the Artists' Diploma, and a prize for best accompanist. She was also the choir director for the Church of Our Lady of Lourdes.

Sara E. Dallas received a bachelor of music from Trinity College, one of the first to obtain one. She was the organist at Central Presbyterian Church and also conducted its choir. She helped at the Presbyterian Ladies' College and played the piano for the Toronto Choral Society. She was one of the few prominent musicians who studied only in Toronto and not abroad. Her sister, Eleanor Dallas, also received a bachelor of music degree at Trinity College with a gold medal. She played the violin as well as the piano and taught theory at the conservatory. She also taught at Havergal and the Ontario Ladies' College. Lucy Franklein, a well-known contralto from England, visited Toronto and was persuaded to stay as a teacher of voice at the Toronto College of Music.

Ada E.S. Hart, a gold medal pianist, studied abroad and toured Canada to great acclaim. It was reported that she also "entertained charmingly." Nora H. Hillary, a vocalist from Dublin, Ireland, was the principal voice teacher at Mrs. Neville's, Miss Dupont's, and Miss Veals's schools; the St. Joseph Convent; and the Toronto College of Music, as well as conductor of the Toronto Ladies' Choral Club. The American Mrs. Klingenfeld also taught voice to a large class of pupils, as did Miss Norma Reynolds, professor of singing at the Toronto Conservatory of Music. Miss Reynolds was also a pianist, the soloist at a number of Toronto churches including St. James Cathedral and the Metropolitan Church, and a member of the Arion Quartette. The German-born mezzo-soprano Mme. Adele Strauss Youngheart came to Toronto in 1892 and sang in *Samson*, initially with the Philharmonic Society.

Emma Albani (1847–1930) was the first Canadian singer to become internationally known. Born Marie-Louise-Emma-Cecile Lajeunesse, she changed her name to be simpler and sound more European. She become not only a famous soloist, but also a harpist and organist. She studied and performed in Italy, Paris, New York, London, Germany, and Canada. One of her last performances was a solo at the funeral service for Queen Victoria. There are streets in Montreal memorializing her and a commemorative Canadian postage stamp was issued in 1980.

Emma Stanton Mellish Dymond (m. 1890) wanted to study at Trinity College in Toronto, but she could not gain admittance because she was a woman. So she tried to pass herself off as a man, but her ruse was discovered.

Mme. Albani, "Canadian Queen of Song," 1897, "Souvenir of Musical Toronto."

In 1886, however, she was one of the first two women to receive the bachelor of music degree at that same university. She had begun teaching piano in 1881. In 1887 she was appointed teacher of theory at the Toronto Conservatory of Music, and in 1888 lecturer of harmony at St. Hilda's College for Women. In 1900 she won a prize in a competition sponsored by *Etude* magazine for her essay "The Educational Value of Concerts." She wrote, in part:

> In spite of the increasingly large number of good concerts given in our cities and towns each year, the proportion of concert-goers is not so great as it might be. When we except those who go because they "must put in an appearance, you know" (which means the putting on of much fine apparel at home, arriving near the middle of the concert, and leaving some time before its close), those who have, unexpectedly, had tickets presented to them "which it would be a pity not to use," those who go out of curiosity to see (not hear) a famous artist, and those who are persuaded to accompany some music-loving friend, there remains a small number who will obtain real benefit as well as pleasure from a high-class concert.[43]

One other prominent musician that G. Mercer Adam highlighted was Mrs. S.R. Bradley, who sang and played piano. "A brilliant soprano," she was a principal soloist at age seventeen in a performance of the *Messiah* in Toronto. Another was Miss Lizzie Higgins, a piano teacher at the conservatory. However, as Adam pointed out, Toronto was not really a "distinctively musical city"; rather, "the masses" were fonder of sport, "sensational drama and the saloon."[44]

Musical Canada, the Toronto monthly review and magazine, listed a number of other prominent women in the musical scene in Toronto. Evidently, women indeed made up a large portion of instrumental musicians and vocal soloists in Toronto in the nineteenth century.

One also needs to remember that there was a female composer and music critic, Susie Frances Riley Harrison, described above under "Poets."

Entertainers

There were dramatists who entertained in the Royal Lyceum on King Street — the Holman Sisters and Charlotte Nickinson, the latter known to the locals as Mrs. Morrison. Several visiting women occasionally gave "dramatic readings" in Toronto, women such as the English actors Mary Frances Scott-Siddons (1844–1896) and Mary Anne Fanny Stirling (1815–1895), who occasionally travelled around North America.[45]

Charlotte Nickinson (1832–1910) made her stage debut at the age of fourteen in New York City. Her father was an actor; he involved all his children in his troupe, but Charlotte was the star. They were Canadian and often played in Canadian cities, and when Charlotte was in Quebec City, her birthplace, she was hailed as "La Jeune Québecoise." Charlotte was tall, slim, and striking, with a "beautiful musical voice" and an infectious laugh; she was very successful. Her family played Shakespeare and other quality fare, but sometimes they did blackface minstrel shows. Even as early as 1840, people protested that form of "entertainment," but evidently nothing was done about it by the city.[46]

When she was twenty-six, Charlotte married a newspaperman, Daniel Morrison, and retired from the stage. They lived in Toronto, where he worked at the *Daily Telegraph*. Daniel died when Charlotte was thirty-eight, and she went back to the stage to support herself. She gathered a troupe together and opened a new theatre in Toronto in 1872, the Grand Opera House, soon known as Mrs. Morrison's Grand Opera House. A four-storey white brick building, it had a seating capacity of 1,644, as well as standing room for 500. By the end of 1878, however, salaries were not being paid, actors were let go, and Charlotte was no longer manager. Rebuilt after a fire in 1885, it was reopened with a performance by the internationally acclaimed actress Miss Adelaide Neilson, but with a new manager and lessee.[47]

Charlotte continued to act with amateur societies, but she directed most of her energies toward charitable and church work. She became an active member of the Women's Canadian Historical Society of Toronto and the National Council of Women of Canada.[48]

Beatrice Gladys Lillie (1894–1989), called "the funniest woman in the world," was born in Toronto to a concert singer (her mother) and a Canadian government official. She, her mother, and an older sister, Muriel, performed as a trio around Ontario until her mother took the girls to London, where Lillie made her West End debut in 1914. From then on, she starred in films, vaudeville, and stage shows in both London and New York. Lillie became Lady Peel after she married Sir Robert Peel in 1920. She discovered upon Peel's death that his finances were in a very disastrous condition.[49]

Mary Pickford (1892–1979) was born in Toronto to Charlotte Hennessey, an Irish immigrant seamstress, and John (Jack) Charles Smith, an alcoholic who abandoned the family when Mary was four. She was baptized Gladys Louise Smith. Her mother took in boarders, one of whom was a stage manager for Cummings Stock Company. Gladys, then seven, and her sister Lottie, a year younger, were both given small theatrical roles at Toronto's Princess Theatre, since destroyed by fire, while their mother played the organ. Gladys went on to more senior roles — her last one in Toronto was the starring role of Little Eva in the Valentine production of *Uncle Tom's Cabin*.

Gladys kept on in the theatre in the 1900s, playing in third-rate productions throughout the United States. Finally, as Mary Pickford, she landed a leading role on Broadway in 1906. She became more and more famous, the first actress to sign a million-dollar contract. Although she lived a long life, it was later one of failed marriages, alcoholism, and loneliness. At her request, she officially became a Canadian citizen just before she died, although authorities thought she had never lost that citizenship. She still owned a house in Toronto.

Photographer

The granddaughter of the well-known settler Susanna Strickland Moodie, grandniece of Catharine Parr Strickland Traill, and a distant cousin of Susanna's husband, John Douglas Moodie, Toronto-born Geraldine Fitzgibbon Moodie (1854–1945) was one of Canada's first female professional photographers. Her studios were in the West, but she and her husband farmed briefly and unsuccessfully in Manitoba and then moved to Ottawa. Her most famous photographs are of Indigenous people in Canada, especially members of the Cree Nation and the Inuit.

Geraldine's husband, John Moodie, had initially worked as a North-West Mounted Police officer, and then with the Canadian Pacific Railway. She often accompanied him on his travels across the country, particularly to the north, photographing people, ranches, and nature. She carted her photographic gear by train, wagon, boat, and dogsled, through six pregnancies. Her husband took photographs, too, featuring his workers.

Geraldine was successful even in a male world and was once commissioned by the prime minister to photograph historic sites in Canada's West. She was always concerned, of course, about proper settings, modifying her techniques because of the snow and harsh weather. She once wrote of a photo shoot:

> This week I have succeeded in getting a picture satisfactorily
> that I have been trying all winter to get, one of the *Arctic*

Dominion Government Ship (DGS) *Arctic* frozen in the ice in Fullerton Harbour, Nunavut, April 1905.

[ship] lying in her winter quarters, from the shore. There has always been such a glare of snow with nothing to relieve that it gave no definition when photographed, and made a poor negative. I tried it under every condition of light, and finally found by stopping my lens very low and taking the photo when the afternoon sun was very bright, throwing strong shadows, that I succeeded in getting a fine negative.[50]

For years, Geraldine's photos lay forgotten, but today they are in several Canadian museums.[51]

CHAPTER 9

PROFESSIONALS

———————— • • ————————

Teachers

I n the nineteenth century many women in Toronto received a basic education. There were a number of privately operated schools for women and girls in York/Toronto, apart from the schools run by religious groups and those that focused on musical or artistic training mentioned earlier. These schools, though, cost a fair amount of money; some were more reasonably priced than others, but probably all were beyond the reach of the poorer classes, especially those with large families. The courses of study also varied from school to school, although some for girls and young ladies were fairly basic. For example, in 1815, Miss Lancaster opened a school for children where apparently only reading, writing, and needlework were taught.

The Misses McCord had one of the most fashionable and best-conducted schools, opened in 1831. In 1833 a girls' school under Rebecca Sylvester taught English, reading, writing, arithmetic, and drawing. The fees were one dollar per quarter, but parents needed to pay for only two children, even if more

The McCord sisters' school.

were enrolled.[1] Fashionable Bay Street had a ladies' school under the Misses Skirving, popular for about fifteen years.

Also early in York, Anne Powell was interested in Mrs. Goodman's school, a new boarding school with a much wider curriculum, for her daughter Anne. Mrs. Goodman had been teaching in Quebec City, but was moving to York. However, in a letter she sent in 1817 to George Murray, Anne Powell felt that while Mrs. Goodman had a good reputation as a teacher, she failed to supervise her students "out of the School Room." She also decried the lack of "distinction of classes" — not because of "Aristocratic pride" she claimed, but from the "vulgar habits of home."

Mrs. Cockburn took over the school in 1822 "under the patronage of the Rt. Honorable Lady Sarah Maitland [sic] and the principal Ladies of Upper-Canada." Her school's classes consisted of "English Language, Gramatically, History, Geography, the use of the Globes, with plain and fancy

Needle-work." For extra fees, there could be "Writing and Ciphering, The French Language, Drawing and Painting on Velvet, Music, Dancing, Flower and Card-work." At this boarding school, "Every Lady" was "to provide a Table, and Tea-spoon, Knife and Fork, Sheets and Towels, and to pay for her own washing."[2]

Entrance to the school was one guinea, and a further fee was charged depending on which subjects the girls chose. The basic quarter-term program as above cost two pounds. Mrs. Cockburn also accepted children five to seven years old for five dollars a quarter. Board and lodging were £8.10.0 per term.[3]

Elizabeth Jane McMurray Turnbull (1837–1935), one of five daughters of an Irish clockmaker, attended a school for young ladies run by a Mrs. Brown. There she learned French and music and how to knit and sew. Evidently that was inadequate for entrance in the Toronto Normal School, and she had to have a tutor later on in order to attend the school, where she spent five months preparing to teach.[4]

The Toronto Normal School for teacher training had opened in 1847 and accepted candidates at least sixteen years of age who could produce a certificate signed by a clergyman that they were of "good moral character." Unfortunately, the Normal School attracted less than a quarter of all Ontario teachers even by 1875, but women formed the majority of the students. The course included nine hours a day of lectures and one hour of observation and practise at a model school, resulting in what Dr. J. Workman of Toronto categorized in 1881 as "morbid results of persistent mental overwork." The school, however, was advanced in design and had a good reputation: it contained a library and art gallery, which Jennie Fleming wanted to see on her trip to Toronto in 1869, along with the garden; "it has so many different varieties of flowers, shrubs and trees," she wrote.

In his *Landmarks of Toronto*, Robertson mentions a number of schools staffed by women. In 1850 Monsieur and Madam Des-Landes rented Pinehurst, a "commodious building" just east of the Grange, and opened a ladies' school "until 1853, when they were succeeded by one of the most ... charming of women, Mrs. Forster." She ran the school until 1866, and then another woman took over. At another location in downtown Toronto, sometime around 1845, Miss McNally from Dublin, Ireland, operated a school assisted by her three sisters. The head lady spoke French, German, and Spanish "with equal facility." Another well-known school was owned by Miss Macartney, from 1854 until she married Mr. Nixon about six years later, but she kept on working as a principal of an Anglican school. The widow Mrs. Crombie, with two of her sons and a daughter, had a school for "small boys and girls."[5]

Edith Firth notes that the Western Auxiliary School was opened in 1859, a one-storey frame building with two rooms — one for girls and one for boys. Mrs. O'Flaherty taught eighty-four pupils there in ten grades, earning a salary of $320 for the year. In the building there were at least two teachers, but by 1871 there were about 250 pupils enrolled, although the truant officer reported that the lack of sidewalks and the bad roads often kept the smaller children at home. Classrooms tended to be crowded. By 1881 Miss Fraser had a room seated for 72 students, a class numbering 107, and an average attendance of about 90. Apparently, the number of pupils always exceeded the space available.[6]

One of the more reputable private schools in the late 1800s was Dufferin House, a three-storey white brick boarding and day school owned by Miss Dupont. According to the compiler J. Timperlake, it offered a "higher, more liberal and more select scholastic training than any other public or private Institution." The historian Mulvany agreed. Miss Dupont, her sister Amy, and a staff of eleven, including three resident governesses, taught French, German, Italian, Latin, music, and drawing.[7]

In 1833 young "Ladies" were accepted even at the York Commercial and Classical Academy. There they could study needlework, with a separate and spacious apartment and a governess of "unquestionable" ability and "respectability," although French and drawing were also listed as potential subjects, presumably costing additional fees.[8] The Bishop Strachan School, built in 1867, accepted "young ladies"; it had a staff of five resident lady teachers and a number of non-residents.[9]

Some of the schools must have been profitable. Miss Eliza Hussey kept a school from as early as 1831 until about 1854, when she sold it to Mr. Ince for about $5,000, equal to about $141,000 today. Her school had an excellent reputation; she was said to be kind as well as strict, and she always kept some kind of lunch on a table for any of the children who were hungry.

Teaching became one of the most common professional activities for women in the nineteenth century in Toronto and throughout Ontario. The formal Ontario public school system dates from the year 1816, when the legislature passed the Common School Act, granting five thousand pounds annually to maintain the schools. Six years later, the province set up a board of education, but it was not until after the Canada East and Canada West Union in 1841 that efficient provision was made to operate the system. By the end of the 1800s, there were six thousand elementary school houses in the province and seven thousand teachers, as well as 115 high schools with more than four hundred teachers.

Children between seven and thirteen were required to attend at least one hundred days a year. In 1857, 2,310 boys and 2,233 girls were registered for Toronto schools, but in fact, only 1,023 boys and 840 girls attended regularly, less than half.[10] As G. Mercer Adam reported in 1889, the "flaw in the ointment" was that the registered attendance in Toronto was 28,287 children, whereas the average daily attendance was only 18,926, a wide discrepancy.[11]

Women became teachers in droves by mid-century. As compulsory attendance resulted in the swelling of the school population, there were many opportunities for women. By 1861 one teacher of every four was a woman; by 1919, they outnumbered men five to one. The classrooms were crowded: most teachers taught from 90 to 100 pupils. In 1871 a teacher might be charged with teaching 105 pupils, but by 1883 that was reduced to 70. In the late 1800s the maximum number of students per class in Toronto schools was calculated to be 75.[12]

In 1883 a male teacher in the Township of York earned an average of $422.56, whereas a female teacher earned an average $234.00. Salaries were higher in the city; in 1885, a man's average salary was $742, a woman's less than half of that. Subjects taught might be spelling, writing, dictation, arithmetic, geography, grammar, composition, Canadian and British history, hygiene, algebra, geometry and measurement, and bookkeeping.[13] As the years progressed, there were more female teachers and fewer males. School boards realized that they could operate the schools more economically with female teachers at less than half salary. So the profession was becoming feminized, at least at the elementary level. Eventually women were appointed as principals.

In 1882 even the Jarvis Collegiate Institute had two female teachers for English, Miss Charlotte E. Thompson and Miss Helen MacMurchy. The Toronto Model School had four female teachers for the girls' school. The principal of the Bishop Strachan School in 1882 was, surprisingly, a woman, Miss Grier, daughter of the late Reverend Mr. Grier, rector of the Anglican Church in Belleville.

Pickering College began as a coeducational Quaker school to develop cultured Canadian men and women. The historian-librarian Ella Rogers Firth was at one time its principal. She had been hired by the school in the 1890s, just after she completed a degree in modern languages from the University of Toronto.[14]

Egerton Ryerson was appointed superintendent of education for all of Ontario in 1846, and his Common School Acts of 1846, 1847, and 1850 promised education "as free as the air and as the right of all men." However, his intent was partly to "civilize" society in the face of non-British immigration. He was also responsible for refusing women's education at Victoria College. In 1842 when he became president of that college, women were no longer permitted to attend, ostensibly because of lack of space. He made allowance, however, for young men who had trouble learning the classics. However, he did ensure that elementary education was free for all young children, paid for through taxation. In 1871 school attendance for children aged seven to twelve was made compulsory for four months a year, recognizing that many children were required at home to help with farm chores, especially at certain times of the year.[15]

Women did well at school, often surpassing male students. Reverend Alex Gale, a Presbyterian minister, was the first principal of the Toronto Academy in 1846. His daughter, one of the students, was renowned for her intelligence. She could translate Greek and Latin at sight and her mental arithmetic abilities were legendary.[16]

Teachers, of course, were of varied ability, especially in the early small private schools before training in the Normal School. The Reverend John Carroll (1809–1884) tells of an incident in a local school he attended, taught by a Mrs. Glennon "who lived in the other end of the house in which [he and his family] lived." Mrs. Glennon was a doctor's widow trying to earn enough money to raise her own children in the early 1800s. She "had no experience or tact in teaching," he wrote, and she was "without skill or authority to govern a school." Her own eldest daughter, Theresa, "became utterly unmanageable" and one of the big girls, Ann Skinner, "offered her services to punish Theresa." Carroll writes, "It soon became a rough and tumble battle through the room, over benches, tables, and chairs, and on to the bed, which stood in the corner, the curtains of which ... were pulled down. It ended in a sort of drawn battle, Theresa getting a pretty thorough slapping and Miss Skinner getting a punch in the eye."[17]

There were, too, a variety of private schools, such as the writing school taught by Mr. Corry, "professor of penmanship." In "six easy lessons of one hour each," Mr. Corry instructed "ladies in an elegant, easy and expeditious mode, particularly feminine; and to the Merchant or Storekeeper a strong, bold and masculine hand, fit for business." There was also a special style for the "private gentleman or the army." Pen-making would also be taught — free to those registered for lessons, but two dollars otherwise.[18]

Mme. Harris had a dance school under the patronage of the Countess of Dalhousie. On September 19, 1810, the *York Gazette* announced the opening of a "Nocturnal School" or night school for "Young Ladies (or men)" who couldn't "conveniently attend in the Day time to Study.... Evening Scholars to furnish severally, 1 lb. Candles per Month; and all Scholars, half a Cord of Fire Wood for the Winter.... The hours of attendance from 6 to 9 P.M. for 5 days of the week only. Regular monthly payments to be made."[19]

While women could attend the Normal School, they struggled to be educated at university level. Eliza May Balmer (ca. 1866–1915) had an unusual background before she taught at Harbord Collegiate in Toronto and at a school in Strathroy, Ontario, from 1888 to 1891. Prevented from attending the University of Toronto, she went to classes anyway, amidst cheers and boos. Eliza had won four scholarships and had written the entrance examinations but was not permitted to attend. By March 1884, however, female students were finally allowed in, and nine took advantage of the legislation: Mary Bell Bald, Ella Gardiner, Margaret Langley, Nellie Spence, Caroline Fair, Alice Jones, Mary Lennox, Jennie Stork, and Eliza Balmer, although some sources suggest that only Mary Bald, Catherine Brown, Margaret Brown, Ella Gardiner, and

Margaret Langley were the first women students who started on October 6, 1884.[20] And Henrietta Charles had graduated earlier, in 1870, although she had not been permitted to attend classes, but wrote the exams after working with a tutor. In any case, the early women had several restrictions placed on them; for example, they were prohibited from using the reading room and library catalogues and from standing at bulletin boards in the hall. Whether or not women should attend university was a hot topic. In 1875 the subject of the first gathering of the University College Literary and Scientific Society was a debate: "Is it advisable that women receive a University or Professional education?" In 1889 that society voted to limit membership to men only.

It wasn't long before school reached down to the youngest children. Adaline Augusta "Ada" Marean Hughes (ca. 1848–1930), an American born in New York State, was recommended as the first kindergarten teacher in Toronto. James Laughlin Hughes, Toronto's chief inspector of schools, had written to Madame Maria Kraus-Boelte, an advocate for "children's garden" — kindergarten — a new kind of class for preschool children; she suggested that Ada would be the ideal candidate. In 1883 Ada began the first class in Toronto. She was later appointed the first woman president of the Ontario Educational Association, and she married Hughes in 1885. Even with her new approach to education, Ada remained a conservative maternal feminist. Describing the "Ideal Woman" in a speech to the Toronto Women's Association in 1896, she said, "Woman's aim in life should be motherhood and her education should be such as would fit her for that estate."[21]

Ada Mary Brown Courtice (1860–1923) was also one of their followers. Growing up a Quaker and educated at Pickering College and the Ontario Ladies' College, Ada taught music and was the choir soloist at the Parliament Street Methodist Church. Andrew C. Courtice was the minister there; they married in 1888. Both Andrew and Ada wanted to found a new school with the aim of developing the students physically, morally, and mentally, promoting self-knowledge, self-control, and a healthy life. At the beginning of the twentieth century they opened the Balmy Beach College and the School of Music and Art.[22] Ada became very involved in reform movements, especially the National Council of Women of Canada and later the Toronto Public School Board and the Toronto Home and School Council.[23]

Some women became principals at elementary schools before the century was over. Charlotte Madeline Churchill was appointed a Toronto school principal in 1876; in 1882 her salary was $700. Also in 1882, forty-year-old Georgina Stanley Riches Reid/Read/Reed (1842–1915) became principal of Palace Street School, later named Sackville Street Public School. This latter appointment was not well-received. Georgina held only a senior third-book class teaching certificate and some teachers with higher qualifications protested her appointment and higher salary. Ratepayers and parents, however, expressed both disapproval and great appreciation for her work. A male board member was appalled that his wife earned only $250 as a teacher while Georgina was to earn $750. "Perhaps that is all she is worth," Georgina suggested. However, Georgina's school was reclassified as a junior third-book school, and her salary was reduced to $650 to solve the problem.[24]

Librarians

In 1810 a Toronto library was set up, but only for private subscriptions. Twenty years later, the first York Mechanics' Institute was founded, the object being "the mutual improvement of its members in useful Scientific knowledge." It was "a Library of reference and circulation … for instruction in various branches of useful study," except that works on "Religion and Politics " were to be excluded. The organizational minutes stated that "suitable accommodations will be provided for the Ladies," but there was no explanation as to what that involved. In 1883 the institute was taken over by the fledgling Toronto Public Library, and in 1884 the first two branches of the public library system opened, the Western Branch and the Northern Branch.[25]

The top librarians of all the Toronto libraries were male in the early years of the nineteenth century. However, women were an integral part of the Toronto Public Library from the beginning. Miss O'Dowd was the head librarian at the Western Branch. By 1886 Mrs. Perkins had been appointed to head the new Northern Branch. There were four branches in 1888, and all were headed by women — Mrs. Thompson in the Eastern Branch, Mrs. Perkins in the Northern Branch, Mrs. Hamilton in the Western Branch, and Miss Kingsmill

Female librarians at the York Mechanics' Institute/Toronto Reference Library, Toronto, 1895. Standing (l. to r.): Eva Davis, Rose Ferguson, Elizabeth Moir, Hattie Petit, Margaret McElderry, Margaret Graham, Frances Staton. Seated (l. to r.): Teresa O'Connor, Mina Wylie.

in the North Western Branch. The Dundas Street Branch was headed by Mrs. Hamilton in 1889, and that year, Miss Moodie headed the Western Branch. Later, when a music library was set up, Ogretta McNeil supervised that division. It should be noted, though, that the system's chief librarian and the assistant librarian/secretary were consistently male for many years and the salaries were quite discriminatory. In 1883 the head librarian earned two thousand dollars, the assistant one thousand dollars, and the branch heads, three hundred dollars. As one wag put it, "Why is it that a male librarian resembles a dead fish?" And the answer: "Because he so quickly rises to the top."[26]

There were, however, several women working in the public libraries; a photo of the reference library staff in 1895 at the York Mechanics' Institute shows nine female librarians: Eva Davis, Rose Ferguson, Elizabeth Moir, Hattie Petit, Margaret McElderry, Margaret Graham, Frances Staton

(1863–1947), Teresa O'Connor, and Mina Wylie. Later, some of these women became branch or department heads, but little is publicly known about them, except for Frances Staton, who headed the reference department for more than fifty years. In writing about Toronto in 1887, G. Mercer Adam noted that the public library was under the supervision of Mr. James Bain Jr. and a "corps of intelligent young women."[27]

Other women worked in libraries of associations. In 1886 Ada M. Read became the first librarian for the County of York Law Association.[28]

Much can be discovered from the public libraries' circulation statistics. The 1891 annual report noted that the number of books taken out rose rapidly during the year to 427,347, an increase of 39,867. The report also stated that the number of works of fiction borrowed during the year actually decreased proportionately, which the library management deemed a good thing. As it said: "The figures amply justify the conclusions at which older Library Boards have arrived, that there is a progressive character in mental culture which is imparted by a taste for reading and which can be fostered by supplying freely the best literature,"[29] referring to non-fiction.

Nurses

In 1617 Marie Rollet Hébert Hubou sailed to New France (Lower Canada) with her husband. But in only ten years, she was a widow. Her husband, Louis Hébert, had been a surgeon and apothecary. Marie had learned a great deal from him, so when he died, she started caring for her neighbours using her new-found medical knowledge. It was not until 1632, however, that trained nurses arrived in Quebec from France, the first women to work in the Hôtel-Dieu de Québec, which was founded in 1639 by the French Duchess d'Aiguillon and the Augustinian Hospitaliers of Dieppe. Then, in 1641, Ursuline-educated Jeanne Mance, another woman from France, founded a second hospital, the Hôtel-Dieu de Montréal. In 1738 the non-cloistered order of Grey Nuns introduced district nursing to many other areas of Canada, but not until the nineteenth century in York/Toronto. The York General Hospital, which opened in 1829 for patients, was the evolution of an 1812 military hospital hurriedly organized to treat the wounded from the war of 1812–1814; it became the Toronto General Hospital in 1856.[30]

But before that, in the summer of 1847, Toronto faced another major medical crisis: almost forty thousand destitute Irish immigrants, many of them ill with deadly contagious typhus or cholera, poured into the city of only twenty thousand men and women. Ship after ship arrived in Toronto from Ireland with sick or dying on board. For example, the bark *Larch* from Sligo, which had 440 passengers on board when it left port, carried 150 sick when it arrived. One hundred and eight had died on the crossing. A smaller ship, *Ganges*, arrived with 80 sick; 45 had died on the voyage. The bark *Wellington* sailed from Liverpool with 435, buried 26 at sea, and arrived with 30 sick.[31] They were met with fear and quarantine. Fever sheds were set up in an attempt to keep these new migrants isolated, and residents complained about the stench from the steady stream of undertaker carts. Farmers refused to hire survivors as labourers or to bring their produce to the markets.[32] However, selfless medical professionals and volunteers gave their lives to care for the sick. English and Irish nurses contracted the diseases themselves and died young: Susan Bailey, thirty-two; English nurse Anne Slocumb, twenty-six; Irish-born Sarah Jane Sherwood, twenty-three; Irish Sarah Duggan, only eighteen; and Catherine Doherty, also from Ireland, fifty-five. It is not known what medical training these women had received or whether they themselves were immigrants that year or earlier. But they are listed, along with male orderlies and a well-known Toronto doctor, as "first responders" who died in the discharge of their duty.[33]

The first training school for Ontario nurses opened in St. Catharines, south of Toronto, in 1874, organized by the Irish-born gynecologist Dr. Theophilus Mack and two nurses who had trained under Florence Nightingale. Initially, most of the nurses were from working-class homes. As Dr. Mack wrote in 1875, "All the most brilliant achievements of modern surgery are dependent to a great extent upon careful and intelligent nursing. Incompetency on the part of a nurse renders nugatory the best efforts of the doctor in the most critical moments, and has frequently resulted in loss of life."[34]

Florence Nightingale (1820–1910), the British reformer and founder of modern nursing, had strict rules and lofty aims for nurses. She wrote:

What strikes one most with many women, who call themselves nurses, is that they have not learnt this ABC of
nurse's education. The A of a nurse ought to be to know
what a sick human being is. The B is to know how to behave
to a sick human being. The C is to know that her patient is
a sick human being and not an animal.... [Nursing] has
been limited to signify little more than the administration
of medicines and the application of poultices. It ought to
signify the proper use of fresh air, light, warmth, cleanli-
ness, quiet, and the proper choosing and giving of diet —
all at the least expense of vital power to the patient.[35]

As nursing developed, the hospitals, too, had images of the ideal nurse: "to
show wifely obedience to the doctor, motherly self-devotion to the patient and a
firm mistress/servant discipline to those below the rung of nurse." The Montreal
General Hospital paid nursing students twelve to fifteen dollars a month in 1889;
their rat catcher earned twenty dollars. Nurses were a cheap form of labour for
the hospital. They worked an average of twelve-hour days or nights and had
to attend lectures after their exhausting shifts. However, the lectures were in-
frequent. Lectures on anatomy; physiology; medical, surgical, and obstetrical
nursing; communicable diseases; and diseases of the eye, ear, throat, and nose
occupied 160 hours over nine months, less than 18 hours a month. Student nurses were the main workers in the hospital, as graduate nurses tended to accept
private nursing opportunities where the conditions were supposedly better.[36]

In 1888 the Toronto Homeopathic Hospital began in a dispensary with a
nursing staff of six — a head nurse and five in training. In 1890 it had eleven
beds but was so popular that it increased its capacity to thirty-two beds the
same year. In 1892 the St. Michael's Hospital School was founded in Toronto,
one of many nursing schools opening up across Canada. The Victorian Order
of Nurses, another source of nurses, was founded in 1897 under the auspices
of Lady Aberdeen, wife of Governor General Earl Aberdeen. The organization
set up hospitals across Canada.

One of the most important influences on nursing in Canada, however, especially in Toronto, was Mary Agnes Snivley (1847–1933), a St. Catharines

schoolteacher who was persuaded by friends to attend New York's Bellevue Hospital Training School for Nurses, modelled on Florence Nightingale's school in England. In 1884 Mary Agnes was hired as superintendent of the Toronto General Hospital Training School for Nurses after her two years' training in the United States. What she found in Toronto was disorganization and unacceptable working conditions: seven nurses for four hundred patients, with twenty-seven nurses in training; no work schedules; no proper record-keeping; no policies for obtaining supplies; nurses sleeping on straw beds and eating meals beside the boiler room in the basement. She immediately expanded the nurses' course of study, increasing it first to two years and later to three; eliminated unnecessary, time-consuming activity for nurses such as washing their own dishes; began the process for a nurses' residence; and encouraged the nurses to found the Alumnae Association of the Toronto General Hospital Training School of Nurses to create a community of graduate nurses and "advance the sphere of nursing." By 1894, ten years after Mary Agnes arrived,

Miss Mary Agnes Snively and graduate nurses, ca. 1895. Graduates in 1910 (inset) had modern caps.

the Toronto General Hospital school had become the largest in Canada. Six hundred and forty-seven young women had applied to the program that year, but only fifty-six could be accommodated. Mary Agnes applauded enthusiasm, courage, and inspiration, and considered nursing a mission:

> The noblest, most womanly, most *Christ*-like, of all the avo-
> cations open to women.... What makes a woman a good
> nurse? Practice. What makes a woman a good woman?
> Practice.... Life is not a holiday, it is an education. The world
> is not a playground, it is a school-room, and character de-
> velops in the stream of the world's life.[37]

Mary Agnes also became president of the Society of Superintendents of Training Schools for Nurses of the United States and Canada in 1897, and later helped found the Canadian Nurses Association. Called "the mother of nurses in Canada," she was remembered for her legacy of higher education, professional ethics, and devotion to duty and for transforming nurses into "both ladies and professional women."[38]

Doctors

As early as 1795, doctors had pressured the legislature of Upper Canada to enact legislation that would limit the practice of medicine to university graduates, and women were not allowed in universities. By 1836 Toronto had fifteen doctors, all male, in a population of six thousand, or one doctor for every four hundred people, nearly twice as many per capita as cities such as Boston. By 1839 the Medical Board of Upper Canada had become an incorporated self-governing and provincially based College of Physicians and Surgeons, "in order to monopolize and standardize licensing" doctors. The board had considerable power: they turned away many whom they felt unqualified, and not being able to read Latin, for example, was not acceptable.[39]

A few women, however, did break the medical glass ceiling in the nineteenth century, many in Toronto. Perhaps the most curious case was that of

Dr. James Miranda Barry (1795–1865), teetotaller and vegetarian. It was only after Dr. Barry's death that it was discovered that she had been female and had actually given birth. Margaret Bulkley, the daughter of a destitute Irish woman and an Irish shopkeeper, received a good education through an inheritance from the estate of her uncle, a well-known painter and supporter of women's rights. Margaret told her brother that if she had been a boy, she would have been a soldier. So it might have been no surprise when Margaret disappeared and James Miranda Barry appeared in her place, a smooth-faced boy taking his uncle's name, like many women over the centuries who have disguised themselves as men in order to receive a good education. Graduating from Edinburgh Medical School, Barry joined the Army Medical Department in 1813 and worked as a doctor in countries such as South Africa, Mauritius, Jamaica, Saint Helena, Trinidad, Malta, and Corfu. He supervised military hospitals and barracks in Canada from 1857 to 1859 in Montreal, Quebec City, Kingston, and Toronto.[40] He made several improvements in the soldiers' living conditions: the installation of ovens to vary their diet, better sewage and drainage in their barracks, separate quarters for married couples, and improved nutrition. He was also a skilled surgeon, performing one of the first Caesareans.[41]

Barry dyed his hair red and wore a dark blue military uniform, but was always without facial hair. He appears to have enjoyed his life as a military doctor for forty years, gaining an excellent reputation for his work. Barry died in London, England, in 1865, seventy years old, having survived a lifelong disguise, a duel, and an altercation with Florence Nightingale.[42]

Most of the Canadian female doctors who graduated in the nineteenth century, however, either took work in the United States in places such as asylums, hospitals, or even universities; worked with women and children at home in institutions such as baby hospitals or as school medical inspectors; or became Christian missionaries, especially to India or China. Some of these were Leonora Howard King (1851–1925), the first Canadian doctor in China; Amelia LeSueur Yeomans (1842–1913) and her daughter Lilian Barbara Yeomans (1861–1942), the first two female physicians in the province of Manitoba; Elizabeth Hurdon (1868–1941), the author of *Gynaecology and Pathology*, associate professor at Johns Hopkins University, and "the most outstanding medical woman of the 20th century";[43] and the feminist Elizabeth Smith-Shortt (1859–1949), who was active in the suffragette cause. Many others across Canada graduated from universities offering medical training for women before the turn of the century.[44] Perhaps the most famous, however, was Emily Stowe.

Emily Howard Jennings Stowe (1831–1903)

Born in 1831 to a Quaker family and the first of six daughters, Emily, who was home-schooled by her mother, became a teacher herself when she was fifteen. Later she attended the Toronto Normal School, and in 1854 she became the principal of an elementary school, the first woman in Canada to be hired in that position. She applied to the Toronto School of Medicine in 1865 to study to become a doctor but was denied admission. The vice-president of the University of Toronto informed her that "the doors of the University are not open to women," and he added, "I trust they never will be." To that, Emily replied, "Then I will make it the business of my life to see that they will be opened, that women will have the same opportunities as men."[45]

Emily turned to the New York Medical College for Women, one of nineteen medical schools in the United States training women in medicine between 1850 and 1895. Graduating as a doctor in 1867, she set up a homeopathic practice in Toronto even though she couldn't get a licence. When she was permitted to take the exams in 1879 in order to get a licence, she refused, because the exams were administered by the men of the Council of the College of Physicians and Surgeons. However, the college suddenly granted her a licence in 1880. In 1886 she joined the staff of the Toronto Homeopathic Hospital and Richmond Street Dispensary.

As a result of her pressure for better education for women, the Women's Medical College opened in 1883, but initially it had a teaching staff of over twenty professional men. Even by the turn of the century, only four of the teaching staff were women. In 1876 or 1877 Emily founded the Toronto Women's Literary Club, reorganized in 1883 as the Canadian Women's Suffrage Association. It served as an educational resource for women who had access to very few educational facilities, featuring speakers on varied subjects such as history, biographies of women, travel, science, current events, and civic improvement. In 1888 Emily became president of another female association, the Dominion Women's Enfranchisement Association. Her work went a long way toward enfranchisement for women; however, she believed, like other maternal feminists, that women should be educated to undertake their duties in the home, not because of gender equality. In 1896 she wrote, "My career has been one of struggle, attended by that sort of persecution which falls to the lot of everyone who pioneers a new movement or steps out of line with established custom."[46]

Dr. Emily Stowe.

Although Emily married a lay Methodist preacher, she herself lost all interest and confidence in organized religion. She said that she had "outgrown all religious creeds." As she had been home-schooled, Emily home-schooled her own daughters, and while she was studying medicine, one of her sisters cared for them.[47]

Emily was charged in 1879 with practising without a licence and performing an abortion, but she was acquitted due to her skill and the backing of the medical community as to her character.[48]

Ann Augusta Stowe-Gullen (1857–1943)

One of Dr. Emily Stowe's daughters, Ann Augusta Stowe-Gullen, was the first woman to graduate from a Canadian medical school, the Faculty of Medicine at Victoria College, in 1883. Augusta helped her mother establish what would later be called Women's College Hospital, where she taught for many years. She also helped found the National Council of Women and was elected a member of the senate of the University of Toronto. She was a trustee on the Toronto Board of Education in 1892. Augusta became president of the Dominion Women's Enfranchisement Association after the turn of the century.[49]

Jennett (Jenny) Gowanlock Kidd Trout (1841–1921)

While Emily Stowe was the first Canadian woman to openly practice medicine, Jenny Trout was the first *licensed* Canadian female doctor. Jenny endured the harassment she received at the University of Toronto and got her degree. Another unfortunate difference was that Jenny helped set up the Women's Medical School at Queen's University in Kingston, Ontario, at the same time that Emily was helping found the Medical College for Women at the University of Toronto. There were not enough students to merit two colleges, so in 1894 they united to form the Ontario Medical College for Women. Unlike Emily, Jenny sustained her Christian faith. "I hope to see the day when each larger town ... in Ontario will have one good true lady physician working *in His [Jesus's] name,"* she wrote in 1881. And like Emily and some of the early nineteenth-century female doctors who graduated from Trinity, such as Eliza Gray, Margaret Blair, and Margaret Wallace Sterling, Jenny taught school before attending medical college. It may be that they needed the money, or perhaps because it was a common career choice at that time for women.

After graduation Jenny and another medical graduate, Emily Amelia Strong Tefft (1816–1890), opened the Therapeutic and Electric Institute in Toronto, specializing in treatments for women. Jenny had benefited from such treatment earlier, and again later on due to poor health. They had so many patients that they opened a branch in Hamilton and one in Brantford as well. Jenny also opened a free dispensary for the poor, but it was not financially viable. She retired in 1882 at the age of forty-one because of ill health. She became increasingly involved in Bible study, foreign missions, and spiritual healing and cared for two young relatives as a result of a family tragedy. In 1919, at age seventy-eight, Jenny was ordained a minister with the fledgling Assembly of God denomination in the United States, eventually living to age eighty.[50]

Isabella S. Wood

A few of the other women who took advantage of the open admission to medical college were especially well-known, such as Isabella Wood. She, too, had a downtown practice, which was described as being much admired. Isabella graduated from the Toronto Model and Normal Schools, then attended the medical college, graduating at the turn of the century. She practised in Boston and St. John before establishing herself in Toronto. Her practice was described as "large and lucrative."

Susanna (Susie) Carson Rijnhart Moyes (1868–1908)

One of the more recognized medical missionaries from Toronto was Susanna Carson. In 1894, six years after she graduated as a doctor from Toronto Women's Medical College at the age of twenty, she married Dutch-born Petrus

Rijnhart, a China Inland Mission missionary. The daughter of a Methodist school inspector, she had wanted to be a missionary from the age of eleven. Petrus had been with his mission since 1890. Most of the Canadian medical missionaries were allied with the Presbyterian, Anglican, or Methodist denominations, but Susie and Petrus, supported by the Disciples of Christ church in Toronto, travelled around Outer Tibet, at one point helping out with the sick and wounded in a Tibetan monastery and opening a medical dispensary. In 1898 they set out on horseback for Lhasa, the capital of Tibet. But on the way, their newborn baby died, their guides left, five of their pack animals were stolen, and they were attacked by bandits. Petrus disappeared while seeking help from some nomads, and Susie eventually made it to a missionary outpost alone, penniless, in rags, with frostbitten feet. Later, in 1900, she was able to return to Toronto. There she recuperated from her ordeal, writing the story of her experience: *With the Tibetans in Tent and Temple: Narrative of Four Years' Residence on the Tibetan Border.*[51]

In 1902 Susie returned to Tibet and married another missionary, James Moyes. They soon returned to Canada because of Susie's poor health; she died in 1908 in Chatham, Ontario.

Optician

Born in London, Ontario, to a family "prominent among the early residents," Helen Cunningham (1883–?) went to a private elementary school, then to Jarvis Collegiate in Toronto. She received an optician's diploma after one year's study and then set up a practice in downtown Toronto. J.H. Beers, who wrote a biographical history of the County of York, considered her prominent enough to be included in a record of Toronto residents that consisted mainly of men. He wrote:

> She has already demonstrated conclusively her ability in her chosen line of work, and in these few years has established herself firmly among the professional workers of the city. She is personally a young woman of superior culture and attainments, and is very popular among her friends.[52]

Midwives

Midwives have been denounced at times, over centuries. Heinrich Kramer and Jacob Sprenger, co-authors of the *Malleus Maleficarum*, the 1487 manual for witch hunters, wrote that of all the evil women they had come in contact with, midwives surpassed all others in wickedness. No one does more harm to the Catholic Church than midwives, they wrote: "If a woman dare to cure without having studied she is a witch and must die." In chapter 13 of their treatise, they listed the "injuries" done to children by "witch midwives": "first by killing them, and secondly by blasphemously offering them to devils." Fortunately, the *Malleus Maleficarum* was no longer influential in the nineteenth century, but a negative attitude toward midwives persisted in some quarters.[53]

In the early years in Upper Canada, the status of midwives was confusing. While ordinary women called upon them to assist with birthing, in 1795, a law specified that "no person ... shall be permitted to vend, sell, or distribute medicines by retail, or prescribe for sick persons, or practise physic, surgery or midwifery within the Province, for profit, until such person or persons shall be duly approved of by a board of surgeons." Legislation passed in 1815 stated that "nothing in this Act contained shall extend or be construed to extend to prevent any female from practising midwifery in any part of this province, or to require such female to take out such license as aforesaid." Later laws either included or omitted these latter phrases; thus, depending on the time, practising midwifery without a licence could be said to be either legal or illegal in Ontario. In 1873 an amendment was prepared to the Ontario Medical Act, but never passed or defeated, stating that midwives "upon satisfactory proof of competence and upon their payment of an annual fee would be granted a licence to practise within a specified district," but "this licence could be revoked if the woman was found incompetent or guilty of misconduct.... It also exempted her from any penalties that the Medical Act may have otherwise imposed."[54]

Toward the end of the century, the editor of the *Ontario Medical Journal*, the official paper of the province's medical association, stated that there were no specific laws in Ontario either prohibiting or supporting midwives. Midwifery, he wrote, was "open to public competition, as if it was something any ignoramus, mule [*sic*] or female could dabble in with impunity."[55] (Whether or not *male* was meant instead of *mule* in the above sentence is not known.)

According to government census data, there were eight midwives in Ontario in 1851, sixteen in 1861, twenty-one in 1871, and sixty-one in 1891. Most of them were probably in cities such as Toronto, but one source states that the numbers refer only to midwives trained in other countries who immigrated to Canada; there were no training opportunities for female midwives anywhere in Canada.[56]

Nevertheless, a few women were listed in the Toronto street directories as midwives, and a number of women advertised their services in various other ways. In 1810 the wife of the King's printer in York had a sign on her residence door: "Isabella Bennet, midwife from Glasgow." In 1828 "Mrs. Bennet, *Midwife*," advertised in the *Colonial Advocate*, stating "that she was moving to new premises." In the same paper, at the end of 1829, Mrs. Sarah Trebbutt was now "ready to attend families … in the Town or neighbourhood of York," having practised for several years as a midwife in England; she was supported by a well-known local doctor. In 1842 Dublin-trained Mrs. Mahon also advertised in the *Colonial Advocate* that she had worked successfully as a midwife for twenty years and would be ready to respond "to any call."[57] Some of the United Empire Loyalists who traditionally had used female healers brought a Mrs. Trull to Canada in 1794. She was knowledgeable about the use of herbs and followed a book she held on midwifery. It was said that "her services were frequently called on over a wide stretch of country and as there were, at that time, no bridges across the numerous streams … she many times had to swim her horse through them on her mission of mercy."[58]

There was no doubt that women were accepted as midwives by many men and women, including some, but not all, doctors. In the 1820s, the Society for the Relief of Women supported pregnant women by providing comfortable clothing, a midwife, good nourishment, and a physician if required. The early settler Mary O'Brien wrote in her diary that a midwife, Mrs. Fraser, helped in the birth of one of her children, and Mary herself acted as midwife at least twice, although once she was concerned and wanted to see a doctor. And the *Globe* editor wrote that it was "notoriously far more decent and becoming that women should be engaged on such occasions than men."[59]

On the negative side, there were a number of people like the anonymous "Country Practitioner" who wrote to the *Globe* in 1875 that in his "twenty years of medical practice he had 'never yet met [a midwife] who had any knowledge of anatomy, who could act whenever the slightest complication occurred, or even knew it had become necessary to send for a surgeon.'" And some were angered because a male who practised midwifery without a licence could be charged, but not a woman. But in spite of the pros and cons, the arguments back and forth, the practice of midwifery appears to have almost died out by the end of the nineteenth century. Government statistics show that in 1899 in Ontario, only 3 percent of all births were attended by midwives, 16 percent attended by no one, and the rest by physicians.[60]

In 1839 the first medical school in Upper Canada, King's College, opened with Dr. George Herrick teaching midwifery and diseases of women and children. He was paid the yearly salary of two hundred pounds. The introductory lectures every year were delivered to the public, and as an eccentric bachelor, Herrick found it embarrassing to present his lecture before the "ladies" in attendance. Considered a bit peculiar, he would have no carpet or gas in his house, he had a nap every day between four and six, and he had a half-dozen younger men "around his hospitable board" every night, with special dinners at Christmas and on his father's birthday. He went to bed regularly at nine. Before his appointment to the hospital, he had a private practice where he gave "gratuitous attendance to the poor afflicted with eye diseases, from 8 to 9 every morning." He was described as tall and stout, a typical Irishman, clever and well-educated in Ireland, London, and Edinburgh.[61]

Lawyer

Clara Brett Martin's (1874–1923) well-to-do Irish Anglican father was determined that his large family of twelve children would be well-educated. All of them went to university for at least some period of time, and a number of them became teachers. Clara's father had been an Upper Canadian township superintendent of education before they moved to Toronto sometime before Clara was born.

Clara began her studies at home with tutors and then attended Toronto's Trinity College in 1888, when she was fourteen. There she majored in mathematics, and she graduated with high honours at age sixteen.

Years later, the *Toronto Star* wrote:

> While a mere girl with Hungarian and Irish blood in her veins, she dared to beard the masculine lion by declining to take any of the admittedly feminine courses on the curriculum.... No. Miss Martin chose to take mathematics. This was in those days manifestly and palpably absurd.... It was with great supercilious regret that the male mathematicians of those days admitted that a woman never could master the binomial theorem or the integral calculus.[62]

Then she stirred up a hornet's nest by applying to study law. Women had been admitted to the bar of the Supreme Court in the United States in 1879. However, it was said in Canada that this would "prove disastrous to the best interests of women" and "that fashion-conscious women would never want to wear the ... official robes." However, in 1892, a compromise was effected, and the law society agreed that women could be admitted to the level of solicitor.[63]

Clara began articling with Mulock, Miller, Crowther, and Montgomery, but she was treated so badly that she changed to Blake, Lash, and Cassels. Lectures at Osgoode Hall were tortuous; both students and lecturers subjected her to verbal abuse, but she passed her examinations handily and went on to receive a bachelor of civil law from Trinity in 1897 and a bachelor of laws from the University of Toronto in 1899. On February 2, 1897, Clara was admitted as a barrister and a solicitor, the first woman in the British Empire, but only after another long battle, in which it was pointed out that the "homes and womanhood of Ontario" would be in grave danger.

Described as an "odd" sort of woman, probably because she rode her bicycle everywhere, Clara remarked, "I was looked upon as an interloper, if not a curiosity. The clerks avoided me and made it as unpleasant for me as they possibly could.... If it were not that I set out to open the bar for others of my sex, I would have given up the effort long ago."[64]

Clara began her practice with Shilton, Wallbridge, and Company, became a partner in 1901, and set up her own office five years later, centred on wills, real estate, and family law. Following in her father's footsteps, she spent time in administrative educational pursuits, serving as a member of the board of the Toronto Collegiate Institute from 1896 to 1899, and becoming a member of the public school board in 1901.[65]

There were also a number of female lawyers in the first few decades of the twentieth century.

CHAPTER 10

REFORMING PHILANTHROPISTS

A s early as 1817 the Society for the Relief of Strangers in Distress was formed in York, primarily to deal with distressed immigrants, some of whom were left destitute as their caregivers had died on the sea voyage or on arrival in quarantine. The organization accepted applications for employment, but kept the wages low so that only those who were really "necessitous" would apply and others would be kept from "burthening the Society." In 1828 the name was changed to the Society for the Relief of the Sick and Destitute. No women were on the committee, but there was an interesting variety of men required: "a catholic clergyman ..., a methodist ditto [sic] ..., an episcopalian archdeacon and his curate ..., a baptist preacher ..., a presbyterian minister ..., a solicitor and attorney general ..., a judge of the king's bench court ..., a member of the legislature ..., an editor of a public journal ..., a physician ..., two cabinet ministers ..., a police magistrate" and a squire.[1]

Another committee, the Society for the Relief of the Orphan, Widow, and Fatherless, reported in 1833 that there were at that time "about 136 widows and nearly 400 children" on their list. Because of the great numbers, the society decided to "dispose" of the orphans and fatherless among the "respectable farmers" and others in the province, "girls to the age of eighteen, and boys to that of twenty-one." One of their plans — to engage the widows in sewing shirts and knitting socks for sale — had to be ended because many of the shirts and socks were made very badly. It was also noted that a number of destitute people from other towns or places found their way to York, increasing the burden on the city.[2]

From 1880 on, a number of women's organizations were established in the City of Toronto and throughout the province and country: missionary societies in various church denominations, non-denominational groups such as the Woman's Christian Temperance Union (WCTU), and secular groups such as the National Council of Women and the Dominion Women's Enfranchisement Association.

The WCTU was founded in 1874, and by the turn of the century it had expanded across Canada with ten thousand members, many more than in the suffragist movements. Its members supported outright prohibition, not simply temperance, as they watched the consumption of alcohol rise. It had been extremely available in the early years of Upper Canada, and by 1871 the yearly alcohol consumption per capita, for people fifteen years and older, was 1.19 imperial gallons. Women and children were too often the victims of drinking husbands, both through family violence and through wasted paycheques. Women believed that if they were to receive the vote, they would be able to control the abuse of alcohol. Women, it was widely accepted, were the moral and spiritual guardians of society, and they had the support of the churches, particularly the Methodist denomination. In fact, it was understood that abstinence was a Christian duty.[3]

"Maternal feminism" was the belief that women's special role was the result of her inherent maternal nurturing qualities, whether she was married or not, a mother or not. The nineteenth-century suffragettes were, for the most part, maternal feminists, reformers who wanted the vote for the stability and reform of the home and community. They firmly believed that if women were given the vote, the world would change for the better. The vote, then, was an enabling tool for social reform, not primarily for gender equality. They believed they would get the necessary reforms passed, and violence, poverty, and other afflictions would be a thing of the past. As social historian Wayne Roberts writes, "The image of the woman 'with a spiritual scrubbing brush in her right hand and moral uplift in her left eye' who aimed 'to make this old Earth into a Spotless Town' also came to be a trademark of the new woman's entrance into public life and reform" at the latter days of the nineteenth century. As one wag said, "I'm glad I picked a committee before all the reforms had been taken."[4]

There are many stories of the poor in the City of Toronto from the beginning, no more so than with the young newsboys trying to help their families survive. The following poem was printed in the *Toronto Telegram*:

> The poor little newsboy that jostles
> The parsons parading the street ...
> ... his language is not the politest;
> He can swear pretty hard if he likes.
>
> Yet a warm heart is his. I remember
> Now, selling her papers, a child
> On King Street, one night in December,
> When the bleak blast from Bay Street blew wild,
>
> Some lost little waif she resembled,
> Her bundle of papers unsold;
> Till one newsboy, who saw how she trembled,
> "See boys!" he said, "Sissie is cold!"
>
> They clubbed all their coppers together,
> They bought every paper she had,
> And they wrapped her up warm from the weather,
> And sent her home hearty and glad.[5]

In 1833 the only charities that women were involved in — to the extent that they were listed in the annual *York Street Guide* — were the York Annual Bazaar "conducted" by Lady Colborne, wife of the governor, and the "ladies" of York; and the lying-in (maternity) hospital charity. In 1833 the bazaar raised £322 (equivalent to a little more than £36,000 today), although historian Henry Scadding suggested it was £311; and the subscription for the hospital raised £50 1s. 5d. (equal to approximately £6,000 today) — significant amounts. Scadding quotes a notice that appeared in *Canadian Magazine* about the bazaar, describing it as attended by "all the fashionable and well-disposed"; a "lady" stood at each table and "all the articles were sold to gentlemen." For the occasion that year, James M. Cawdell, Osgoode Hall librarian, wrote "The Raven Plume," a song dedicated to Miss Mary Powell, daughter of Chief Justice Powell, and sung by the well-known international musician John Edward Goodson, who happened to be in York at the time.[6]

By the 1830s there was no lack of crime. As Anna Jameson reported in her writings, in Toronto "from the spring assizes of 1832 to the assizes of the present year, (1837,)" 424 men and 25 women were tried for various crimes — of the men, 10 for murder and 23 for "manslaughter and other violent crimes," and of the women, 2 for manslaughter and the rest for "larcenies and petty crimes." Jameson reported that the mayor had complained about the increase in crime, "and particularly the increase in street beggars and juvenile depredators."[7]

The infamous Brook's Bush Gang was headed by a woman — a vicious English prostitute called Jane Ward. A group of prostitutes, pickpockets, thieves, and petty criminals lived and operated east of the Don River, with their headquarters in a barn in an area now known as Withrow Park. Ellen McGillock, "a 'tall, strapping' figure of six feet," was also involved. They were not above murder with the view to robbing their victims — from a poor Black boy sent to buy hay on Broadview Avenue to a member of the legislative assembly trying to cross the Don River.[8]

By 1850 the number of charities had increased, as had the number of urban women with enough time to do volunteer work. The Ladies' Committee of Management, with the Countess of Elgin and Kincardine as patroness, looked after the Toronto General Dispensary and Lying-in Hospital, which was established in 1848 and received 103 women a year. There were, of course, male doctors and a house committee of seven men who were an integral part of the management. The same countess was also the patroness for the Provincial Lying-In Hospital and Vaccine Institution, which was free of charge to poor women and managed by nine male directors and eleven female "directresses." The Female Emigration Society was working with a society in England, directed by a committee of nineteen gentlemen and eighteen ladies in Toronto.[9]

The historian J. Timperlake noted that by 1857 "disorderly houses" were "alarmingly and unblushingly" on the increase in the city, and there was obviously a need for intervention. He pointed out that one in nine people had been arrested that year — 2,031 males and 673 females — for being drunk and disorderly. The Baptist Church had set up the Young Women's Association (and Young Men's for men) to "provide a suitable home" for girls coming into the city to work, to protect them "against the dangers and temptations consequent on leaving the parental roof." That this was necessary is evident by other statistics that 170 girls had been rescued by the Girls' Home, set up for girls' rescue and care, and the Magdalen Asylum, which "rescued fallen women."[10]

Other facilities that the ladies of Toronto reportedly took a charitable interest in were the Provincial Lunatic Asylum, the Asylum for the Incurable, and the Infants' Home. According to the census of 1851–52, there were a number of "supposed causes" of insanity including disappointed affection, slander, heredity, jealousy, fright, and over-study. The number of men and women in the asylum were roughly evenly divided.

G. Mercer Adam also listed a number of facilities where women helped out as active volunteers: the Home for Incurables, the House of Industry, the St. Nicholas Home, the Infants' Home and Infirmary, the Hillcrest Convalescent Home, the Wayfarers' Home, the Prisoners' Aid, the Ladies' Mission and Review Society, the Haven for Discharged Female Prisoners, the Industrial Refuge, the Sunnyside Children's Home, the Industrial Refuge for Girls, the Mercer Reformatory for Females, the Boys' Home, the Girls' Home, and the Orphans' House.[11]

There were also ladies' educational associations from the 1860s on, organized to get women into local universities.

In 1821 the first report of the Female Society for the Relief of Poor Women in Childbirth noted that seventeen women "experienced the benevolence of the Society." During the first month of operation, the society helped one woman whose husband had drowned just a few months earlier, leaving her with an infant and a second child about to be born. The 1825 meeting on

Isolation Hospital seen from the Don River. Date unknown, but taken after 1896, when the Valentine and Sons company began to produce postcards.

January 19 reported that there had been only two deaths among the mothers, and "few or none" among the fifty-four children that had been born. Two new orphans were nursed by funds from the society.[12]

While most charitable organizations were staffed by fairly well-to-do female volunteers, other women played a large part in these social reforms, such as the ones described below.

Ellen Toyer Abbott (1801–1876)

Ellen Toyer Abbott organized the Queen Victoria Benevolent Society to help Black women with such basics as education, settling into the city, and paying for funerals — anything that they might need. And the needs were great for women such as the remarkable Ann Martin Jackson (1809–1880), who managed to flee from her Delaware slaveholder with seven of her children, aged three to sixteen years, and find her way to Ontario; or Lucie Blackburn (1805–1895), who escaped with her husband, Thornton, from Louisville, Kentucky, as Lucie was about to be sold. Thornton Blackburn set up Toronto's first horse-drawn cab company. The Queen Victoria Benevolent Society also sponsored an employment centre where local employers could post jobs they were trying to fill. A free Black woman, Ellen had come to Toronto from Alabama with her husband, Wilson Ruffin Abbott, around 1835. They left a prosperous grocery business in Mobile because it had been ransacked and they both wanted freedom. Their son, Anderson Ruffin Abbott (1837–1913), became the first Black doctor in Canada.

The Queen Victoria Benevolent Society had strict rules. For example, a woman could not be admitted if she were addicted to alcohol, she could have only one husband, and she could not own a brothel. It was important to protect the society's image.[13] Later Ellen became active in the Toronto Methodist Episcopal Church.

Louella/Luella/Lewelyn Cooper Price (1858–1935)

The Queen Victoria Benevolent Society was not the only charitable organization initiated and maintained by Toronto's Black women. While not well-known because it was kept fairly private, the Eureka Club helped a large number of Black citizens even into the twentieth century. An article in the *Toronto Star* in 1980 by columnist Lotta Dempsey noted:

> The Eureka group has done everything: Assisting with rent, hospital or funeral payments, visiting shut-ins, distributing food and clothing, supplying glasses for children, making cancer pads; awarding scholarships to students entering university, donating a wheelchair to Bloorview Children's Hospital, assisting churches in purchasing hymnals.... Thank God for such a wonderful helping and caring group as the Eureka Club.... I was graciously assured there would be no discrimination, if I cared to attend the celebration [of the 70th anniversary of the club with a gala dinner].[14]

Louella/Luella/Lewelyn Price was an active member of the Eureka Club. She and a few other women met, often in Louella's house, to discuss how to help someone in their community — one person at a time. Their motto was "Not for ourselves, but for others." As the *Globe* newspaper reported on June 5, 1923, "Effective Work Being Done ... It is evident that those of the colored people who have achieved prominence in the affairs of the community are not losing sight of the needs of their less fortunate countrymen."

And Louella and her husband were some of the more prominent. Louella/Luella/Lewelyn Cooper had been born in either Virginia or Maryland in 1858. In 1875 she married a tall, dark waiter, Granison/Grandison Thomas Price, who became a sergeant in the U.S. Army, but was apparently a messenger for the U.S. government at the time. They had a son in 1877, but he died in infancy, so they adopted Robert C. Lynch, who became a waiter on the railroad.

By 1887 the Prices were living in the downtown core of Toronto, where Luella was an active member of the First Baptist Church. Grandison became a barber and then a railroad porter. Luella worked in a variety of occupations. She was a dressmaker and ran a boarding house and then her own restaurant downtown, on York Street. They moved east of the Don in 1910, building their own house. That year, she started or became involved in the Eureka Club, or the Eureka Friendly Club as it was sometimes called, the oldest Black women's organization in Ontario.

One of her friends and co-workers was Eureka president Viola Deas, whose husband, Horatio, was also a railroad porter. It seems as if this commonality drew them together, for all the women in the Eureka Club — never more than eighteen at any one time — were members of a variety of churches in Toronto.

In 1915 the *Toronto Star* reported that Luella Price had secured a permit for a three-storey brick apartment house costing $9,500 in the east end, near their home. Grandison was still alive, but not in good health; he died in 1921. Louella and Grandison had evidently worked hard and saved their money for years. Louella even managed a trip to the south aboard the steamer *Bermudian* in 1914.[15]

Elizabeth Jennet Wyllie McMaster (1847–1903)

Elizabeth had volunteered visiting the poor long enough to realize the need for a hospital for children in Toronto. So in 1874 she publicized an anonymous donation of ten dollars (her own gift), beginning an avalanche of other donations, enough to rent a building for the Hospital for Sick Children. She immediately set up a committee of prominent society women, serving as president herself from 1884 to 1891. The women were deeply involved in the hospital's management. They oversaw the daily operations, supervised staff, visited patients, offered religious instruction, found new buildings as the number of patients increased, and helped found a training school for nurses. In fact, Elizabeth decided to train as a nurse herself and became the first superintendent of the hospital. It is no surprise that, on several occasions, she found herself in conflict with the board of trustees. She contracted diphtheria in 1891 and had to leave, but later she organized the Hospital of the Good Samaritan in Los Angeles and reorganized the Children's Home in Schenectady, New York.[16]

Hester/Esther How (1846–1915)

Hester was a frequent visitor at the judge's chamber at city hall to discuss some of her students. She had been asked to take on a new school on Centre Street in downtown Toronto, set up for delinquent and neglected boys, because she'd had earlier success with reaching troubled boys. Finally, the judge decided to go to the school every Wednesday afternoon. This was the beginning of juvenile court in Toronto. Hester provided free hot lunches for poor children, as well as supper after school, craft classes, and holidays at a farm. She set up a daycare centre for working mothers, a penny bank account for children, and classes in practical subjects such as cooking and sewing.[17]

Elizabeth Jane Harvie Creighton (1860–1932)

Elizabeth Harvie was from a prominent family in Toronto. Her husband worked for the Northern Railway. The Haven opened its doors in 1878 with about eight beds, providing assistance to 178 women that year. In 1893 it increased its capacity to seventy-five beds and admitted 741 women. Initially it was a shelter for women released from prison, but in 1879 it admitted any woman in need, "the odds and ends of humanity." As its 1885 annual report stated, the Haven "makes provision for all classes and grades of fallen women.... The doors of The Haven always stand open to receive any poor, homeless, friendless, miserable wanderer." A number of women from prominent Toronto families administered the program, with twenty-four of the thirty-two founding members being women. For example, Elizabeth Harvie was involved with the Haven from its beginning until her death, and served as president for seventeen years. Like many other nineteenth-century women involved in charitable work, she was a staunch lay member of a Protestant evangelical church — in this case, the Presbyterian Church's foreign mission committee. She had even travelled overseas to observe missionary activity. Also, like many other affluent Toronto women, she was involved in several causes. She was a founding member of the Ontario WCTU and of the Women's Medical College, and at one time, president of the Hospital for Sick Children.[18]

At first the Haven's residents were helped to find "honourable positions" in society, such as seamstresses, house servants, or nursery matrons. But gradually the home turned inward, and the residents provided a stable workforce for the charity itself with the women working in the laundry or ironing or sewing for the Haven. There were very strict house rules, even to the point where the superintendent read all the women's mail before passing it on. The house also catered more to the "feeble-minded." It lost its initial connection to religious organizations and churches in the beginning of the twentieth century, with liaisons more often with professional social workers.[19]

—·—

In the nineteenth century, not all men and women espoused maternal feminism, and some very prominent men fought for the equality of men and women, and therefore suffrage for women. The influential British philosopher John Stuart Mill (1806–1873), a champion of social reform, advocated for equality of women and men, noting the ridiculous and unreasonable aspects of maternal feminism. If women were spiritually and morally superior to men, he argued, then "the better" were required to obey "the worse." Besides, he wrote, the subordination of one sex to another was wrong in itself.[20]

Mill also attacked the idea that women were naturally worse at some things than men and should therefore be forbidden from doing them. He noted that society simply didn't know what women were capable of because there was no evidence. If women could not do something by nature, he wrote, it was unnecessary to stop them from doing it. He believed that the emancipation and education of women would benefit men as well — it would result in the greater intellectual development of everybody.[21]

One of the strongest early Canadian supporters of women's suffrage was the nineteenth-century prime minister the Right Honourable John A. Macdonald. In a speech to the legislature on April 27, 1885, Macdonald began:

> With respect to female suffrage, I can only say that, personally, I am strongly convinced, and every year for many years, I have been more strongly convinced, of the justice of giving women otherwise qualified [owning sufficient property, as was then the standard requirement] the suffrage.... I am strongly of the opinion, and have been for a good many years, and I had hoped that Canada would have the honour of first placing women in the position she is certain, eventually, after centuries of oppression, to obtain ... of completely establishing her equality as a human being and as a member of society with man.[22]

The reaction was swift and unfortunately predictable. Joseph Royal, member from Provencher, the first to speak against the motion, declared:

Woman has been created for another kingdom. Her kingdom is powerful enough. They are supreme in almost everything.... It is all very well where a lady of property and rank may object that her butler has a vote while she has not. But that is due to the fact that the lady is a woman and the butler is a man. That is all. The reason is very plain.[23]

(In 1888, on the advice of Sir John A. Macdonald, Joseph Royal was appointed lieutenant-governor of the North-West Territories.)

A second attempt was made in 1895, when a little-known newspaper publisher, Sir Mackenzie Bowell, was prime minister. On May 8, Irish-born Nicholas Flood Davin, a fifty-two-year-old bachelor and the backbencher member of Parliament for Assiniboine West, moved that "in the opinion of the House, the privilege of voting for candidates for membership thereof should be extended to women possessing the qualifications which now entitle men to the electoral franchise." Speaking to his motion, he noted:

The hon. member for Bothwell (the Hon. David Mills) says that woman is an aesthetic product, and that we would interfere with her aesthetic character.... I do not admit that. If we look into history, we find that those gifted women who have been great politicians and great rulers did not lose their fascination by taking an active part in politics. Will politics degrade women? I hold on the contrary, that this reform would give women such a position in the world that man would regard her as something more than one of the supreme objects of beauty to be admired and desired.

James McMullen, member from Wellington North, was the first to respond. He noted that "woman's proper sphere" was "the home" and that there she had an influence over her children and husband which could not "be overestimated." If she were to get mixed up in politics, this influence "would be lessened." Instead her role was to make the home comfortable for her husband.

Davin's motion was defeated on June 5, 105 votes to 47.[24]

CHAPTER 11

EPILOGUE

—————•◦•—————

I f one reads early male-authored histories of nineteenth-century Upper
Canada/Ontario, one often wonders if the female species actually existed,
for the historical works are either largely devoid of women or full of anonymous women. For example, it was written that a school organized by the
Anglican priest Dr. Okill Stuart in 1807 was attended by "boys who became
rich and celebrated men, and ... girls who blossomed into the belles of the
growing capital." Twelve names of the boys are given. Then it noted that
"among the girls' names are many afterward distinguished in the society of
Upper Canada," but who they were, the reader was left to guess.[1]

The same is true, of course, of some modern historical accounts. Yet the
early Toronto street directories give an exciting glimpse into some of the occupations, professions, and vocations that women held, and where they worked.

By the end of the nineteenth century, Toronto women, or women connected to Toronto in some way, were active in the arts, education, journalism,
medicine, agriculture, religion, hospitality, entertainment, finance (bookkeeping), science (botany), and photography. They were involved in some
areas more than others, even in politics if one counts the suffragette movement
in that category, and in law very marginally. However, acceptance into any

profession that required a university degree, such as medicine and law, did not come without a horrendous struggle.

Women's accomplishments were even more remarkable when one considers all the obstacles put in their way. As Anne Rochon Ford entitled her book on the history of female University of Toronto graduates, their "path [was] not strewn with roses." However, it was full of thorns! Women bore the names of their husbands, fathers, or brothers, and most women were answerable to them and dependent on them. Even though this phenomenon continued into the next century, it was more difficult for women in the 1800s. The concept of maternal feminism, which required women to focus on the home, permeated society for the whole of the century. Yet women owned shops, hotels, and other businesses and managed them successfully, obviously outside the home.

Women were generally judged by how they looked, rather than by their abilities. John Howison's assessment of Canadian women in 1821 was that some of them were "extremely pretty," but their chief attraction was in the naïveté of their manners and in their "beautifully dark and sparkling eyes." He noted that they lost their teeth and good looks eight or ten years sooner than European women, but he didn't know why.[2] His attention was focused on women's attractiveness or looks, not on their achievements.

Women had smaller families as the century progressed, and this may have allowed many of them to enter the workforce. Why this happened is not known. But in the marriage registers in churches in East Toronto/Riverdale from 1897 on, women were older than their male marital partner in 20 to 30 percent of all the marriages registered.[3] In those cases, the women would have started their families later, resulting in fewer children.

However, there were very few labour-saving devices in the nineteenth-century home that would allow women to finish their household chores more quickly, giving them more time for work outside the home. Most of these devices, such as efficient vacuums or electric clothes washers and dryers, are inventions of the twentieth century, as were easy-to-care-for synthetic fabrics. Some of the women, however, had servants. As well, if they had sufficient money, they could purchase most of what they needed or wanted in the variety of shops that existed in Toronto in the nineteenth century — owned by workers such as milliners, tailors, and producers of foodstuffs. As the century progressed, an even greater variety of goods could be bought, some made in Canada, others imported, giving women much more time to devote to outside employment.

Still, women displayed an astonishing breadth of involvement in the community. They were resourceful and resilient in spite of the restrictions placed upon them and attitudes such as their place of "curiously subordinated equality" mentioned in the 1860 *Christian Journal*. All in all, nineteenth-century women in Toronto were very much freer and much more involved outside the home in a variety of businesses, vocations, and professions, especially by the end of the century, than is usually supposed. This was likely also true in other large Ontario cities, although perhaps not as much in the country and smaller communities; research would be necessary to determine whether or not this was the case.

There was a somewhat different kind of labour for women in the first half of the century than later on, after industrialization reached Upper Canada. Initially, women generally laboured alongside men on early farms, although they also owned a variety of shops, other businesses, and hotels. In the second half of the century, as more and more factories and industries changed the shape of the cities, women had more opportunities to work outside the home and enter professions such as medicine and law, albeit after a supreme struggle. Nevertheless, throughout the whole century, women were much more involved outside the home than most previous accounts allow.

ACKNOWLEDGEMENTS

My thanks to the following people who have provided me with information:

- Dee Muir Allaert, independent computer whiz
- Chris Bateman, Heritage Toronto
- Daryl Betenia, Director of Collections, Glenbow Museum
- Neil Brochu, City of Toronto
- Ann Brown, Chair, Ontario Genealogical Society
- Philip Cheong, City of Toronto
- Christopher Coutlee, Toronto Reference Library
- Sarah Fairley, Colborne Lodge Museum
- Heather Gardiner, Archivist, Women's College Hospital
- Kim Geraldi, University of Calgary Archives
- Elizabeth Carswell Gillan, private researcher
- Sophie Granger, McCord Museum
- Sally Han, City of Toronto
- Major Mike LeBlanc, Assistant Director, Salvation Army Archives
- Cal Lorimer, Women's Art Association of Toronto

- Geraldine Loveys, Victoria University Library
- Adria Lund, Glenbow Museum
- Gabrielle Major, City of Toronto
- Lauren McCallum, Museums and Heritage Services, City of Toronto
- Dr. Adam McCulloch, Baptist Archives
- James Gillan Muir, independent computer whiz
- Barbara Myrvold, Local History Senior Services Specialist, Toronto Reference Library
- Leigh Naturkach, Women's College Hospital Foundation
- Ani Orchanian-Cheff, Toronto University Health Network Archives
- Patrick Osborne, Library and Archives Canada
- Laurel Parson, Anglican Church of Canada Archives
- Eric Schwab, Toronto Reference Library
- Paul Sharkey, City of Toronto Archives
- Rebecca Shaw, Archivist, Music Library, University of Toronto
- Katherine Taylor, author
- Gordon Thompson, Chair, Canadian Friends Historical Association
- Alan Walker, Beau Levitt, and the incredible team of librarians who spent countless hours searching for information and photographs in Special Collections, Toronto Reference Library
- Linda Wicks, Archivist, Sisters of St. Joseph of Toronto

I am also greatly indebted to Terry Gregg for reading the manuscript and pointing out ways to improve it, and to Lynda Newmarch for her excellent suggestions and enhancements to the text. Pancheta Barnett took time from her busy schedule to help ferret out information about Black people in nineteenth-century Toronto, a major feat. All three gave immensely of their time and talents. Thank you.

Kathryn Lane, Elena Radic, and Susan Fitzgerald — my editors — and Ashley Hisson — my proofreader — were diligent, helpful, and creative, spotting errors before they became a permanent part of the text; and the members of the Dundurn design and production team produced an attractive and readable manuscript. My thanks to all of them.

My thanks also to the reviewers who graciously agreed to read the entire manuscript and write a brief review for publicity: Warren Clements, Dr. Rose Dyson, Dr. Bruce Grant, Rick Mercer, Katherine Taylor, and Dr. Elizabeth Trott.

There are also names at the end of Appendix A of people who searched their files and provided information about street names of women in Toronto.

I apologize if I have inadvertently omitted people who should be listed here as well.

APPENDIX A

SELECTED TORONTO AND AREA STREETS COMMEMORATING OR CONNECTED TO NINETEENTH-CENTURY WOMEN

ADELAIDE STREET: Historians believe this street memorializes Princess Adelaide of Saxe-Meiningen, wife of King William IV. Named by Peter Russell in 1797.

AGGIE HOGG GARDENS: Agnes (Aggie) Hogg was the daughter of John and Janet Hogg. They owned a general store and John was postmaster for the Don Post Office. After her father's death, Agnes operated the post office, a new brick general store, and the first Don Mills library.

AGNES LANE: Commemorates Agnes Thomson Muir (1837–1865), who married the schoolteacher Alexander Muir around 1858. They had three children, John George Muir, James Joseph Muir, and Colonette Campbell Muir.

ALBERTA AVENUE: Named after the province of Alberta, which, in turn, was named after Queen Victoria's fourth daughter, Louise Caroline Alberta (1848–1939). She married Douglas Sutherland Campbell, Canada's governor general from 1878 to 1883, and was the first British princess to live in Ottawa's Rideau Hall.

AMELIA STREET: Named after Amelia Luton Rogers, wife of Levi Rogers, who had a farm between Yonge and Main Streets. Other historians are definite that the name commemorates Amelia Playter (1808–1902), granddaughter of Toronto settlers George Henry Playter and Elizabeth Welding; Amelia married first John

Scadding Jr., in 1830, and possibly, secondly, the Toronto publisher William Joseph Coates.

ANNETTE STREET: Possibly named after relatives of Jacques Baby, an early resident of the area known as Baby Point.

BARBARA CRESCENT: One of the first lots sold from the Taylor estate was to a young man in love with a woman named Barbara. He asked the executors of the estate to name a road for her. Barbara and the young man never married.

CARLTON STREET: Ann Wood McGill Strachan named this street after her brother Guy Carlton Wood, who was named after Guy Carleton, Lord Dorchester.

CAROLINE STREET: Commemorates Caroline Davis Leslie (1814–ca. 1853), who married George Leslie in 1836. George Leslie founded the famous Leslie Nurseries in the eastern part of Toronto.

CAVELL AVENUE: A British nurse, Edith Cavell (1865–1915) was shot by the Germans for helping about two hundred Allied soldiers escape from German-occupied Belgium during the Second World War. She became an international hero.

CHERRY NOOK GARDENS: Frank Britton and Minnie Duff married and raised prize-wining Irish terriers at Cherry Nook Gardens, so when they subdivided their land, they named a new street Cherry Nook Gardens.

CONNORVALE AVENUE: Named after the O'Connor family, John and Ellen O'Connor, who bought 12 Connorvale Avenue, and their eight daughters, who formed the famous O'Connor Sisters act in vaudeville and on radio and television. The street was originally called O'Connor Avenue.

CONSTANCE STREET: Marion Murray and her husband, Colonel Walter O'Hara, Assistant Adjutant General of Upper Canada Militia from 1827 to 1846, immigrated to Canada in 1826. Over the years they acquired 120 hectares of land in the Brockton and Parkdale villages and several streets are named after their family. Constance was one of their daughters.

CURZON STREET: Sarah Anne Vincent (1833–1898) married city hall clerk Robert Curzon in 1858. A writer and historian, she was a founding member of the Toronto Women's Literary Club and first president of the Women's Canadian Historical Society of Toronto. Detractors called the women historians "amateur historians and housewives."

DAGMAR AVENUE: Named for Princess Dagmar of Denmark (1847–1928), who married Czar Alexander III of Russia. She was the sister of Queen Alexandra, who married King Edward VII.

DARTNELL AVENUE: Named for Georgina Dartnell, daughter of George Russell Dartnell, a painter and surgeon. She married Frederick Wells, who was the son of Colonel Joseph Wells, owner of the Davenport estate. Georgina died giving birth to Nina Federica, a second daughter.

DEER PARK: Sarah Lockwood Heath, widow of the American brigadier general William Heath, bought land in 1836 with her son Charles. Deer roamed there, so they called it Deer Park.

DELISLE AVENUE: Named for Harriet de Lisle from Guernsey, wife of Weymouth Schreiber, who in 1874 subdivided his property, which he had bought from Charles Heath.

DELMA DRIVE: Named after developer Rex Heslop's wife, Delma. They had two children, Marilyn and Rex Jr. Heslop developed communities in Alderwood and Rexdale.

DENTON AVENUE: In 1897 Walter Massey, president of the Massey-Harris Company, named a farm in East York and Scarborough after his wife, Susan Marie Denton Massey (1861–1938). They had four children, Ruth Lillian, Madeline, Dorothy, and Denton.

DIXON AVENUE: Annie Noble Duggan (1865–?) married realtor John Joseph Dixon in 1892, but the avenue is named in her honour. Annie inherited Woodbine Park racecourse and adjacent property from her father, Joseph Duggan.

DOROTHY KERR: Named after a woman who married into the Price family.

DUCHESS LANE: Named after Frederica Charlotte of Prussia (1767–1820), the Duchess of York and Albany.

ELINOR DRIVE: Named after Bert Gooderham's daughter.

ELLERBECK AVENUE: Sarah Ellerbeck (1777–1865) married Captain John Playter in 1796. He was one of settlers Elizabeth Welding and George Henry Playter's sons. They had eight children. The Ellerbeck daughters of Lieutenant Emmanuel Ellerbeck, a cavalryman and a mariner, visited back and forth between Kingston and York. Both the Playters and Ellerbecks were United Empire Loyalists.

FLORENCE WYLE LANE and **FRANCES LORING LANE:** Americans Florence Wyle (1881–1968) and Frances Loring (1887–1968), both noted sculptors, came to Canada together in 1913, where they both became successful artists in the twentieth century.

GERTRUDE PLACE: Commemorates Gertrude (Gerty) Frankland (1881–1926), daughter of Mr. Henry Robertshaw Frankland. The Frankland family settled at Pape and Danforth in 1858. Frankland became a prominent livestock exporter.

GREENWOOD AVENUE: Named for hotel owner Catherine Kate Dwyer Greenwood (1822–1897), who took over the Puritan Hotel at Queen Street and Greenwood's Lane on the death of her husband, John, in 1868. They had opened the hotel four years earlier.

HARRIET STREET: Commemorates Harriet Wharfe, who married a Morley, a brick maker in the 1850s.

IVY STREET: Named after a member of the Morley family.

JACKMAN AVENUE: Named for Mary Jane (Minnie) Jackman (1850–1929), who married John Lea Playter in 1875. The Jackmans emigrated to Canada from England in 1836 on the *Heber*.

JANE STREET: Possibly named after a relative of Jacques Baby, an early resident of the area now known as Baby Point.

LAVINIA STREET: Named after Lavinia Coe. The Coes were farmers in the Swansea area.

LEUTY AVENUE: Named for Emma Mary Leuty (1841–1909), who married Walter Sutherland Lee in 1859.

LEWIS STREET: Named for Catherine Lewis, wife of John Saulter, a local farmer in the east of Toronto. They were married in St. James Anglican Church in 1805.

MARION STREET: Marion Murray and her husband, Colonel Walter O'Hara, Assistant Adjutant General of Upper Canada Militia from 1827 to 1846, immigrated to Canada in 1826. Over the years they acquired 120 hectares of land in the Brockton and Parkdale villages and several streets are named after their family.

MARJORY STREET: Named for the daughter of John Edward Russell, a developer and contractor.

MARY GAPPER CRESCENT: Mary Sophia Gapper O'Brien was an early settler; see page 41 in chapter 3.

MAUGHAN CRESCENT: Named after the Maughan family. Fidelia Jane Maughan was Mary Armstrong's daughter-in-law.

McGILL STREET: Named after Ann Wood, daughter of Dr. George Wood. She was the wife of Andrew McGill, fur trader, and secondly, of John Strachan.

MYRTLE STREET: Thought to be a member of the Morley family, east-end brick makers.

NINA STREET: Named for Nina Frederica Wells (1875–?), daughter of Frederick Wells, who inherited the Davenport estate. She married Adam Urias de Pencier, curate at St. Alban's Church, in 1895.

NORMA CRESCENT: Possibly named after Norma Love, a relative of the developer in the area near Bloor and Runnymede.

O'CONNOR DRIVE: Named after the late Senator Frank Patrick O'Connor, the founder of Laura Secord chocolates — a tenuous connection!

QUEEN STREET and **QUEEN VICTORIA STREET**: Commemorate Queen Victoria (1819–1901) who reigned over Great Britain and Ireland from 1837 to 1901 and was Empress of India from 1876 to 1901.

ROSEHILL: Named for Jesse Ketchum's daughter Anna, who married Walter Rose.

ROYAL DRIVE: Commemorates the 1939 visit of Queen Elizabeth (1900–2002) and King George VI (1895–1952).

ST. CLAIR STREET: Named for Clara of Assisi/Ciara Offreduccio (1194–1253), who became the abbess of San Damiano and founder of the Order of the Poor Clares.

STANTON AVENUE: Memorializes Virginia (Virna) Stanton Sheard (1862–1943), a Canadian poet and novelist who flourished in the twentieth century. Her first novel, *Trevelyan's Little Daughters*, was published in 1898.

SWANWICK AVENUE: Commemorates Mary Swanwick Hutton Morton (1830–1908), second wife of East Toronto developer Benjamin Morton. Mary donated the land for St. Saviour's Anglican Church, built by and for the workers at Union Station, the first railroad station east of Toronto.

WALKER AVENUE: Probably named after Emily Walker, who had a large shop for brick makers' supplies on the west side of Yonge Street at Walker Avenue.

WINEVA AVENUE: Named after Winnie, the only daughter of William James Hambly and Dora Elizabeth Parks (1870–1945), and Eva Rogers, a daughter-in-law. Winnie died in childbirth.

WINNIFRED AVENUE: Named for Winnifred Radcliffe, a Victorian author who wrote stories about fairies.

Emily Walker's brick moulds and wheelbarrow factory — wagons made and repaired.

SOURCES FOR STREET NAMES

Armstrong, C.H. *The Origin and Meaning of Place Names in Canada*. Toronto: Macmillan, 1930.

Bonnetta, Glenn. North York Historical Society.

Bradburn, Jamie. "Test Your City Knowledge." *Toronto Star*, February 14, 2021, TO10.

Chisolm, George. President, Oakville Historical Society.

Doucette, Joanne. *Leslieville Historical Society Newsletter*, September 2017.

———. *Pigs, Flowers and Bricks: A History of Leslieville to 1920*. Toronto: J. Doucette, 2011.

Ellis, John. The Beach and East Toronto Historical Society.

Harris, Denise. "Alderwood Street Names." Etobicoke Historical Society, n.d. etobicokehistorical.com/alderwood-street-names.html.

Huot, Gilles. Board member, Cabbagetown Preservation Association.

Jarvis, Mary Hoskin. *Historical Street Names of Toronto*. Toronto: Mary Hoskin Jarvis, 1960.

Lemos, Coralina R. *Corktown: The History of a Toronto Neighbourhood and the People Who Made It*. Toronto: Coraline R. Lemos, 2018.

Mayer, Adam. "Soldier's Story Forever Etched in City Streets." *Toronto Star*, August 21, 2007.

McKnight, Alanna M.M. "Shaping Toronto: Female Economy and Agency in the Corset Industry 1871–1914." Ph.D. diss., Ryerson University and York University, 2018.

Michailidis, John. "East York Street Names." *East York Tidbits*, June 2006.

Mourer, Sharon. Davisville Village.

Muir, Elizabeth Gillan. *Riverdale: East of the Don*. Toronto: Dundurn Press, 2014.

Roden, Bob, and Susan. Swansea Historical Society.

"Street Names of Scarborough." Scarborough Historical Society, n.d. scarboroughhistorical.ca/local-history/street-names-of-scarborough.

Toronto Public Library. *Toronto and Early Canada: A Catalogue of the Toronto and Early Canada Picture Collection in the Toronto Public Library*. Toronto: Baxter Publishing, 1964.

Whyte, Gerald Arthur. *The Streets of Riverdale: An Illustrated History*. Toronto: Riverdale Historical Society, 2012.

Wise, Leonard, and Alan Gould. *Toronto Street Names: An Illustrated Guide to Their Origins*. Richmond Hill, ON: Firefly Books, 2011.

APPENDIX B

HISTORICAL PLAQUES IN TORONTO AND AREA COMMEMORATING OR CONNECTED TO NINETEENTH-CENTURY WOMEN

———————— • ————————

MAY BALD, ELLA GARDINER, MARGARET LANGLEY, ELIZA BALMER, NELLIE
SPENCE, CAROLINE FAIR, ALICE JONES, MARY LENNOX, AND JENNIE
STORK: The first women to attend University of Toronto classes, in 1884. The
very first woman to attend a lecture, however, was said to be Catherine Brown,
one of George Brown's daughters. The founder of the *Globe* newspaper, George
Brown was a close friend of Daniel Wilson, president of the university. Catherine
begged Wilson to allow her to attend lectures. He replied that when she was
as tall as he was, she could attend. Catherine did grow tall — an inch above
Wilson. So he allowed Catherine and her older sister Margaret to listen to his
anthropology lectures through the open door of his office next to the lecture
room. Afterward, they were tutored in their own home and they graduated in
1885 with bachelor of arts degrees in modern languages. Plaque located at the
University of Toronto.

LUCIE/RUTHIE BLACKBURN (1805–1895): In the 1830s, Lucie and her husband,
Thornton Blackburn, both slaves, escaped to Upper Canada from Kentucky.
Lucie wore clothes exchanged with Mrs. George French from her church.

Thornton escaped during a jail riot. In Canada, they became very active in the Underground Railroad, began the first horse-drawn taxicab company in Toronto, and helped build Little Trinity Anglican Church. Lucie looked after the books for Thornton's taxi company, as wives often did for their husbands. For example, Torontonian Mildred Lewis (1871–1905), from the Riverdale area of the city, moved to Alberta in her teens. She met and married a former slave in 1892, rancher and well-known steer wrestler John Ware, who owned a ranch and two hundred head of cattle. He increased his herd to one thousand and bought a second ranch, while Mildred did all the bookkeeping for his businesses as well as teaching their children to read and write. Thornton plaque located at 19 Sackville Street.

Mildred and John Ware and early family, ca. 1896.

MARY ANN SHADD CARY (1823–1893): A journalist, newspaper editor, and publisher. Plaque located at 143 King Street East.

KATHLEEN BLAKE COLEMAN (1856–1915): A noted journalist. Plaque located at 234 Front Street East.

RHODA SKINNER TERRY CORNELL (1775–1834): A Toronto settler, Rhoda was the mother of thirty-seven children by two marriages, although nineteen were stepchildren. She and her family operated mills on the Don River. Plaque located at Cornell House in Thomson Memorial Park.

ISABELLA VALANCY CRAWFORD (1850–1887): One of the finest Canadian poets. A small garden park in downtown Toronto at Front and John Streets, near the CN Tower, has been named the Isabella Valancy Crawford Park. Dublin-born, Isabella immigrated with her parents to Ontario around 1858. She became fascinated by backwoods life and First Peoples' legends. Plaque located at 299 Front Street West.

ELIZABETH FISHER CUMMER (1775–1854): Elizabeth married Jacob Cummer when she was sixteen, and in 1797 they immigrated to Upper Canada from Pennsylvania, to a site on the east side of Yonge Street, now part of Willowdale (North York). Originally Lutheran, the family founded an Episcopal Methodist Church in Toronto and built a sawmill, a woollen mill, and a gristmill. They had six sons. Plaque located at the corner of Doris Avenue and McKee Avenue.

SARAH ANN CURZON (1833–1898): Part of the Toronto Women's Literary Club, Sarah was one of the more active of the group's fifty members. She also helped found the Women's Canadian Historical Society and the Women's Art Association, as well as being a columnist for the *Canada Citizen,* a temperance and reform journal. Plaque located at 274 Carlton Street.

ELIZABETH CUTHBERT: Elizabeth Cuthbert owned three properties on Wellesley Street in downtown Toronto (Cabbagetown) in the late 1870s, one of them a fancy goods store. While she owned the store, James Cuthbert operated it. The 1878 assessment roll indicates that she was a spinster and that James resided at the store. Since she was not married, James was likely her brother. The house she lived in was a two-storey roughcast with outbuildings at the rear. At the time, Cabbagetown was working class. Plaque located at 333 Wellesley Street East.

MAZO DE LA ROCHE (1879–1961): Writer. Plaque located in Wesley Brooks Memorial Park, Water Street and Main Street, Newmarket.

MATILDA RIDOUT EDGAR (1844–1910): Toronto-born historian Matilda Ridout Edgar, mother of nine children, began her literary career in her mid-forties after her children were grown.

SUSIE FRANCES RILEY HARRISON (1859–1935): Susie Riley was a Canadian poet, but she also worked as a novelist, music critic, and composer in Ottawa and Toronto under the pen names Seranus and Gilbert King. Plaque located at Exhibition Place.

ADELAIDE HUNTER HOODLESS (1858–1910): In 1897, she organized the first Women's Institute for rural women. There are blue provincial and maroon Parks Canada plaques for her located in the Brantford area.

EMILY PAULINE JOHNSON (1861–1913): A poet, writer, singer-songwriter, and performer, Pauline was born in Six Nations territory. Her father was a Mohawk Clan chief; her mother had immigrated to the United States from England in the 1830s. Her Mohawk name was Tekahionwake ("Double Wampum" or "Double Life"). Plaque located at 1037 Highway 54, Six Nations of the Grand River Territory.

BEATRICE LILLIE (1894–1989): Beatrice Lillie grew up in Toronto, eventually becoming "the funniest woman in the world." She entertained in three countries on two continents: Canada, the United States, and England. In 1920 she married Robert Peel, the heir of Lord Peel, but when he died, she was left with extensive debt. Plaque located at Queen Street West and Lisgar Street.

AGNES MACPHAIL (1890–1954): Agnes was born in the nineteenth century, but her work took place in the next. She was the first woman elected to the House of Commons in 1921, and in 1943 was elected member of provincial Parliament for East York. Plaque located at 2 Donegall Drive (at Millwood Road).

MAUD LEONORA MENTEN (1879–1960): Although she was born in the nineteenth century, Maud graduated from the University of Toronto in 1907 and four years later became a medical doctor. Plaque located at the University of Toronto.

LUCY MAUD MONTGOMERY (1874–1942): An acclaimed novelist. Plaque located at 222 Riverside Drive.

CHARLOTTE SCHREIBER (1834–1922): First woman elected to the Royal Academy of Arts. Plaque located on the University of Toronto Mississauga Campus.

ELIZABETH POSTHUMA SIMCOE (1762–1850): Plaque located at Rosedale Heights School of the Arts, 711 Bloor Street East.

GLADYS MARIE/LOUISE SMITH, A.K.A. MARY PICKFORD (1892–1979): Born in Toronto, Gladys Smith first appeared on a Toronto stage when she was five. She had a dazzling career on Broadway and in Hollywood, and she changed her name after she began to experience success. She received an Academy Award in 1929. Plaque located on the grounds of the Hospital for Sick Children, 555 University Avenue.

MARY AGNES SNIVELY (1847–1933): A nurse, teacher, and administrator. Plaque located at 200 Elizabeth Street.

ANN AUGUSTA STOWE-GULLEN (1857–1943): First woman graduate in medicine. Plaque located in front of Mount Pleasant Public School, 667 Mount Pleasant Road.

FLOS JEWELL WILLIAMS (1893–1970): Flos was born in Toronto, attended Jarvis Collegiate and Toronto Normal School, and taught around and in Toronto. Eventually she moved to Calgary, where she began a writing career. She married David Williams in 1915. Plaque located at 5 Rose Avenue.

NOTES

PREFACE

1   "Women in the 1800s," *Fact File* No. 616443, pp. 52–53, Scholastic, web.archive
    .org/web/20210118111837/http://www.scholastic.ca/education/magazines
    /elt_pdfs/little-women-factfile-616443.pdf.

CHAPTER 1
Toronto: A "New World" City

1   We now know that other Indigenous Peoples lived in the territory in what is
    now the City of Toronto. The land acknowledgement of the City of Toronto
    states that the city "is on the traditional territory of many nations including the
    Mississaugas of the Credit, the Anishnabeg, the Chippewa, the Haudenosaunee
    and the Wendat peoples, and is now home to many diverse First Nations, Inuit,
    and Métis peoples."

2   Filey, *Toronto Sketches 5*, 100; Duncan, *Hoping for the Best*. According to Bruce
    West, writing in the *Globe and Mail* on October 18, 1968 (as quoted in Duncan,
    65–66), a Yorkshire man, John Denison, told John Graves Simcoe that he was
    fed up with pioneer life and was returning to England. Simcoe suggested that
    he try the new capital first: the town of Dublin. "Dublin," cried Denison. "You
    have your audacity to ask a Yorkshire man to set foot in a place called Dublin."
    Simcoe replied that Denison could call the place anything he liked as long as

he remained in Canada. "In that case," replied Denison, "call it York. I said I was going to York. Call it York and I will go there and settle." Also Adam and Mulvany, *History of Toronto and County of York*, 77 and n.p.; Scadding, *Toronto of Old*, preface and introduction.

3　Duncan, *Hoping for the Best*, 79; Leslieville Historical Society, *History of an East End Neighbourhood*, 2.

4　Jameson, *Winter Studies and Summer Rambles*, vol. 1, 2; Mulvany, *Toronto Past and Present*, 47.

5　Aoki, *Revisiting "Our Forest Home*,*"* 13.

6　As quoted in Muir, *Riverdale*, 21.

7　As quoted in Duncan, *Hoping for the Best*, 80–81.

8　Aoki, *Revisiting "Our Forest Home*,*"* 77, 98.

9　Lefroy, *Recollections of Mary Warren Breckenridge*, 1–2; Duncan, *Hoping for the Best*; Cattermole, *The Advantages of Emigration to Canada*, 16, 18; Mulvany, *Toronto Past and Present*, 15.

10　Mulvany, *Toronto Past and Present*, 15–16.

11　Muir, *Riverdale*, 10ff; Ramara Historical Society, "The Name 'Toronto'"; Mulvany, *Toronto Past and Present*, 9ff; Kyte, *Old Toronto*, 143.

12　Adam and Mulvany, *History of Toronto and County of York*.

CHAPTER 2
Women in Nineteenth-Century Toronto:
Their Work and Station

1　Danforth United Church [*sic*], "Marriage Register, 1909–1921." Danforth United was originally a Methodist Church and would have been known as Danforth Methodist Church until church union in 1925.

2　Skelton, *The Backwoodswoman*, 225.

3　Lefroy, *Recollections of Mary Warren Breckenridge*, 1–2; Duncan, *Hoping for the Best*, 81–82.

4　As quoted in Duncan, *Hoping for the Best*, 92.

5　Skelton, *The Backwoodswoman*, 232–33.

6　Aoki, *Revisiting "Our Forest Home*,*"* 42.

7　Danforth United Church, "Marriage Register, 1909–1921."

8　Walton, *York Commercial Directory*, iv.

9　Firth, *The Town of York*, 310.

10　Mosser, *Upper Canada, Minutes of Town Meetings and Lists of Inhabitants 1796–1823.*

11　Walton, *York Commercial Directory.*

12 Walton, *York Commercial Directory*, n.p.

13 Jameson, *Winter Studies and Summer Rambles*, vol. 1, 144.

14 Thomas and Marchant, *When Milk Came in Bottles*.

15 A photo from Toronto Archives notes that the factory burned down in 1833, a discrepancy in dates.

16 Timperlake, *Illustrated Toronto*, 287.

17 Mark Kearney and Randy Ray, *The Great Canadian Trivia Book 2* (Toronto: Hounslow, 1998), 225.

18 Adam and Mulvany, *History of Toronto and County of York*, 461, 469.

19 Doucette, *Pigs, Flowers and Bricks: A History of Leslieville to 1920*, 174.

20 J. Armstrong, *Rowsell's City of Toronto and County of York Directory*; Jameson, *Winter Studies and Summer Rambles*, vol. 1, 269–70.

21 Acton, Goldsmith, and Shepard, *Women at Work*, 38ff.

22 Sager, "The Transformation of the Canadian Domestic Servant," 510.

23 Light and Prentice, *Pioneer and Gentlewomen of British North America*, 202.

24 Duncan, *Hoping for the Best*, 102; Scadding, *Toronto of Old*, ch. 14.

25 Adam and Mulvany, *History of Toronto and County of York*, n.p.

26 Robertson, *Robertson's Landmarks of Toronto*, vol. 3, 59, 63, 65.

27 Kealey, *Hogtown*, 9.

28 Kealey, *Hogtown*, 6–7.

29 Fraser, *A History of Ontario*, 80.

30 Miller, *The Journals of Mary O'Brien*; George Henry as quoted in Firth, *The Town of York, 1815–1834*, 325.

31 Muir, *Riverdale*, 51; Doucette, *Pigs, Flowers and Bricks*.

32 Robertson, *Robertson's Landmarks*, vol. 1, 197.

33 Muir, *Riverdale*, 47.

CHAPTER 3
Early Settlers

1 "William Holmes Peake," Genealogy and Local History, Deckerville Public Library; Firth, *The Town of York, 1815–1834*.

2 Leslieville Historical Society, *History of an East End Neighbourhood*, 3.

3 Fowler, *The Embroidered Tent: Five Gentlewomen in Early Canada*, 77.

4 From Joanne Doucette, storyteller.

5 "Jesse Ashbridge"; "Jesse Ashbridge House."

6 Firth, *The Town of York, 1793–1815*, 256–57.

7 Firth, *The Town of York, 1815–1834*, 235.

8 Firth, "Murray, Anne."

9   Innis, *Mrs. Simcoe's Diary*, 25.

10   Innis, *Mrs. Simcoe's Diary*, 32ff.

11   Jarvis, *Recipes and Remedies in Upper Canada*.

12   Craig, *Upper Canada*, 49.

13   Adam and Mulvany, *History of Toronto and County of York*, 210.

14   Adam and Mulvany, *History of Toronto and County of York*, n.p.; Scadding, *Toronto of Old*, ch. 20.

15   Firth, *The Town of York, 1793–1815*, 229–30.

16   Elizabeth Gillan, "My Great-Grandmother," unpublished manuscript.

17   Scadding, *Toronto of Old*, ch. 1.

18   Scadding, *Toronto of Old*, ch. 25.

19   Kyte, *Old Toronto*, 216–17.

20   Muir, *Riverdale*, 26–27.

21   Muir, *Riverdale*, 27.

22   Darke, *"A Mill Should Be Built Thereon,"* 65ff.

23   Jameson, *Winter Studies and Summer Rambles*, vol. 1, 98–99.

24   Adam and Mulvany, *History of Toronto and County of York*, n.p.

25   Heward and Wallace, "An American Lady in Old Toronto."

26   Heward and Wallace, "An American Lady in Old Toronto."

27   Heward and Wallace, "An American Lady in Old Toronto."

28   Miller, *The Journals of Mary O'Brien*.

29   Langton, *A Gentlewoman in Upper Canada*.

30   Langton, *A Gentlewoman in Upper Canada*, 8, 32.

31   Langton, *A Gentlewoman in Upper Canada*, 60.

32   Langton, *A Gentlewoman in Upper Canada*, 99.

33   Langton, *A Gentlewoman in Upper Canada*, 128, 95.

34   Langton, *A Gentlewoman in Upper Canada*, 44.

35   C.H. Armstrong, *Seven Eggs Today*, 1ff.

36   C.H. Armstrong, *Seven Eggs Today*, 9ff; Kyte, *Old Toronto*, 101.

37   Armstrong, *Seven Eggs Today*, 13.

38   Armstrong, *Seven Eggs Today*.

39   McCalla, *Consumers in the Bush*.

40   Fleming, *Diary 1869–1872*.

41   Fleming, *Diary 1869–1872*.

42   Moodie, *Roughing It in the Bush*, 563.

43   Skelton, *The Backwoodswoman*, 180.

44   As quoted in Guillet, *Pioneer Days in Upper Canada*, 9.

45   As quoted in Morris, *Gentle Pioneers*, x.

46   Morris, *Gentle Pioneers*.

47   Cattermole, *The Advantages of Emigration*, 173–74; Morris, *Gentle Pioneers*, 70.

48   Morris, *Gentle Pioneers*, 52–53.

49   Ballstadt, "Strickland, Susanna (Moodie)."

CHAPTER 4
Adventurers

1   The "Holy Land" is considered to be the Middle Eastern area where Christianity originated, an area roughly located between the Jordan River and the Mediterranean Sea, which also includes the eastern bank of the Jordan River.

2   Muir, *A Women's History of the Christian Church*, 137–38, 264, 369.

3   Philbrick, *The Englishwoman in America*; "The Diaries of William and Elizabeth Peters."

4   As quoted in Fowler, *The Embroidered Tent*, 148.

5   Scadding, *Toronto of Old*, ch. 17.

6   Fowler, *The Embroidered Tent*, 32.

7   Innis, *Mrs. Simcoe's Diary*, 42.

8   Mulvany, *Toronto Past and Present*, 11; Cattermole, *The Advantages of Emigration*, 13.

9   Lucille Campey, *Seeking a Better Future*, 20.

10   Mulvany, *Toronto Past and Present*, 12.

11   Fowler, *The Embroidered Tent*, 21.

12   Innis, *Mrs. Simcoe's Diary*.

13   Innis, *Mrs. Simcoe's Diary*, 43.

14   Noori, "The Complex World of Jane Johnston Schoolcraft."

15   Scadding, *Toronto of Old*, ch. 3.

16   Jameson, *Winter Studies and Summer Rambles*, vol. 1, ix.

17   Mulvany, *Toronto Past and Present*, 79.

18   Guillet, *Pioneer Days in Upper Canada*, 49–50.

19   Bird, *My First Travels in North America*, ix.

20   Philbrick, *The Englishwoman in America*, "Historical Introduction."

21   Philbrick, *The Englishwoman in America*, xxxvi.

22   Bird, *My First Travels in North America*, 140ff; Philbrick, *The Englishwoman in America*.

23   Philbrick, *The Englishwoman in America*, 191ff.

CHAPTER 5
The De Grassi Girls and Other Spies

1   Darke, *"A Mill Should Be Built Thereon,"* 80; Muir, *Riverdale*, 119–20; Da Silva and Hind, *Rebels Against Tories*, 96ff.

2   Darke, *"A Mill Should Be Built Thereon,"* 81.

3   Muir, *Riverdale*, 119.
4   Muir, *Riverdale*, 39.
5   Kyte, *Old Toronto*, 118.
6   Morgan, *Public Men and Virtuous Women*, 41–42.
7   Skelton, *The Backwoodswoman*, 89–90.
8   Muir, "Laura Secord." Used with permission.
9   Morgan, *Public Men and Virtuous Women*, 39–40.

CHAPTER 6
Women and Religion
1   Innis, *Mrs. Simcoe's Diary*; Playter, *Diary 1801–1853*.
2   Adam and Mulvany, *History of Toronto and County of York Ontario*, 71.
3   *Christian Guardian*, November 21, 1829, 5, c. 2; June 5, 1830, 230, c. 3; Muir, "The Bark Schoolhouse," 33.
4   Antliff, *Woman*, 33–34.
5   Muir, *A Women's History of the Christian Church*, 216.
6   Muir, *Petticoats in the Pulpit*, 86ff.
7   Cattermole, *The Advantages of Emigration*, 20.
8   Muir, *Petticoats in the Pulpit*, 85ff.
9   Muir, *Petticoats in the Pulpit*, 85ff.
10 Kyte, *Old Toronto*, 97.
11 Hopper, *Old-Time Primitive Methodism in Canada*, 52.
12 Russell, "Wage Labour Rates in Upper Canada," 77.
13 Campey, *Seeking a Better Future*, 148.
14 Muir, *Petticoats in the Pulpit*, 104ff.
15 Walton, *York Commercial Directory*, 122.
16 Muir, "The Bark Schoolhouse," 32.
17 "The 'Honeymoon' Diary of Eliza Barnes Case"; Light and Prentice, *Pioneer and Gentlewomen of British North America*, 190.
18 Sadlier with Clarke, *The Black Church in Canada*.
19 Dorland, *The Quakers in Canada*, 22.
20 Muir, *A Women's History of the Christian Church*, 255ff.
21 Healey, *From Quaker to Upper Canadian*, 14ff.
22 Batho, *Durham Biographies*, n.p.
23 Healey, *From Quaker to Upper Canadian*, 85.
24 Healey, *From Quaker to Upper Canadian*.
25 Dorland, *Former Days and Quaker Ways*, 115.
26 Fuller, "Alma Gould Dale (1854–1930)."

27 Dorland, *The Quakers in Canada*, 167.
28 Dorland, *The Quakers in Canada*, 167–68.
29 Dorland, *Former Days and Quaker Ways*, 116.
30 Dorland, *The Quakers in Canada*, 195ff.
31 Trewhella, *The Yonge Street Quakers*.
32 Brown, *"What God Hath Wrought?,"* 19.
33 Muir, *A Women's History of the Christian Church*, 277ff.
34 Collins, *The Holy War of Sally Ann*, 3.
35 Brown, *"What Hath God Wrought?,"* 31.
36 Muir, *A Women's History of the Christian Church*, 282.
37 Brown, *"What God Hath Wrought?,"* 37.
38 Marks, *"'The Hallelujah Lasses,'"* 76–77, 88.
39 Marks, *"'The Hallelujah Lasses,'"* 92.
40 Brown, *"What God Hath Wrought?"*; Collins, *The Holy War of Sally Ann*, 24.
41 Marks, *"'The Hallelujah Lasses,'"* 96.
42 Porter, "A Quartet and an Anonymous Choir," 92.
43 Porter, "A Quartet and an Anonymous Choir," 98.
44 Porter, "A Quartet and an Anonymous Choir," 98–99.
45 "That Sacred Spot - Canadian Traditional/Folk Song Midi and Lyrics," Traditional Folk Songs: Filipino, American, Canadian, Irish, English, Scottish, Kids Songs, filipinofolksongsatbp.blogspot.com/2011/06/that-sacred-spot-canadian.html.
46 Sadlier, *Harriet Tubman and the Underground Railroad*.
47 "New Plaque Honours Black Community That Helped 'Forge the Identity' of Leslieville," CBC News, November 19, 2019, cbc.ca/news/canada/toronto/new-plaque-honours-black-community-that-helped-forge-the-identity-of-leslieville-1.5364692.
48 Craig, *Upper Canada*, 111.
49 Howison, *Sketches of Upper Canada*, 135.
50 Muir, *Petticoats in the Pulpit*; Craig, *Upper Canada*.
51 For example, see Muir, *A Women's History of the Christian Church*, 186–95.
52 Barnes, *Our Heritage Becomes Our Challenge*, 16.
53 Sisters of St. Joseph of Toronto, "1851: Mother Delphine Fontbonne," 2020.
54 Young, "Fontbonne, Marie-Antoinette."
55 Young, "Fontbonne, Marie-Antoinette."
56 Sisters of St. Joseph of Toronto, "1851: Mother Delphine Fontbonne."
57 Muir, *A Women's History of the Christian Church*, 245–46.
58 "Project Canterbury," 2.
59 *A Journey Just Begun*.

60 *A Journey Just Begun.*
61 Brouwer, "Far Indeed from the Meekest of Women."
62 Kemper, "Deaconess as Urban Missionary and Ideal Woman."

CHAPTER 7
Proprietors of Boarding Houses, Taverns, and Hotels

1 Guillet, *Pioneer Days in Upper Canada,* 145.
2 Johnson, *In Duty Bound,* 105.
3 Jameson, *Winter Studies and Summer Rambles,* vol. 1, 80–81.
4 As quoted in Kyte, *Old Toronto,* 212.
5 Guillet, *Pioneer Days in Upper Canada,* 145.
6 Richardson, *The Temperance Lesson Book,* 220.
7 McBurney and Byers, *Tavern in the Town,* 12.
8 Playter, *Diary.*
9 Johnson, *In Duty Bound,* 105.
10 McBurney and Byers, *Tavern in the Town,* 11, quoted from W.P. Lett, *Recollections of Baytown and Its Old Inhabitants.*
11 Roberts, "Women, Men, and Taverns," 382.
12 Walton, *York Commercial Directory,* 145.
13 Duncan, *Hoping for the Best,* 97.
14 Adam and Mulvany, *History of Toronto and County of York,* 89.
15 Robertson, *Robertson's Landmarks,* vol. 1, 540.
16 Jameson, *Winter Studies and Summer Rambles,* vol. 1, 76.
17 McBurney and Byers, *Tavern in the Town,* 8.
18 Jameson, *Winter Studies and Summer Rambles,* vol. 2, 111.
19 McBurney and Byers, *Tavern in the Town,* 12.
20 Archibald, "In the Matter of the Ontario Heritage Act."
21 McBurney and Byers, *Tavern in the Town,* 100; there is some disagreement as to when Moses Furlong became involved.
22 Doucette, "Mystery of the Hanging Cat of Greenwood & Queen"; Muir, *Riverdale,* 78.
23 Muir, *Riverdale,* 78.
24 Robertson, *Robertson's Landmarks,* vol. 3, 35.
25 Robertson, *Robertson's Landmarks,* vol. 1, 249ff.
26 Armstrong, Stevenson, and Wilson, *Aspects of Nineteenth-Century Ontario,* 91–92.

CHAPTER 8
Visual, Literary, and Performing Artists

1 Guillet, *Pioneer Arts and Crafts.*
2 Stagg, "Allamand, Jeanne-Charlotte Berczy."
3 Keefe, "John and Jemima Howard."
4 *Catalogue of the First Exhibition of the Society of Artists & Amateurs, 1834.*
5 Lackner, "Toronto Psychic Examines Local Landmarks Rumoured to Be Haunted."
6 "View of Toronto, 1855: A Great Work for a Lady," Distillery District Heritage, April 6, 2008, distilleryheritage.com/snippets/58.pdf.
7 "View of Toronto, 1855."
8 Firth, *Toronto in Art*, 29–30; "View of Toronto, 1855."
9 Staton, *Toronto Women*, 67ff.
10 Ungar and Bach, "Morrell, Charlotte Mount Brock (Schreiber)."
11 Cronin, "Science on a Salad Plate?"
12 "Gertrude Eleanor Spurr Cutts, (1858–1941)," Cowley Abbott, n.d., cowleyabbott .ca/artist/gertrude_eleanor_spurr_cutts/portfolio.
13 "Ford, Harriet Mary," Canadian Women Artists History Initiative.
14 "Biography of Laura A. Lyall Muntz," Galerie Jean-Pierre Valentin, Montreal, n.d., galerievalentin.com/contemporary-artists/laura-a-lyall-muntz/biography.php.
15 Forster, *100 Canadian Heroines*, 73–74.
16 Forster, *100 Canadian Heroines*, 75–76.
17 "E. Cora Hind: Biographical Sketch."
18 Morgan, *Public Men and Virtuous Women*, 225.
19 Silverman, "Mary Ann Shadd and the Search for Equality," 102.
20 Silverman, "Mary Ann Shadd and the Search for Equality," 102–3.
21 Howe, *The Refugees from Slavery.*
22 Howe, *The Refugees from Slavery.*
23 Sadlier, *Mary Ann Shadd.*
24 Tripp, "Mary Miles Bibb," 16.
25 Forster, *100 Canadian Heroines*, 68–69.
26 Freeman, "Ferguson, Catherine (Kit Coleman)."
27 Dean, "Duncan, Sara Jeannette (Cotes)."
28 Lefebvre, *A Life in Print.*
29 Barclay, "Married to Matilda," 41ff.
30 Brault, "Ridout, Matilda."
31 Curzon, *Laura Secord, the Heroine of 1812*, 23.
32 Bird, "Sarah Anne Curzon."

33 Magee, "The Growth of Canadian National Feeling as Reflected in the Poetry and Novels of English Canada" (master's thesis, University of British Columbia, 1946).

34 Livesay, "Crawford, Isabella Valancy."

35 Harrison, *Pine, Rose and Fleur de Lis*, 168.

36 Keller, *Pauline Johnson*, 3–4.

37 Keller, *Pauline Johnson*, 1ff.

38 Garvin, *Canadian Poets*, 189.

39 Forster, *100 Canadian Heroines*, 68–69.

40 Beers, *Commemorative Biographical Record*, 646–47.

41 Beers, *Commemorative Biographical Record*, 581; Adam and Scadding, *Toronto, Old and New*, 136.

42 Beers, *Commemorative Biographical Record*, 612.

43 Adam and Scadding, *Toronto, Old and New*, 137; Dymond, "Fourth Prize Essay."

44 Adam and Scadding, *Toronto, Old and New*, 135ff.

45 Adam and Scadding, *Toronto, Old and New*, 134.

46 Skene, "Toronto's First Theatre Impresario."

47 Timperlake, *Illustrated Toronto, Past and Present*, 240; Adam and Mulvany, *History of Toronto and County of York*, 298.

48 Gardner, "Nickinson, Charlotte."

49 Dugan, "Ungilded Lillie."

50 Musial, *North of Ordinary*.

51 White, *In Search of Geraldine Moodie*.

CHAPTER 9
Professionals

1   Kyte, *Old Toronto*, 323.

2   Firth, *The Town of York, 1815–1834*, 144–45, 151.

3   Acton, Goldsmith, and Shepard, *Women at Work*, 167.

4   Gillan, "My Great-Grandmother."

5   Robertson, *Robertson's Landmarks*, vol. 3, 33–34.

6   Firth, *Toronto in Art*, 80.

7   Timperlake, *Illustrated Toronto, Past and Present*, 376.

8   Walton, *York Commercial Directory*, n.p.

9   Timperlake, *Illustrated Toronto, Past and Present*, 216.

10 Timperlake, *Illustrated Toronto, Past and Present*, 134.

11 Adam and Scadding, *Toronto, Old and New*, 116.

12 Acton, Goldsmith, and Shepard, *Women at Work*, 180.

13 Timperlake, *Illustrated Toronto, Past and Present,* 376.

14 Dorland, *Former Days and Quaker Ways,* 145ff.

15 Muir, *Petticoats in the Pulpit,* 207; Acton, Goldsmith, and Shepard, *Women at Work,* 169–70.

16 Kyte, *Old Toronto,* 321.

17 Firth, *The Town of York, 1815–1834,* 139.

18 Firth, *The Town of York, 1815–1834,* 173–74.

19 Firth, *The Town of York, 1793–1815,* 209.

20 "Women at the University of Toronto," Toronto Historical Board plaque, 1985.

21 Staton, *Toronto Women,* 46.

22 Staton, *Toronto Women,* 23.

23 Kiefer, "Brown, Ada Mary (Courtice)."

24 Kiefer, "Reid (Reed, Read) Georgina Stanley (Riches)."

25 Firth, *The Town of York, 1815–1834,* 324–25.

26 Annual reports of the Toronto Public Library, 1883–1888; Penman, *A Century of Service.*

27 Adam, *Toronto of Today with a Glance at the Past,* 7.

28 "History of Toronto Public Library."

29 *Eighth Annual Report of the Toronto Public Library,* 1891, n.p.

30 Baker et al., *Nursing Education from the 16th to the 21st Century,* 2.

31 "Coffin Ships: Death and Pestilence on the Atlantic."

32 Bradburn, "19th-Century NIMBYism and the Typus Epidemic in Ontario."

33 Doyle, "New Park Honours Those Who Helped Sick Irish Arriving in Toronto"; Baker et al., *Nursing Education,* 3.

34 Baker et al., *Nursing Education,* 4.

35 Baker, et al., *Nursing Education,* 6.

36 Acton, Goldsmith, and Shepard, *Women at Work,* 139.

37 Mansell, "Snively, Mary Agnes."

38 Mansell, "Snively, Mary Agnes."

39 Rainer, "The Medical Profession in Upper Canada Reconsidered."

40 This discussion uses masculine pronouns when referring to James Barry, as Barry did to refer to himself.

41 Moore, "*Dr. James Barry: A Woman Ahead of Her Time* Review."

42 Forster, *100 Canadian Heroines,* 40ff.

43 Downy and Hart, "Elizabeth Hurdon."

44 Strong-Boag, "Canada's Women Doctors: Feminism Constrained," in Kealey, ed., *A Not Unreasonable Claim,* 109ff.

45 Baros-Johnson, "Emily Stowe."

46 Baros-Johnson, "Emily Stowe."

47 Feldberg, "Jennings, Emily Howard (Stowe)."

48 "Spotlight: Dr. Emily Stowe," All About Canadian History, April 14, 2015, cdnhistorybits.wordpress.com/2015/04/14/dr-emily-stowe.

49 Baros-Johnson, "Emily Stowe."

50 Dembski, "Gowanlock, Jenny Kid Trout."

51 Austin, "Susanna Carson Rijnhart."

52 Beers, Commemorative Biographical Record, 466.

53 Muir, A Women's History of the Christian Church, 121–22.

54 Connor, "'Larger Fish to Catch.'"

55 As quoted in Connor, "'Larger Fish to Catch,'" 108.

56 Acton, Goldsmith, and Shepard, Women at Work, 163.

57 Connor, "'Larger Fish to Catch,'" 110.

58 Acton, Goldsmith, and Shepard, Women at Work, 130.

59 Connor, "'Larger Fish to Catch,'" 112.

60 Connor, "'Larger Fish to Catch,'" 118.

61 Caniff, The Medical Profession in Upper Canada, 426.

62 Toronto Star, April 24, 1914.

63 Backhouse, "Martin, Clara Brett."

64 Staton, Toronto Women, 107ff.

65 Backhouse, "Martin, Clara Brett."

CHAPTER 10
Reforming Philanthropists

1 Firth, The Town of York, 1815–1834, 224–25, 232.

2 Firth, The Town of York, 1815–1834, 254–57.

3 Mitchinson, "The WCTU: 'For God, Home and Native Land': A Study in Nineteenth-Century Feminism," in Kealey, ed., A Not Unreasonable Claim, 151ff.

4 Roberts, "'Rocking the Cradle for the World': The New Woman and Maternal Feminism, Toronto 1877–1914," in Kealey, ed., A Not Unreasonable Claim, 17.

5 Mulvany, Toronto Past and Present, 68; Walton, York Commercial Directory, n.p.; Adam and Mulvany, History of Toronto and County of York, n.p.

6 Armstrong, Rowsell's City of Toronto; Scadding, Toronto of Old, ch. 2; Robertson, Robertson's Landmarks, 682–83.

7 Jameson, Winter Studies and Summer Rambles, vol. 1, 256–57.

8 Duffy, "Historicist: The Real Bandits in the Valley."

9 Armstrong, Rowsell's City of Toronto.

10 Scadding, *Toronto of Old*, n.p.

11 Adam and Scadding, *Toronto, Old and New*, 114.

12 Firth, *The Town of York, 1815–1834*, 226–27.

13 Staton, *Toronto Women*, 132–33.

14 Dempsey, "Eureka Celebrates 70 Years of Caring"; Leslieville Historical Society, "Not for Ourselves, but for Others"; Leslieville Historical Society, "Weaving Our History."

15 Doucette, "Coxwell and Gerrard, Hello friends and neighbours."

16 Feldberg, "Wyllie, Elizabeth Jennett (McMaster)."

17 Staton, *Toronto Women*, 104–5.

18 Graham, "The Haven, 1878–1930."

19 Graham, "The Haven, 1878–1930."

20 Mill, *The Subjection of Women*, 82.

21 Mill, *The Subjection of Women*, 82.

22 Gwyn, "How Macdonald Almost Gave Women the Vote"; Grittner, "Macdonald and Women's Enfranchisement."

23 "Canadian Legal History: 1885, Women Suffrage — Act I."

24 "Canadian Legal History: 1895, Women Suffrage — Act II."

CHAPTER 11
Epilogue

1 Kyte, *Old Toronto*, 306–7.

2 Howison, *Sketches of Upper Canada*, 267.

3 Simpson Avenue Methodist/United Church Marriage Register 1897– and Riverdale Avenue Methodist/United Church Marriage Register 1902–.

BIBLIOGRAPHY

PRIMARY SOURCES

Adam, G. Mercer, and C. Pelham Mulvany. *History of Toronto and County of York, Ontario: Containing an Outline of the History of the Dominion of Canada; a History of the City of Toronto and the County of York, with the Townships, Towns, Villages, Churches, Schools; General and Local Statistics; Biographical Sketches, Etc., Etc.* Toronto: C.B. Robinson, 1885.

Adam, G. Mercer, and Henry Scadding. *Toronto, Old and New: A Memorial Volume, Historical, Descriptive and Pictorial.* Toronto: Mail Printing Company, 1891.

Antliff, William. *Woman: Her Position and Mission.* London: T. King, 1856.

Aoki, Jodi Lee, ed. *Revisiting "Our Forest Home": The Immigrant Letters of Frances Stewart.* Toronto: Dundurn Press, 2011.

Armstrong, J., ed. *Rowsell's City of Toronto and County of York Directory from 1850–1.* Toronto: Henry Rowsell, 1850.

Armstrong, Jackson W., ed. *Seven Eggs Today: The Diaries of Mary Armstrong, 1859 and 1869.* Waterloo: Wilfrid Laurier University Press, 2004.

Beers, J.H. *Commemorative Biographical Record of the County of York, Ontario, Containing Biographical Sketches of Prominent Representative Citizens and Many of the Early Settled Families.* Toronto: J.H. Beers & Company, 1907.

Bird, Isabella L. *My First Travels in North America.* Mineola, NY: Dover, 2010.

"Canadian Legal History: 1885, Women Suffrage — Act I." Duhaime.org. Last updated April 6, 2014. duhaime.org/LawMuseum/Canadian-Legal-History /ID/158/1885-Women-Suffrage-Act-I.

"Canadian Legal History: 1895, Women Suffrage — Act II." Duhaime.org. Last updated April 6, 2014. duhaime.org/LawMuseum/Canadian-Legal-History /ID/164/1895-Womens-Suffrage-Act-II.

Caniff, Wm. *The Medical Profession in Upper Canada 1783–1850: An Historical Narrative, with the Original Documents Relating to the Profession, Including Some Brief Biographies.* Toronto: William Briggs, 1894.

Catalogue of the First Exhibition of the Society of Artists & Amateurs of Toronto, 1834. Toronto: T. Dalton, 1834.

Cattermole, William. *The Advantages of Emigration to Canada: Being the Substance of Two Lectures Delivered at the Town-Hall, Colchester, and the Mechanics' Institution, Ipswich.* London: Simpkin and Marshall, 1831.

Census of the Canadas, 1851–2. Vol. 1. Quebec: J. Lovell, 1853.

Clarke, Wm. F., and R.L. Tucker. *A Mother in Israel or Some Memorials of the Late Mrs. M.A. Lyle.* Toronto: W.C. Chewett, 1862.

"Coffin Ships: Death and Pestilence on the Atlantic." Irish Genealogy Toolkit, n.d. irish-genealogy-toolkit.com/coffin-ships.html.

Curzon, Sarah Anne. *Laura Secord, the Heroine of 1812: A Drama and Other Poems.* Toronto: C. Blackett Robinson, 1887.

Danforth United Church [*sic*]. "Marriage Register, 1909–1921." Toronto: United Church of Canada Archives, n.d.

Dempsey, Lotta. "Eureka Celebrates 70 Years of Caring." *Toronto Star,* October 16, 1980.

"The Diaries of William and Elizabeth Peters (1830)." A Living Past. alivingpast .ca/petersdiary.htm.

Drew, Benjamin. *The Refugee: Or the Narratives of Fugitive Slaves in Canada Relayed by Themselves.* Boston: John P. Jewett, 1856.

Dymond, Emma Stanton. "Fourth Prize Essay — The Educational Value of Concerts." *Etude,* June 1900.

Firth, Edith G., ed. *The Town of York 1793–1815.* Toronto: University of Toronto Press, 1962.

———. *The Town of York 1815–1834: A Further Collection of Documents of Early Toronto.* Toronto: University of Toronto Press, 1966.

Fleming, Jennie. *Diary of Jennie Fleming 1869–1872.* Transcribed by Ruth Larmour and Gwen Harris. Derby Township: Ruth Larmour Collection, 2016.

Fraser, Alexander. *A History of Ontario: Its Resources and Development.* Toronto: Canada History Co., 1907.

Godfrey, H. H. *A Souvenir of Musical Toronto*. 2 vols. Toronto: Office of Minister of Agriculture, 1897–1898.

Harrison, S. Frances. *Pine, Rose and Fleur de Lis*. Toronto: Hart, 1891.

Heward, S.A., and W.S. Wallace., eds. "An American Lady in Old Toronto: The Letters of Julia Lambert, 1821–1854" in *Royal Society of Canada Trans.*, 3rd Ser., 40 (1946), sect II: 101–42.

"History of Toronto Public Library." Toronto Public Library. torontopubliclibrary .ca/about-the-library/library-history/.

"The 'Honeymoon' Diary of Eliza Barnes Case, August 6–September 30, 1833." *Hay Bay Guardian* 7 (1999): 27. Oldhaybaychurch.ca/wp-content/uploads /2017/05/1999-vol-7.pdf.

Howe, S.G. *The Refugees from Slavery in Canada West: Report to the Freedmen's Inquiry Commission*. Boston: Wright and Potter, 1864.

Howison, John. *Sketches of Upper Canada*. Edinburgh: Oliver & Boyd, 1821.

Innis, Mary Quayle, ed. *Mrs. Simcoe's Diary*. Toronto: Dundurn Press, 2007.

Jameson, Anna. *Winter Studies and Summer Rambles in Canada*. 3 vols. London: Saunders and Otley, 1838. Reprint, Toronto: Coles, 1970–1972.

Jarvis, Hannah Peters. *Recipes and Remedies in Upper Canada*. Edited by Elizabeth Oliver-Malone. Kentville, NS: Gaspereau Press, 2015.

Langton, H.H., ed. *A Gentlewoman in Upper Canada: The Journals of Anne Langton*. Toronto: Clarke Irwin & Company, 1950.

Lefroy, Catherine F., ed. *Recollections of Mary Warren Breckenridge*. Women's Canadian Historical Society of Toronto Transaction 3. Toronto: Women's Canadian Historical Society of Toronto, n.d.

Light, Beth, and Alison Prentice, eds. *Pioneer and Gentlewomen of British North America, 1713–1867*. Toronto: New Hogtown Press, 1980.

Mill, John Stuart. *The Subjection of Women*. Amherst, NY: Prometheus Books, 1861.

Miller, Audrey Saunders, ed. *The Journals of Mary O'Brien, 1828–1838*. Toronto: Macmillan, 1968.

Moodie, Susanna. *Life in the Backwoods*. Reprint, New York: BiblioLife, 2008.

———. *Roughing It in the Bush*. Reprint, New York: W.W. Norton & Co., 2007.

Mosser, Christine, ed. *Upper Canada, Minutes of Town Meetings and Lists of Inhabitants 1796–1823*. Toronto: Metropolitan Toronto Library, 1984.

Mulvany, C. Pelham. *Toronto Past and Present (Until 1882)*. Toronto: W.E. Caiger, 1884.

Murney, Maria. "History of the Arrival of the Baldwin Family in Canada 1798, recollection of Mary Warren Breakeneridge written by her daughter Maria Murney — from her Mother's own words, in 1859." n.p., n.d.

Musial, Geraldine, coordinator. *North of Ordinary: The Arctic Photographs of Geraldine and Douglas Moodie*. Calgary: Glenbow Museum, 2018–2021.

Philbrick, Thomas, ed. *The Englishwoman in America*. Chicago: R.R. Donnelley & Sons, 2012.

Playter, Ely. *Diary 1801–1853*. Toronto: Archives of Ontario, n.d.

Roberts, Phoebe. "Phoebe Roberts' Diary of a Quaker Missionary Journey to Upper Canada." Edited by Leslie R. Gray. *Ontario Historical Society* 42 (January 1950): 7–46.

Robertson, J. Ross. *Robertson's Landmarks of Toronto*. Vol. 1, *A Collection of Historical Sketches of the Old Town of York from 1792 Until 1833 and of Toronto from 1834 to 1893*. Toronto: J. Ross Robertson, 1894.

———. *Robertson's Landmarks of Toronto*. Vol. 2, *A Collection of Historical Sketches of the Old Town of York from 1792 Until 1833 and of Toronto from 1834 to 1895*. Toronto: J. Ross Robertson, 1896.

———. *Robertson's Landmarks of Toronto*. Vol. 3, *A Collection of Historical Sketches of the Old Town of York from 1792 Until 1833 and of Toronto from 1834 to 1898*. Toronto: J. Ross Robertson, 1898.

Scadding, Henry. *Toronto of Old*. Toronto: Adam, Stevenson & Co., 1873.

Simpson Avenue Methodist/United Church Marriage Register 1897– and Riverdale Avenue Methodist/United Church Marriage Register 1902–. United Church Archives, Toronto.

Tiffany, Orrin Edward. *The Canadian Rebellion of 1837–38*. Buffalo, NY: Buffalo Historical Society, 1905.

Timperlake, J. *Illustrated Toronto, Past and Present, Being an Historical and Descriptive Guide Book*. Toronto: Peter A Gross, 1877.

Toronto Directory for 1889 Containing an Alphabetical Directory of the Citizens and a Street Directory; Also a Classified Business Directory to Which Are Added a Directory of Ben Loman, Broxton, Don Mount, Doncaster, Leslieville, Parkdale, Seaton Village and Yorkville, Corrected to January 1st, 1880. Toronto: Might and Taylor, 1888.

Traill, Catharine Parr. *The Backwoods of Canada*. Toronto: McClelland & Stewart, 1966.

———. *The Canadian Settlers' Guide*. Toronto: Old Countryman Office, 1855. Reprinted, Toronto: McClelland & Stewart, 1969.

Walton, George. *York Commercial Directory, Street Guide, and Register, 1833–4: with Almanack and Calendar for 1834; Being Second After Leap-Year, and the Fifth Year of the Reign of His Majesty King William IV*. York: Thomas Dalton, 1833.

SECONDARY SOURCES

Acton, Janice, Penny Goldsmith, and Bonnie Shepard, eds. *Women at Work, Ontario, 1850–1930*. Toronto: Canadian Women's Educational Press, 1974.

Archibald, Christine. "In the Matter of the Ontario Heritage Act, R.S.O. 1990

Chapter 0.18 and 1204 Queen Street West, Notice of Intention to Designate." City Clerk's Office, City of Toronto, November 16, 2004.

Armstrong, F.H., H.A. Stevenson, and J.D. Wilson. *Aspects of Nineteenth-Century Ontario*. Toronto: University of Toronto Press, 1974.

Austin, Alvyn. "Susanna Carson Rijnhart." In *Biographical Dictionary of Christian Missions*, edited by Gerald H. Anderson, 571–72. New York: Macmillan Reference, 1998.

Backhouse, Constance. "Martin, Clara Brett." In *Dictionary of Canadian Biography*. Toronto: University of Toronto/Université Laval, 2005.

Baehre, Rainer. "The Medical Profession in Upper Canada Reconsidered: Politics, Medical Reform, and Law in a Colonial Society." *Canadian Bulletin of Medical History* 12 (1995): 101–24.

Baker, Cynthia, Elise Guest, Leah Jorgenson, Christine Crosby, and Joni Boyd. *Nursing Education from the 16th to the 21st Century*. Ottawa: Canadian Association of Schools of Nursing, 2012.

Ballstadt, Carl P.A. "Strickland, Susanna (Moodie)." In *Dictionary of Canadian Biography*. Toronto: University of Toronto/Université Laval, 1982.

Barclay, Arlis. "Married to Matilda: A Late Nineteenth-Century Companionate Marriage." *York Pioneer* 110 (2015): 41–43.

Barnes, Esther. *Our Heritage Becomes Our Challenge*. Etobicoke, ON: Canadian Baptist Women of Ontario and Quebec, 2013.

Baros-Johnson, Irene. "Emily Stowe." *Dictionary of Unitarian and Universalist Biography*. N.p.: Unitarian Universalist History and Heritage Society, 2004. uudb.org/articles/emilyjenningsstowe.html.

Batho, G.R., ed. *Durham Biographies*. Vol. 1. Durham City, UK: Durham County Local History, 2000.

Bird, Kym. "Sarah Anne Curzon." In *The Canadian Encyclopedia*. Last updated December 16, 2013. thecanadianencyclopedia.ca/en/article/sarah-anne-curzon.

Black Creek Brewery. "Mixed Company: Women and Taverns." *Black Creek Growler*, October 2, 2014. blackcreekbrewery.wordpress.com/2014/10/02/mixed-company.

Bradburn, Jamie. "19th-Century NIMBYism and the Typhus Epidemic in Ontario." *TVO*, March 26, 2020. tvo.org/article/19th-century-nimbyism-and-the-typhus-epidemic-in-ontario.

Brault, Erin. "Ridout, Matilda." In *Dictionary of Canadian Biography*. Toronto: University of Toronto/Université Laval, 1994.

Brouwer, Ruth Compton. "Far Indeed from the Meekest of Women: Marion Fairweather Mission in Central India 1873–1880." In *Canadian Protestant and Catholic Missions, 1820s–1960s: Historical Essays in Honour of John Webster Grant*, edited by John S. Moir and C.T. McIntire, 121–49. New York: Peter Lang, 1988.

Brown, Major Arnold. *"What God Hath Wrought?": The History of the Salvation Army in Canada.* Toronto: Salvation Army Printing and Publishing House, 1952.

Byrne, Angela. "Dubliner Frances Stewart, one of the first women pioneers in Canada." *Irish Times*, March 12, 2019.

Campey, Lucille H. *Seeking a Better Future: The English Pioneers of Ontario and Quebec.* Toronto: Dundurn Press, 2012.

Collins, Robert. *The Holy War of Sally Ann: The Salvation Army in Canada.* Saskatoon, SK: Western Producer Prairie Books, 1984.

Connor, James T.H. "'Larger Fish to Catch Here Than Midwives': Midwifery and the Medical Profession in Nineteenth Century Ontario." In *Caring and Curing*, edited by Dianne Dodd and Deborah Gorham, 103–34. Ottawa: University of Ottawa Press, 1994.

Cooper, Barbara. "O'Neill, Margaret." In *Dictionary of Canadian Biography*. Toronto: University of Toronto/Université Laval, 2005.

Craig, Gerald M. *Upper Canada: The Formative Years, 1784–1841.* Toronto: McClelland and Stewart, 1963.

Cronin, Keri. "Science on a Salad Plate? Thinking About the Representation of Natural History in the Canadian Historic Dinner Service Project." *Scientia Canadensis* 31, no. 1–2 (2008): 113–30.

Da Silva, Maria, and Andrew Hind. *Rebels Against Tories in Upper Canada 1837.* Toronto: James Lorimer, 2010.

Darke, Eleanor. *"A Mill Should Be Built Thereon": An Early History of the Todmorden Mills.* Toronto: Natural Heritage, 1995.

Dean, Misao. "Duncan, Sara Jeannette (Cotes)." In *Dictionary of Canadian Biography*. Toronto: University of Toronto/Université Laval, 2005.

Dembski, Peter E. Paul. "Trout, Jenny Kidd Gowanlock." In *Dictionary of Canadian Biography*. Toronto: University of Toronto/Université Laval, 2005.

Dorland, Arthur G. *Former Days and Quaker Ways: A Canadian Retrospective.* Belleville, ON: Mika Studio, 1972.

———. *The Quakers in Canada: A History.* Toronto: Ryerson Press, 1968.

Doucette, Joanne. "Coxwell and Gerrard, Hello friends and neighbours." Coxwell and Gerrard Facebook group. facebook.com/groups/702749939738437/permalink.

———. "Mystery of the Hanging Cat of Greenwood & Queen." Leslieville Historical Society, November 17, 2017. leslievillehistory.com/2017/11/17/mystery-of-the-hanging-cat-of-greenwood-queen.

———. "Not for Ourselves but for Others." Leslieville Historical Society, February 10, 2017. leslievillehistory.com/2017/02/10/not-for-ourselves-but-for-others.

————. *Pigs, Flowers and Bricks: A History of Leslieville to 1920.* Toronto: J. Doucette, 2011.

————. "Weaving Our History: The Isaac Price House and the Underground Railroad." Leslieville Historical Society, February 1, 2016. leslievillehistory.com/2016/02/01 /weaving-our-history-the-isaac-price-house-and-the-underground-railroad.

Downy, Kathleen, and William Hart. "Dr Elizabeth Hurdon." *International Journal of Gynecology and Pathology* 19, no. 1 (January 2000): 85–93.

Doyle, John. "New Park Honours Those Who Helped Sick Irish Arriving in Toronto." *Globe and Mail,* June 18, 2017.

Duffy, Dennis. "Historicist: The Real Bandits in the Valley." *Torontoist,* September 30, 2017. torontoist.com/2017/09/historicist-real-bandits-valley.

Dugan, James. "Ungilded Lillie." *Maclean's,* July 15, 1948.

Duncan, Dorothy. *Hoping for the Best, Preparing for the Worst: Everyday Life in Upper Canada, 1812–1814.* Toronto: Dundurn Press, 2012.

"E. Cora Hind: Biographical Sketch." Archives of the Agricultural Experience, University of Manitoba Archives and Special Collections, n.d. umanitoba.ca /libraries/units/archives/exhibits/agric_exper/women/hind_index.html.

Errington, Elizabeth Jane. *Women and Their Work in Upper Canada.* Ottawa: Canadian Historical Association, 2006.

"Evangeline Booth." Last updated January 9, 2022. en.wikipedia.org/wiki /Evangeline_Booth.

Feldberg, Gina. "Jennings, Emily Howard (Stowe)." In *Dictionary of Canadian Biography.* Toronto: University of Toronto/Université Laval, 2003.

————. "Wyllie, Elizabeth Jennett (McMaster)." In *Dictionary of Canadian Biography.* Toronto: University of Toronto/Université Laval, 2003.

Filey, Mike. *Toronto Sketches 5: The Way We Were.* Toronto: Dundurn Press, 1997.

Firth, Edith G. "Howard, John George." In *Dictionary of Canadian Biography.* University of Toronto/Université Laval, 2003.

————. "Murray, Anne." In *Dictionary of Canadian Biography.* University of Toronto /Université Laval, 2003.

————. *Toronto in Art: 150 Years Through Artists' Eyes.* Toronto: Fitzhenry and Whiteside, 1983.

Ford, Anne Rochon. *A Path Not Strewn with Roses: One Hundred Years of Women at the University of Toronto, 1884–1984.* Toronto: University of Toronto Press, 1985.

"Ford, Harriet Mary." Canadian Women Artists History Initiative. Last updated November 28, 2013. cwahi.concordia.ca/sources/artists/displayArtist.php ?ID_artist=19.

Forster, Merna. *100 Canadian Heroines: Famous and Forgotten Faces.* Toronto: Dundurn Group, 2004.

Fowler, Marian. *The Embroidered Tent: Five Gentlewomen in Early Canada.* Toronto: Anansi Press, 1982.

Freeman, Barbara. "Ferguson, Catherine (Kit Coleman)." In *Dictionary of Canadian Biography,* Toronto: University of Toronto/Université Laval, 1998.

Fuller, Sandra McCann. "Alma Gould Dale (1854–1930): Quaker Minister and Social Evangelist." *Canadian Quaker History Journal,* no. 69–70 (2004–5): 57–90.

Gardner, David. "Nickinson, Charlotte." In *Dictionary of Canadian Biography.* Toronto: University of Toronto/Université Laval, 1994.

Garvin, John William, ed. *Canadian Poets.* Toronto: McClelland and Stewart, 1916.

Graham, John R. "The Haven, 1878–1930: A Toronto Charity's Transition from a Religious to a Professional Ethos." *Histoire Sociale-Social History* 25, no. 50 (November 1992): 283–306.

Grittner, Colin. "Macdonald and Women's Enfranchisement." In *Macdonald at 200: New Reflections and Legacies,* edited by Patrice Dutil and Roger Hall, 27–57. Toronto: Dundurn Press, 2014.

Guillet, Edwin C. *Pioneer Arts and Crafts.* Toronto: University of Toronto Press, 1940.

———. *Pioneer Days in Upper Canada.* Toronto: University of Toronto Press, 1933.

———. *Pioneer Inns and Taverns.* Vol. 1, *Ontario with Detailed Reference to Metropolitan Toronto to Yonge Street to Penetanguishene.* Toronto: Edwin Guillet, 1954.

Healey, Robynne Rogers. *From Quaker to Upper Canadian: Faith and Community Among Yonge Street Friends, 1801–1850.* Toronto: McGill-Queen's University Press, 2006.

Hendrick, George, and Willene Hendrick. *Black Refugees in Canada: Accounts of Escape During the Era of Slavery.* Jefferson, NC: McFarland, 2010.

Hill, Lawrence. *The Book of Negroes.* Toronto: HarperCollins, 2007.

Hopper, Jane Agar. *Old-Time Primitive Methodism in Canada: 1829–1884.* Toronto: William Briggs, 1904.

Ireland Park Foundation. "First Responders, 1847: Remembering Their Sacrifice." Toronto, 2020.

"Jesse Ashbridge." Toronto: Mount Pleasant Group, 2020.

"Jesse Ashbridge House." Toronto: Ontario Heritage Trust Property Files, n.d.

Johnson, J.K. *In Duty Bound: Men, Women, and the State in Upper Canada, 1783–1841.* Montreal/Kingston: McGill-Queen's University Press, 2014.

Kealey, Gregory S. *Hogtown: Working Class Toronto at the Turn of the Century.* Toronto: New Hogtown Press, 1974.

Kealey, Linda, ed. *A Not Unreasonable Claim: Women and Reform in Canada 1880s–1920s*. Toronto: Women's Educational Press, 1979.

Kearns, Robert. "Health Care Workers Sacrificed Themselves to Help Irish Migrants." *Globe and Mail*, July 16, 2020.

Keefe, Kathleen. "John and Jemima Howard." High Park Nature. n.d. highparknature.org/article/john-and-jemima-howard.

Keller, Betty. *Pauline Johnson*. Toronto: Betty Keller and XYZ Publishing, 1999.

Kemper, Alison. "Deaconess as Urban Missionary and Ideal Woman: Church of England Initiatives in Toronto 1890–1895." In *Canadian Protestant and Catholic Missions, 1820s–1960s: Historical Essays in Honour of John Webster Grant*, edited by John S. Moir and C.T. McIntire, 171–90. New York: Peter Lang, 1988.

Kiefer, Nancy. "Brown, Ada Mary (Courtice)." In *Dictionary of Canadian Biography*. Toronto: University of Toronto/Université Laval, 1998.

———. "Reid (Reed, Read) Georgina Stanley (Riches)." In *Dictionary of Canadian Biography*. Toronto: University of Toronto/Université Laval, 1998.

Kyte, E.C. *Old Toronto*. Toronto: Macmillan, 1954.

Lackner, Chris. "Toronto Psychic Examines Local Landmarks Rumoured to Be Haunted." *Globe and Mail*, October 28, 2013.

Lefebvre, Benjamin, ed. *The L.M. Montgomery Reader*. Vol. 1, *A Life in Print*. Toronto: University of Toronto Press, 2013.

Leslieville Historical Society. *History of an East End Neighbourhood, Ashbridge's Bay*. Toronto: Leslieville Historical Society, n.d.

Livesay, Dorothy. "Crawford, Isabella Valancy." In *Dictionary of Canadian Biography*. Toronto: University of Toronto/Université Laval, 2003.

Lucky, Natalie. "McNicoll, Helen Galloway." In *Dictionary of Canadian Biography*. Toronto: University of Toronto/Université Laval, 2003.

Mansell, Diana. "Snivley, Mary Agnes." In *Dictionary of Canadian Biography*. Toronto: University of Toronto/Université Laval, 2003.

Marks, Lynne. "'The Hallelujah Lasses': Working-Class Women in the Salvation Army in English Canada, 1882–92." In *Gender Conflicts: New Essays in Women's History*, edited by Franca Iacovetta and Mariana Valverde, 93–116. Toronto: University of Toronto Press, 1992.

McBurney, Margaret, and Mary Byers. *Tavern in the Town: Early Inns and Taverns of Ontario*. Toronto: University of Toronto Press, 1987.

McCalla, Douglas. *Consumers in the Bush: Shopping in Rural Upper Canada*. Montreal: McGill-Queen's University Press, 2015.

McKillop, A.B. *The Spinster and The Prophet*. Toronto: Macfarlane Walter & Ross, 2000.

McKinley, Steve. "Canada to Honour Abolition of Slavery." *Toronto Star*, June 20, 2021.

McKnight, Alanna M.M. "Shaping Toronto: Female Economy and Agency in the Corset Industry, 1871–1914." Ph.D. diss., Ryerson and York Universities, 2018.

Moore, Wendy. "Dr. James Barry: A Woman Ahead of Her Time Review — An Exquisite Story of Scandalous Subterfuge." *Guardian*, November 10, 2016.

Morgan, Cecilia. *Public Men and Virtuous Women: The Gendered Languages of Religion and Politics in Upper Canada, 1791–1850.* Toronto: University of Toronto Press, 1996.

Morris, Audrey Y. *Gentle Pioneers: Five Nineteenth-Century Canadians.* Toronto: Hodder and Stoughton, 1966.

Muir, Elizabeth. "The Bark School House: Methodist Episcopal Missionary Women in Upper Canada, 1827–1833." In *Canadian Protestant and Catholic Missions, 1820s–1960s: Historical Essays in Honour of John Webster Grant*, edited by John S. Moir and C.T. McIntire, 23–47. New York: Peter Lang, 1988.

Muir, Elizabeth Gillan. "Eliza Case 1769–1887." In *Canada Portraits of Faith*, edited by Michael D. Clarke. 2nd ed. Chilliwack, BC: Reel to Real, 1998.

———. "Laura Secord." *The Maple Leaf Rag*, Fall 2012.

———. *Petticoats in the Pulpit: The Story of Nineteenth-Century Methodist Women Preachers in Upper Canada.* Toronto: United Church Publishing House, 1991.

———. *Riverdale: East of the Don.* Toronto: Dundurn Press, 2014.

———. *A Women's History of the Christian Church: Two Thousand Years of Female Leadership.* Toronto: University of Toronto Press, 2019.

Murray, Heather. *Come, Bright Improvement! The Literary Societies of Nineteenth-Century Ontario.* Toronto: University of Toronto Press, 2002.

"The Name 'Toronto' Came from 'The Narrows.'" Ramara Historical Society, n.d. ramarahistoricalsociety.ca/how-toronto-got-its-name/.

Nicholson, Murray W. "Irish Catholic Education in Victorian Toronto: An Ethnic Response to Urban Conformity." *Histoire Sociale/Social History* 18, no. 34 (November 1984): 287–306.

Noori, Margaret. "The Complex World of Jane Johnston Schoolcraft." *Michigan Quarterly Review* 47, no. 1 (Winter 2008). hdl.handle.net/2027/spo .act2080.0047.121.

Penman, Margaret. *A Century of Service: Toronto Public Library 1883–1983.* Toronto: Toronto Public Library Board, 1983.

Porter, Wendy J. "A Quartet and an Anonymous Choir." In *Canadian Baptist Women*, edited by Sharon M. Bowler, 89–112. Hamilton: Canadian Baptist Historical Society Series, 2016.

Richardson, Benjamin Ward. *The Temperance Lesson Book: A Series of Short Lessons on Alcohol and Its Action on the Body.* New York: National Temperance Society, 1880.

Roberts, Julia. "Women, Men, and Taverns in Tavern-Keeper Ely Playter's Journal." *Histoire Sociale/Social History* 36, no. 72 (November 2003): 371–406.

Sadlier, Rosemary. *Harriet Tubman and the Underground Railroad: Her Life in the United States and Canada.* Toronto: Umbrella Press, 1997.

———. *Leading the Way: Black Women in Canada.* Toronto: Umbrella Press, 1994.

———. *Mary Ann Shadd: Publisher, Editor, Teacher, Lawyer, Suffragette.* Toronto: Umbrella Press, 1995.

Sadlier, Rosemary, with Fiona Raye Clarke. *The Black Church in Canada.* Burnstown, ON: Burnstown Publishing House, 2015.

Sager, Eric W. "The Transformation of the Canadian Domestic Servant, 1871–1931." *Social Science History* 31, no. 4 (Winter 2007): 509–37. doi.org/10.1017/S0145553200013845.

Sager, Eric W., and Peter Baskerville, eds. *Household Counts: Canadian Households and Families in 1901.* Toronto: University of Toronto Press, 2007.

Silverman, Jason H. "Mary Ann Shadd and the Search for Equality." In *A Nation of Immigrants: Women, Workers, and Communities in Canadian History, 1840s–1960s,* edited by Franca Iacovetta, Paula Draper, and Robert Ventresca, 101–14. Toronto: University of Toronto Press, 1998.

Skelton, Isabel. *The Backwoodswoman: A Chronicle of Pioneer Home Life in Upper and Lower Canada.* Toronto: Ryerson Press, 1924.

Skene, Angus. "Toronto's First Theatre Impresario." *Toronto Star,* May 17, 2015.

Stagg, Ronald. "Allamand, Jeanne-Charlotte Berczy." In *Dictionary of Canadian Biography.* Toronto: University of Toronto/Université Laval, 1988.

Staton, Pat. *Toronto Women: A Walk Through History.* Toronto: Green Dragon Press, 2012.

Stephenson, Mrs. Frederick C. *One Hundred Years of Canadian Methodist Missions 1824–1924.* Toronto: Missionary Society of the Methodist Church, 1925.

Taylor, John Doug. "Toronto's Unique Wheat Sheaf Tavern." Historic Toronto, August 6, 2012. tayloronhistory.com/2012/08/06/torontos-unique-wheat-sheaf-tavern.

Taylor, Katherine. *Toronto City of Commerce 1800–1960.* Toronto: James Lorimer, 2021.

Thomas, Dave, and Bob Marchant. *When Milk Came in Bottles: A History of Toronto Dairies.* Cobourg, ON: Cowtown, 1997.

Toronto Public Library. *Toronto and Early Canada, A Catalogue of the Toronto and Early Canada Picture Collection in the Toronto Public Library Landmarks of Canada.* Vol. 3. Toronto: Baxter Publishing, 1964.

Trewhella, Ethel Wilson. *The Yonge Street Quakers.* Aurora, ON: J.M. Walton, 1937.

Tripp, Bernell E. "Mary Miles Bibb: Education and Moral Improvement in the *Voice of the Fugitive*." Presented at the Association for Education in Journalism and Mass Communication Convention, Kansas City, MO, 1993.

Ungar, Molly Pulvar, and Vicky Bach. "Morrell, Charlotte Mount Brock (Schreiber)." In *Dictionary of Canadian Biography*. Toronto: University of Toronto/Université Laval, 1998.

"U of T Grad Excelled at Reaching New Heights." *The Engineering Newsletter*. University of Toronto Faculty of Applied Science and Engineering, 2008.

Wencer, David. "Historicist: Sticky Business." Torontoist, March 28, 2015. torontoist .com/2015/03/historicist-sticky-business.

———. "Historicist: Straitlaced Toronto." Torontoist, October 12, 2013. torontoist .com/2013/10/historicist-straight-laced-toronto.

White, Donny. *In Search of Geraldine Moodie*. Regina: University of Regina Press, 1998.

Winks, Robin W. *The Blacks in Canada: A History*. Montreal: McGill-Queen's University Press, 1997.

"Women at the University of Toronto." Toronto Historical Board plaque, 1985.

Young, Mary Bernita. "Fontbonne, Marie-Antoinette." In *Dictionary of Canadian Biography*. Toronto: University of Toronto/Université Laval, 2003.

IMAGE CREDITS

92 Toronto City Archives, Series 841, File 48, Item 4.
110 Edwin C. Guillet, *Pioneer Inns and Taverns* (p. 97)/Early Toronto photos, Toronto Reference Library.
111 Edwin C. Guillet, *Pioneer Inns and Taverns* (p. 97)/Toronto Reference Library/ J. Ross Robertson, *Landmarks of Toronto*, vol. 1 (p. 541).
113 City of Toronto Archives. Inset: Courtesy of James Muir.
115 Edwin C. Guillet, *Pioneer Inns and Taverns*/Toronto Reference Library.
118 Toronto Reference Library.
119 Toronto Reference Library, JRR 831.
122 Courtesy of the City of Toronto.
123 From *Canadian Wildflowers with Botanical Descriptions* by C.P. Traill, 1868, printed and published by John Lovell, Montreal.
124 Toronto Reference Library.
126 Toronto Reference Library, X3-2Cab 1.
127 Toronto Reference Library, JRR 4387.
141 Toronto Reference Library.
145 Music Library, University of Toronto, Archives Collection 2: Kathleen Parlow.
147 Music Library, University of Toronto Archives.
151 Photo by Geraldine Moodie/Glenbow Archives, NC-81-39.
154 Toronto Reference Library, X76-2.
162 Toronto Reference Library, R-5973.
166 City of Toronto Archives, Series 1201, Subseries 5, File 7. Inset: Courtesy of the University Health Network, Toronto.
170 Photo by Dufresne, King Street West, Toronto/Women's College Hospital Archives, Photograph Collection, L-02304.
184 Valentine and Sons' Publishing Company, Great Britain and Montreal. From the postcard collection of Joanne Doucette.
203 Toronto Reference Library, R-2037.
206 Glenbow Archives, NA-263-1.

INDEX

Page references in italics indicate a figure.

ABOUT THE AUTHOR

Elizabeth Muir was brought up in a farming community in the Ottawa Valley and lived for many years in Montreal.

Muir has studied extensively at Queen's University, the Harvard Business School, and McGill University, where she earned a Ph.D. She subsequently taught women's studies at the Faculty of Religious Studies, McGill University. Muir has taught Canadian studies at St. Paul's College, University of Waterloo, and Emmanuel College, University of Toronto. A historian, Muir has focused on women in Canada and the worldwide Christian Church. Her most recent publications are *A Women's History of the Christian Church: Two Thousand Years of Female Leadership*; *Air-Crazy, Too: More Fascinating Stories of Canadian Women in the Air*; *Air-Crazy: Fascinating Stories of Canadian Women in the Air*; *Canadian Women in the Sky: 100 Years of Flight*; *Riverdale: East of the Don*; *Changing Roles of Women Within the Christian Church in Canada* (co-editor and contributor); and *Petticoats in the Pulpit: The Story of Early Nineteenth-Century Methodist Women Preachers in Upper Canada.*

Muir has two children, who help her with the technical aspects of writing today, and three grandchildren. She spends her summers sailing and gardening, and the winters reading mystery stories and writing non-fiction.